DATE DUE		

Building a successful customer-service culture

A guide for library and information managers

Edited by
Maxine Melling and Joyce Little

facet publishing

© This compilation: Maxine Melling and Joyce Little 2002
© The articles: the contributors 2002

Published by
Facet Publishing
7 Ridgmount Street
London WC1E 7AE

Facet Publishing (formerly Library Association Publishing) is wholly owned by
CILIP: the Chartered Institute of Library and Information Professionals.

First published 2002
Reprinted 2003

British Library Cataloguing in Publication Data

A catalogue record for this book is available from the British Library.

ISBN 1-85604-449-1

Typeset from editors' disks by Facet Publishing in 11/13 Elegant Garamond
and Humanist 521.
Printed and made in Great Britain by MPG Books Ltd, Bodmin, Cornwall.

Contents

The contributors

Sheila Corrall

Sheila Corrall is Director of Academic Support Services at the University of Southampton with responsibility for co-ordination of computing, library and related activities and development of the institutional information strategy. She has worked in university, national and public libraries and also as a trainer and consultant, specializing in strategic planning, staff development and managing change. She has published three books and more than 50 articles on these and other topics. She has also served on the committees of professional and government bodies and is currently President of the Chartered Institute of Library and Information Professionals.

Alix Craven

Alix Craven is Project and Administration Manager of the Information Services National Training Organisation, having joined the Organisation in 2000 as Administrator. She was formerly in sales in a consumer goods firm, and prior to that she was in banking.

Mary Fleming

Mary Fleming has recently taken up post as Cultural Development Manager with Gateshead Council, which will also involve leading on human resource and customer service issues across the newly formed Cultural Development Service (incorporating Libraries, Arts, Tourism and Leisure). Previously, she had worked in a number of posts in Gateshead Library Service and had a special interest in, and responsibility for, staff training and development, customer care, enquiries, ICT training and quality/service improvement.

Robert Gent

Robert Gent is Assistant Director of Libraries and Heritage in Derbyshire County Council, with particular responsibility for resources, information services and ICT. He has project managed Derbyshire's innovative DELTA service, which attracted three consecutive awards from the DCMS/Wolfson Public Libraries Challenge Fund and was twice winner of the Government Computing Award for Innovation. He is Vice Chair of The Combined Regions and worked previously for Nottinghamshire, where he was seconded to the Chief Executive's Department to lead on Customer Care initiatives for the County Council. He has been involved closely in the design and delivery of the Leadership Masterclass programme for the Society of Chief Librarians.

Grace Kempster OBE

Grace Kempster is Director of Information Services Management for the British Council, the UK's cultural relations organization. She moved to the Council after over 20 years in local government, notably running the library and information service in Leeds where she started the award-winning City Council website and also Leeds Word Arena. Before joining the Council she was Head of Libraries, Information, Heritage and Cultural Services for Essex County Council and led a range of innovative service developments. She was involved in the development of the People's Network, both as a member of the original task group and as Chair of the Training Task Force. She took part on the SCL Masterclass on Leadership in January 2001 and was honoured for services to librarianship and information services in 2000.

R. David Lankes

Dr R. David Lankes is Director of the Information Institute of Syracuse (IIS) and an Assistant Professor at Syracuse University's School of Information Studies where he directs the ERIC Clearinghouse on Information & Technology. He co-founded the award-winning AskERIC project in 1992. AskERIC is an internet service for educators that offers resources and personal assistant for thousands of teachers a week. He founded the Virtual Reference Desk project, which is building a national network of expertise for education. He is also one of the architects of GEM, a standards-based system for describing and finding educational materials on the internet. He is currently a board

member of the Onondaga County Public Library, a visiting fellow at the
National Library of Canada, and a former visiting scholar at Harvard's
Graduate School of Education.

Joyce Little

Joyce Little is Head of Liverpool Libraries and Information Services, which
gained Charter Mark in 1999 and Beacon Council Status in 2002. Previously she
undertook a number of roles in the public library service in Liverpool including
Central Library Manager and Manager, Community Library Services. She
chairs Libraries North West (the successor organization to the North West
Regional Library System) and is an active member of the Society of Chief
Librarians North West, the Merseyside Public Libraries Partnership and
Libraries Together; Liverpool Learning Partnership, the city-wide cross-sectoral
consortium of libraries in the city. In 2001 she was awarded a National Customer
Service Award for Leisure and Tourism.

Andrew McDonald

Professor Andrew McDonald is Director of Information Services and Professor
of Information Management and Strategy at the University of Sunderland. As
well as planning innovative new libraries at Sunderland and Newcastle, he sits
on the Funding Council's Space Management group and chairs SCONUL's
Advisory Committee on Buildings. An active member of the IFLA's section on
buildings, he has directed several international seminars on library planning for
the British Council and has undertaken consultancy work all over the world.
His publications, conference papers and research interests span several professional areas including library planning and design.

Bill Macnaught

Bill Macnaught is Head of Cultural Development in Gateshead Council. He
started his career in Stirling, Scotland, moving to Gateshead in 1984 as
Information Services Librarian, becoming Director of Libraries and Arts in
1991. He initiated the 'Angel of the North' project and also conceived the project to convert an old flour mill silo on the Gateshead side of the River Tyne into
the largest space for contemporary art outside London. He has been very active
in the public library world, being the first Honorary Secretary of the Society of
Chief Librarians, and he was one of the three public librarians on Matthew
Evans' working party, which produced 'New Library: the People's Network'.
His proudest achievement with Gateshead's library service was leading it to

become the first three-star Best Value library service. He was the inaugural Chair of the Gateshead Lifelong Learning Partnership and he led the Gateshead side of the Newcastle/Gateshead joint bid to become European Capital of Culture in 2008. In 2002 he added sport and leisure to his responsibilities within Gateshead Council, but he remains a champion for the public library service.

Graham Matthews

Dr Graham Matthews is Director of Research, Faculty of Computing, Information and English, University of Central England in Birmingham (UCE). Previous academic posts include Head, School of Information Studies, UCE, lecturer, Department of Information and Library Studies, Loughborough University, Senior Lecturer, School of Information Science and Technology, Liverpool Polytechnic. Prior to this he worked in public and academic libraries in Liverpool. His research activities involve working closely with colleagues in the Centre for Information Research (CIRT) at UCE, much of whose research is user-focused, and sector-wide. Teaching and research interests include the education and training of information workers, management of information and library services, and access to information.

Maxine Melling

Maxine Melling is Director of Learning and Information Services at Liverpool John Moores University where she is responsible for the management of a converged library and computing support service. Her professional background is in further and higher education library services and, in addition to strategic management, has included responsibility for areas such as information skills teaching, staff training and development, and quality management systems. Her wider professional activities include chairing the SCONUL Advisory Committee on Performance Improvement, involvement in CILIP as a scrutineer, and associate membership of the Library and Information Research Group and of the North West branch of the Multimedia and Information Technology Group. She has published on a number of topics including customer service and quality management systems.

John M. Pluse

John Pluse is Chief Executive of the Information Services National Training Organisation. He was formerly a freelance training and development consultant, with clients in Cumbria, Hertfordshire, Powys, Renfrew, Shropshire,

Middlesbrough, Newham, Wolverhampton, British Airways and a number of health authorities. Prior to that he was Assistant City Librarian of Bradford. He has written and given conference papers on a wide range of human resource topics.

Christopher West

Christopher West has worked at the University of Wales Swansea since 1994, and has been Director of Library and Information Services since 1999. His previous posts at Swansea were as Deputy Director and Sub-Librarian (User Services). Prior to that, he worked in a variety of posts at Leicester University Library for 18 years and for three years at the National Library of Wales. His professional interests include marketing and communicating with customers (Swansea's policy for customer communication won a Library Association/T. C. Farries award in 1996), user satisfaction measures and library co-operation.

Introduction

The language and concepts of customer service have become common in the library and information sector, as have many of the techniques associated with the provision of customer-focused services. However, customer service can often be viewed as a 'bolt-on' to the existing core provision, a dangerous assumption being that as long as we offer feedback mechanisms, provide informative leaflets, and run customer-training sessions for staff then we've covered customer service. One of the challenges facing managers is not an acknowledgement of the importance of a customer focus but rather acquiring an understanding of how this focus can be embedded in the culture of our services via their strategic and operational management.

This guide presents contributions from authors with extensive experience in the management of public and academic library and information services, who address the challenge of building a culture of customer focus into our core service provision. Each chapter aims to present a good practice guide to an element of strategic or operational management while addressing the challenge of seeing this element of management with the customer placed at centre stage. Where better to start a volume on the development of a service culture than from the viewpoint of the service user? The first chapter therefore provides an overview of evidence gathered from research reports, the professional literature and service websites to show how we are perceived by the users of our library services. Some of the evidence provided, such as the impact of ICT on library provision, the perception of a middle-class bias in our services, and the identification of a generation of customers for whom 'instant gratification' is a key requirement, raises interesting challenges for managers of library and information services. This chapter also sets the scene for the more focused contributions that follow and certainly highlights the need for many of the skills and techniques discussed.

Chapters 2 and 3 consider strategic management issues, providing approaches that aim to build a customer focus into strategic management. Chapter 2 considers how customer service can be managed strategically by putting a customer focus into planning systems. A useful review of the tools and techniques associated with strategic management is provided with a firm focus on how these tools can be used to facilitate cultural change or to strengthen the existing culture. Chapter 3 refers to many of the specific issues addressed by authors in subsequent chapters, providing a contextual focus in terms of customer-focused organizations. This chapter considers the different approaches to leadership style, linking the changing perception of leaders as service providers and enablers, rather than experts, to a greater focus on customer needs.

The very specific management skills associated with human resource planning, marketing and quality control are considered in the following three chapters, again with a customer focus. Chapter 4 highlights the important role played by all staff in the provision of an exemplary service and the human resource management model needed to achieve this end. This chapter provides a practical and informative guide to the building blocks of human resource management with a clear focus on the importance of good practice in customer-focused organizations. Chapter 5 presents a consideration of marketing theory and its relevance to not-for-profit organizations while highlighting the techniques and procedures that can be used to gain a customer focus. The examples given in this chapter are largely from the academic library sector. However, the theoretical approaches considered are relevant to all sectors. In Chapter 6 the major quality management systems are considered from the viewpoint of how these systems can be used to ensure direct benefit to service users. The focus in this chapter is mainly on public libraries. Again, however, the emphasis is on principles that can be transferred to all publicly funded library and information services.

In Chapter 7 a detailed overview is provided of the stages involved in planning new academic library buildings. This chapter emphasizes the importance of space that is planned around the needs and expectations of the people who will be using it, considering vision, strategy, communication, change management and the technical knowledge involved. Chapter 8 provides an overview of partnership activity in library and information services, giving examples of the benefits to service users ranging from improved access and support to better resource discovery and social inclusion. This chapter argues that users of our services can only benefit from greater partnership working, providing locally developed models and basic principles that managers can adapt to local circumstances. The final chapter poses questions about how we ensure a customer focus in the provision of virtual services, arguing for the importance of the human face of the virtual service provider. This chapter raises questions about the branding of electronic services as well as models of good practice in providing digital reference services. This chapter is written from an American perspective and provides examples of developments that have been piloted very largely in the USA.

Where possible, contributors have drawn on examples of good practice from across the range of the publicly funded library sector. However, some bias – based on the contributors' own backgrounds and knowledge – is inevitable and some chapters concentrate largely on one sector. It is hoped that the management approaches and techniques provided are largely transferable.

1

The users' perspective: a personal view

Graham Matthews

Introduction

This chapter provides a selective and personal view of users' perspectives of library and information services (LIS), based on a review of recent research reports, the professional literature and websites. In recent years, there has emerged an LIS profession-wide need, increasingly a requirement, to find out more about users' perspectives of LIS. Whether it is to do with quality management, greater accountability, more formal service planning and review (factors that are considered elsewhere in the book), a brief look at the literature and LIS websites does seem to confirm that there is more of it about, and more to come!

In terms of scope, this chapter limits itself to:

- Who are the users of LIS?
- What influences their perspectives of LIS?
- What is the user (and non-user) perspective of LIS?
- Are there any lessons to be learned from the users' perspective for future development of services?

Who are users?

Client, customer, reader, patron, visitor, are all used to refer to those who use LIS in one way or another. Particular words may be used in certain instances to convey a specific approach or environment, for instance to highlight that an LIS is a user-oriented and user-accountable provider, to underline that an LIS provides more services than just books for reading. The terms thus may have certain connotations attached to them at different times and for different purposes. The more 'neutral' term user is used here. It is used in the sense of potential user, too, as any consideration of users' perspectives of LIS should also consider non-users, who are potential or maybe 'lapsed' users. Users are diverse (for example in university libraries, they include full- and part-time students, both in attendance and distance learners, research students and researchers, teaching staff, and non-university affiliated users from the local community; see Brophy, (2000, 55–69), for a discussion of academic library users and stakeholders. In public libraries, they include children and young people, students, the elderly, local businesses, local government officers, etc. – potentially, anyone in the community (UNESCO, 1994). These different users and user groups use different services, and their needs and expectations change over time.

Line (1988, 69) reflected the traditional view that public libraries have the most diverse range of users, with academic and special libraries having more closely determined user groups: 'In industrial libraries, and to a lesser extent in academic libraries, the clientele is already defined for the librarian, but this is not so in public libraries, for whom most non-users are potential users.' While public libraries still have the widest range of users, 'The population served by any library authority is not homogenous but comprises numerous large and small minority interest groups' (Great Britain. Department for Culture Media and Sport, 2001, para. 23). Both academic and special libraries now have a growing range of user groups – 'Libraries exist to serve their users, but the population is increasingly heterogeneous' (Brophy, 2000, 68) – and Maher (2001, 309) states that:

> user group(s) and information needs change. Let's take an example – in the mid-1980s a typical large UK law firm's library would be catering solely for the fee-earning departments. Now, the legal profession is operating in a more aggressive marketplace and in addition to the fee-earning departments the library is providing services to business development and human resources teams, inhouse support lawyers and, increasingly, external clients. These new groups require different information needs and so the library services have to adapt accordingly.

Users are diverse, and thus have different perspectives or views of the library.

Influences on users' perspectives

Users' perspectives will be influenced by their expectations of LIS, the demands they make of them, and how well LIS provide what they want. It is interesting to note the six key reasons identified by the People Flows project (Thebridge, Nankivell and Matthews, 1999, 68), which investigated individuals' cross use of publicly funded libraries, through questionnaires to and interviews with users, as crucial to their choice of library to visit:

1. Where the library is – location, transport routes to it, parking facilities, proximity to home, work or place of study
2. The resources within the library – books, journals, IT facilities and study space – and their quality, range and appropriateness
3. When the library is open
4. Who staffs the library – their knowledge, helpfulness and approachability
5. How the resources within the library are organized – catalogues, classification systems, signposting, etc.
6. The library environment – how comfortable people find it, the lighting and heating, and provision of such facilities as toilets, phones and a café.

All of these are areas that will affect users' perspectives, from first experiences ('first expressions count') to ongoing satisfaction or otherwise. They can also be affected by external factors, i.e. those outside the LIS, but within the authority or organization (Lilley and Usherwood, 2000, 17): 'In the case of public library services knowledge is not solely confined to experience of the service itself or even similar services. As a publicly funded institution the library service is often affected by the way that the local authority as a whole, other local government departments, or even other publicly funded institutions are perceived.' Beyond this (Lilley and Usherwood, 2000, 17) 'The research has also found evidence . . . that life experience affects the perception that is held of the public library service. There will be times in a user's life where the service is perceived differently, depending on their circumstances.' Moreover (Lilley and Usherwood, 2000, 17):

> Personal experience impacts on perception creation. Similarly, there are factors that impact on personal experience that can further influence the way that an individual's perceptions of the library service are formed . . . Internal factors affecting perception might include family, schooling and the area lived in . . . Identifying external factors that impact on users' perceptions of the library service is slightly more complicated. They include outside agencies, newspapers and television.

We live in changing times – perceptions of LIS must be seen in the context of the world around us and other sources of information or leisure providers, and what can be expected from them, i.e. alternatives or competitors. This situation should also be considered in the light of the often expressed, negative stereotypical image of the librarian.

An informative discussion of the relationship between user expectations and satisfaction and library performance is provided by Millson-Martula and Menon (1995). Williams (2000, 109), commenting on a recent user survey of the Law Society Library, illustrates another factor referred to above in this: that an individual's perspective will obviously be affected by their knowledge and awareness of the library's services: 'This research and another recent qualitative study for the Law Society have both shown widespread ignorance about many of the services on offer.' The SCONUL Advisory Committee on Performance Indicators (West, 2001, 9) discussed the relationship between expectation and satisfaction, and noted 'that users with a low expectation of a service may be pleasantly surprised if it delivers the required service well. Alternatively, if users have high expectations of a service, then they may be ultra-critical of any deficiencies'.

User perspectives

What follows is a selection of sources of users' perspectives. It has not been possible to attempt a comprehensive overview of all such sources. Instead, key, recent research reports have been identified and scanned for what they reveal, with a focus on publicly funded libraries, specifically public and university libraries, where there appears to be more recent information on this subject. The users' perspectives identified are in some cases third hand, and have been selected by others. Reading the reports of others results in one impression here, mine – a snapshot, of snapshots, in some cases – of significant user perspectives on publicly funded libraries in the UK.

Public libraries

New Library: the People's Network (Library and Information Commission, 1997)

This was in part informed by a small-scale qualitative research programme undertaken June–July 1997. In Chapter 2 (2.3), Listening to the people, it reports that 'In general, people's starting position was full of goodwill towards the current service, even though there was dissatisfaction with cutbacks in opening hours and with spend on bookstocks. A principal concern was that the introduction of IT could be unrealistic in a regime of tight finances.'

Further interesting findings, reported in Appendix 2, Qualitative research on library users, include:

The public library was perceived to be a keystone in each local community, and there was a common understanding as to its role and purpose. The library was seen mainly as a place to borrow books, but there was tremendous respect and appreciation of the special space it provides.

(Perceived role, A2.4)

A few younger respondents held the view that the library tended to have a 'downbeat' image and to be full of people killing time when they had nothing to do. They thought that it needed to become much more mainstream, pushing itself forward and leading with new media rather than lagging.

(A2.7)

The public library was perceived to be under increasing financial pressure, as evidenced by restricted opening hours, closure of small libraries, and apparent lack of newly published titles in bookstock.

(A2.9)

New measures for the new library: a social audit of public libraries (Linley and Usherwood, 1998)

'This report describes the use of a "social process audit" to evaluate the impact of libraries in the City of Newcastle upon Tyne and the County of Somerset.' (p.4) The project, based at Sheffield University and funded by the British Library Research and Innovation Centre, tried to match the social objectives of the two authorities by cross-checking 'the views and perceptions of selected stakeholders to ascertain how far these objectives have been achieved' (p.7).

Key social and caring roles of the library identified by the project were personal development, social cohesion, community empowerment, local image and identity, health and well-being. The library was described as 'part of the cement of the social fabric' (p.48). But it also noted that 'financial issues were observed to affect all aspects of the library service' (p.74), for example, cuts in opening hours, feasibility of using libraries for homework centres, inadequate buildings, lack of resources, space for private study, IT facilities. Additionally:

There was support, from all categories of respondent, for the library as a centre of cultural life. ... This support, however, was largely expressed as a general perception of the value of *local* promotion of, and participation in, cultural activities, and of the library as an appropriate centre for these activities.

(p.28)

As with the educational impact of the library, the effect of its information provision was influenced by the availability and accessibility of other provision. In Newcastle other information providers, like neighbourhood housing centres, had a key role in local information provision, although the importance of the City Library for career and employment information was frequently referred to. In Somerset, there was evidence that many libraries acted as a general noticeboard and information point for the local community. In both areas, many respondents saw a 'contingency' value for the library.

(pp.28–9)

Provision of leisure material is important:

Focus groups suggested the enduring popularity of leisure reading. The library remains important as a source of *free* reading material. These benefits were especially seen by and for economically inactive people, who were seen as having both lower incomes and more leisure time.

(p.28)

But services need to be publicized:

Awareness, or more correctly lack of awareness, of services emerged again and again as a factor influencing the effectiveness of libraries. Some respondents were unaware of basic library facilities.

(p.75)

The project also acknowledged the negative impact library rules and culture can have:

For some non-users, the image of the library as 'not for them' was a very powerful one. Their perception of library rules and culture – usually based on past, not recent experience, was a negative one.

(p.77)

The report found that 'recognized and established functions of the public library' – culture, education, reading and literacy, leisure and information – remain important.

Open to all? (Muddiman et al., 2000)

This reports the findings of an 18-month research project funded by the Library and Information Commission, based at Leeds Metropolitan University and conducted in partnership with the London Borough of Merton Libraries, Sheffield Libraries, Archives and Information Services and an independent consultant. One of its investigations (Muddiman, 2000), focusing on exclusion:

> highlighted a number of areas of dispute and disagreement about the relevance of public library services to the disadvantaged and working class users. The dispute continues effectively between those researchers who stress the value of public libraries to working class disadvantaged communities and those who see them mainly catering for the middle class.
>
> (p.186)

> It is clearly the case that libraries are used and valued by a large number of working class people, but that these are a minority of the working class as a whole. Among those who do value them, their worth is largely conceptualized in terms of a) individual or personal development, which is often associated with educational and social mobility, and b) also with 'escape', or a yearning for an exit route (often imaginative) to a wider world. These factors explain, for example, both the high popularity of children's libraries among working class parents who aspire to a wider world for their children and the continuing popularity among working class adults of fiction services.
>
> (p.186–7)

> However, what will fairly immediately become clear to the reader is the relative inadequacy of research/evidence about how 'excluded' 'non-users' perceive library services, or even indeed, their own library related needs.
>
> (p.180)

> Non users of public libraries consistently point to their *institutional culture* as a problem which leads to the effective exclusion of many working class and disadvantaged people . . . working-class non-users generally often perceive the public library to have a middle class image.
>
> (p.187)

> New initiatives and projects which emphasise social and community roles are often appreciated and popular with people who have previously made little use of the public library. However, people are unlikely to demand these services – there is substantial evidence now that people have enormous difficulty in conceptualizing library services in ways other than traditional book borrowing and reference.
>
> (p.187)

A mass observation of the public library project (Black and Crann, 2000)

Funded by the Library and Information Commission, this provides a preliminary analysis by academics at Leeds Metropolitan University of data collected by the Mass-Observation Archive, University of Sussex, based on written observations from 231 of the Archive's volunteer observers undertaken during summer 1999.

> The commonplace image of the local public library is of a historic and stuffy institution, staffed by formal and officious librarians who spend most of their time merely stamping or re-shelving books of light fiction and ensuring that at all times their much-cherished rule of silence is strictly observed. Of course the real picture is far removed from this stereotyped representation.
>
> (p.1)

But, referring to England and Sumsion's *Perspectives of public library use. A compendium of survey information* (1995), it notes that 'Nearly half the population does not possess a library ticket . . . and around another 30% can be classed as infrequent users' (p.1). This analysis concludes (pp.24–5):

> The public library is an institution replete with ambiguities. Generally, the public library is:
>
> - liked and even cherished, yet also viewed with indifference or derision
> - popular in respect of the materials it stocks, yet saddled with the cultural signification of stuffy learning
> - an institution for liberation, yet one that is weighed down by a controlling, bureaucratic image
> - modern, yet with an ambience that is yesteryear
> - pledged to customer care and frequently viewed as user friendly, yet staffed by personnel often seen as distant and unhelpful
> - for many welcoming and homely, yet for others, cold and institutionalized
> - public places potentially productive of anti-social behaviour challenging of authority
> - free, yet increasingly liable to charge for its services
> - devoted to the printed word, yet ready to take on new information and communication technologies.

Academic libraries

There is less current research looking at general user perspectives of academic libraries. Following development work in recent years relating to performance and quality measurement (see, for example, Brockman, 1997; Brooks, Revill and Shelton (1997); Spiller, (2000); Winkworth, 2001), many university libraries now undertake general satisfaction surveys which give some indication of this (and, SCONUL has recently provided guidance and templates aiming for wider application (West, 2001)). Research however seems to focus on more specific issues, in particular at the moment relating to the development of digital libraries, provision of electronic services, and gauging staff and student experience and attitudes to them; see, for example, Armstrong et al. (2001); Bremner (1999); Crawford (2000); Garrod (1998); Lock and Nordon (1998); Palmer and Robinson (2001); Rowley (2001) and Wynne (2000).

The findings of The People Flows (Thebridge, Nankivell and Matthews, 1999) (see above) are echoed:

> Numerous studies, both published and unpublished have identified that access to library and information services geographically close and convenient to their place of work, and/or their home, is the prime requirement of students. This applies particularly to students separated by distance or by available time from the institution at which they are registered for a course of study.
>
> (Heap, 2001, 5)

Dugdale (2000) offers a pragmatic view of students' perspectives of higher education (HE) libraries:

> Today's UK students pay fees and expect value for money. Some expect to be spoon-fed information. They are part of the consumerist society that demands instant gratification. Consequently they often have unrealistic expectations of what their library staff should provide; expecting access to print copies of all core texts whenever they choose to ask for them.
>
> Many are computer literate and aware of the potential availability of a wealth of digital information. These students expect instant access to up-to-date digital information.

A random glance at university library websites reveals that in some, user satisfaction surveys would seem to bear out this view. The information provided on these websites also serves as an example of how university libraries are trying to find out about their users, their levels of satisfaction with services, and what LIS managers are doing with the information they gather through such surveys.

As well as general surveys and comments and suggestions invited electronically via the website and paper forms and books, LIS in HE also undertake occasional topic- or user-group-specific surveys; see, for example, the University of Birmingham Information Services Distance & Part-Time Gateway, *Distance Learning Survey* (www.is.bham.ac.uk/dlsurvey/).

Results of surveys and consequent actions are published so users as well as staff can see them; see, for example, University of Bath Library and Learning Centre, *Library Survey 2001* (general user satisfaction) (2001); *Electronic Journals Survey 2000*; *Reading List and Academic Reserves Usage Survey 2000*. For the first of these, there is brief commentary on response to the survey, and areas of satisfaction and of concern, followed by a statistical breakdown of responses with charts (www.bath.ac.uk/library/about/general/surveys/2001-lib/).

Some academic libraries also publish the minutes of library committees on their website; see, for example, *Lancaster University Library*. *Library Users Forum*, which gives details of membership, minutes, dates of meetings, and how to contact the forum (http://libweb.lancs.ac.uk/luf.htm); and on the Library's *What's New* pages, *Results of our User Satisfaction Survey* (http://libweb. lancs.ac.uk/survres.htm).

Advice on how to tell the library what you think about it is available; see, for example, Newcastle University Library *How to tell us what you think about the Library*, with its advice on how to do this (speak with staff at main counter, telephone the library, use feedback form, hardcopy or electronic, e-mail (the Library, the Deputy Librarian, the Chair of Library Committee), or use the message facility on the Library's web-based catalogue) and including reference to the Library's Customer Care Policy and links to an analysis of comments received 1999–2000 and details of action taken as a result of comments, etc. 1999–2000 (www.ncl.ac.uk/library/tellus.html).

Advance notice of surveys is provided; see, for example, University of Nottingham Information Services Directorate, Library Services, *Special projects and developments* (www.nottingham.ac.uk/library/services/about/projects.html), which advises that

> During the 2001-2002 session, Library Services will carry out a survey of researchers in the University to see how we can better support them in their work. . . . The research support survey follows on from the large scale general user survey during the academic year 2000–2001 to gain a picture of opinions about library services in order to identify ways of improving the services in the future. The responses to this survey were mostly from taught course students.

There are links to updates, news and developments (May 2001 and November 2001) on the *User Survey Report*, including, 'What you asked for and what we are doing about it' (www.nottingham.ac.uk/library/news/survey2.html).

Information about why the surveys are necessary is also provided. See, for example, University of Sunderland Information Services, *Information Services annual performance report 2000/2001*: (www.library.sunderland.ac.uk:8080/is/zfeedback/annual_performance_report_2000-2001?zfeedback)

> The future: We need to revise and simplify our service standards and performance indicators in the light of some five year experience and to reflect current changes in the University. For example, more detailed information of performance indicators, such as a breakdown of core services by site and by services would help with future planning and location of staff. We also need to develop better information on the use of e-journals, specific databases and our networked systems.

One thing in common these sites report is that a high percentage of respondents seem generally satisfied with LIS provision. They also indicate several areas of common concern: electronic services and equipment (for example, the need for more computers and speedy maintenance/repair); photocopying facilities (for example, the need to reduce queues); library environment (for example, noise, temperature, lighting, space); a desire for more copies of key texts on reading lists. But these are first impressions of just a few sites and do not take into account the individual circumstances at each of the institutions.

Recent research projects throw further light on users' perspectives and indicate certain similarities with the situation regarding public libraries, for example the impact of users' previous experience and expectations.

Agora: the hybrid library from a users perspective (Palmer and Robinson, 2001, 5)

An eLib, JISC-funded project, led by the University of East Anglia, with partners UKOLN, Fretwell Downing Informatics, and the Centre for Information Research Management (CERLIM) at Manchester Metropolitan University, this notes:

> Users approach their information requirements from a range of different perspectives, expectations and experiences and the success of any future HLMS [Hybrid Library Management System] will depend on it being made understandable across the range of user types and user expectations.

This is echoed by Rowley (2001, Executive summary, 0.3.4):

The levels of IT and information skills amongst staff and students are extremely varied ranging from very limited to very sophisticated.

Also:

In all, the case studies showed that the users of library systems have embraced the concept of the hybrid library and are ready for an operational HLMS. The problem seems to be, not so much rejection of the idea of the HLMS, but rather impatience that present systems, including Agora, cannot deliver the vision that users themselves already possess.

(Palmer and Robinson, 2001, 5)

Hylife (Wynne, 2000)

This is an eLib project funded by JISC, involved CERLIM at Manchester Metropolitan University, the University of Newcastle, University of Central Lancashire, University of Northumbria, University of Plymouth, and the University of Highlands and Islands project. Reporting on the University of Plymouth's participation in the project, Garrod (1998, 68) comments with regard to designing an interface to the hybrid library for nursing students:

these users do not see library resources as something accessed by a mouse and keyboard. Their concept of a resource utopia features: an onsite library; instant, easily accessible, full text articles on a range of topics from the general to the highly specific; highly flexible borrowing arrangements, and multiple copies of key texts. This library should also be quiet, conveniently situated, open at times which fit in with their working and study patterns; dedicated to their exclusive use, and, lastly, be able [to offer] a personal service using trained subject specialists.

Nurses interviewed as part of the project 'voiced concern that assumptions were being made as to their IT expertise in relation to using a Web-based interface' (Garrod, 1998, 71). It was noted that 'although some users are aware that there "is a lot of stuff out there on the Internet", they tend to see it as a vast amorphous mass of information, much of which is USA oriented, and which requires them to have Web-based search and retrieval skills'.

(Garrod, 1998, 71)

JISC User Survey: Trends in Electronic Information Services (JUSTEIS) (Rowley, 2001)

Armstrong et al. (2001) report the findings from the first annual cycle of a three-year research programme funded by JISC and undertaken at the University of Wales,

Aberystwyth. The research surveyed academics, library staff and students at 25 universities to investigate the range and nature of electronic information systems (EIS) use. Interestingly, the research discovered that 'One immediate difficulty with perceived benefits of EIS is that of the different level of expectations of users' (p.258). And from the user perspective, 'The benefits of using EIS appear to focus around saving time, access to resources that cannot be easily located elsewhere was also important and, possibly, the ease of use of manipulating the information into project and assignment materials' (p.260).

Among Lock and Nordon's findings (1998, 244) from a questionnaire survey undertaken as part of the Continuing-Vocational-Education-funded 'Library Support for Distance Learners' initiative at the George Edwards Library, Surrey University, was that 'service demands are very different amongst distance learning students'.

Barriers discouraging access to libraries as agents of lifelong learning (Hull, 2000)

This research, funded by the Library and Information Commission, and based at the University of Teesside, investigated the extent of use made by FE and HE students of institutional library resource centres and public libraries, and their attitudes towards them. One interesting finding relating to HE students was that:

> The most evident overall barrier to Information Retrieval is the *mismatch* between respondents' stated estimation of their skills and the evident problems they appear to experience in assessing materials. Of the 239 who agreed with the statement, 'I can usually find the information I need without any bother', over half (122) also agreed with 'I don't know where to find specific journal articles.'

> (Hull, 2000, 19)

What does this mean for the management and delivery of LIS?

It is not easy to establish common themes from the increasing amount of data, quantitative and qualitative, which is becoming available. This is perhaps not surprising – LISU's *Perspectives of public library use 2. A compendium of survey information* (Bohme and Spiller, 1999) makes no attempt to analyse the surveys it includes; it presents them for the interested user to read and digest.

There are some themes, however, that emerge from this overview of users' perspectives. How they are revealed, relates as much to the methods used to identify them and the reasons for doing so, as to the actual perspectives. All of these will have an effect on service delivery and its management. These themes are addressed here under three main headings: perspectives, methodologies, and management.

Perspectives

Impact of ICT

One overriding area of conspectus is the impact of ICT on all kinds of LIS and their users. In a recent article on the 'digital information consumer', Nicholas et al. (2002, 33) note that 'Total access and speed of delivery appear to be the consumer's key requirements when seeking information' and they put consumer relationships at the heart of this: 'It is likely that information vendors and providers (libraries included) will have to engage in the same processes as other providers of goods and services, and put customer relationship management at the centre of the information experience rather than at its periphery (or, commonly, nowhere at all)' (p.34).

But ICT can help achieve this too. Rowley (2002, 44) argues that 'The digital or hybrid library needs a philosophy that involves the proactive management of relationships with users through the library website'. She goes on to say how this might be achieved, through, for example, e-mail, e-helpdesk operations, message and bulletin boards, and development of online communities. She concludes (p.45) 'that relationship development involves consideration of communication, profiling, relationships and communities. The challenge facing libraries is to embrace and interpret these concepts in such a way that they are in a position to travel with users through the next generation of innovations.' Dutch and Muddiman (2001), too, look beyond the implementation of ICT applications for the modernization of current services towards more active engagement with local communities and disadvantaged users so that the public library will be open to all.

Diversity of user groups

The users and potential users of libraries are diverse and their perspectives reflect this. 'Far from being a "simple" institution, the public library is sociologically complex – a complexity which its planners, managers and professionals ignore to their disadvantage' (Library and Information Commission, 2000). The SCONUL vision for 2005 predicts that 'A focus on user needs, for the present and future, will be critical to service success in a situation characterized by increasing diversity and choice, which creates both opportunities and threats for library staff' (SCONUL, 2001, 5).

The diversity of user groups seems likely to increase; for example, social inclusion initiatives have increased the need for public library managers to identify the different groups who make up their local community profile; changes in access to higher education and new methods of learning have increased the number of non-traditional users and the need to develop and monitor innovative methods of service delivery to them. Technology, applied to service delivery, management information and surveys, offers the possibility to identify and monitor different user groups and sub-groups. It is becoming easier to break down the user base. The apparent increase in the number and complexity of user surveys, etc. seems to be contributing to an increase in identifiable groups, both new ones and sub-groups of existing groups. Library managers need to think about the impact of this in planning balanced and equitable service.

Increased effort to address non-use will be required. This is generally accepted as difficult to achieve and will need new approaches. This is reinforced by the findings of a recent survey of Buckinghamshire's library users' views: 'Attempts to elicit a response from non-users were unsuccessful – even those filling in the simplified questionnaire in the free Community Voice newspaper were almost all library users' (What users really want, 2002, 8).

Cross-use

Another emerging factor related to the diversity of groups is the cross-use of publicly funded libraries. Increasing co-operation between public and university libraries, for example, will lead to more unaffiliated users of university libraries (Courtney, 2001). Already users of different universities have reciprocal borrowing rights; here, arrangements for access to traditional services are established. The management of access to electronic services with regard, for instance, to institutional/provider licence agreements will need to be resolved. If users have access to libraries other than 'their own', they will want access to services and resources irrespective of their format and the sort of access they enjoy in 'their own' library. The move away from open access to items on the shelf to ID/password-protected access to electronic resources will exacerbate this from a management point of view.

Expectations

Another issue relating to these is the increased expectations of users and how LIS can keep up with this. The *SCONUL vision for 2005* notes: 'There will be tensions between financial and service imperatives arising from the need to enhance the student experience in a fee-paying consumerist environment and "24 x 7" society' (SCONUL, 2001, para. H2). And, 'There will be an increasing requirement to serve the widest possible audiences and to work with business and the local community (including public libraries and museums) as part of the national infrastructure for economic regeneration, lifelong learning and social cohesion' (SCONUL, 2001, para. H6). Lilley and Usherwood (2000, 18) note 'a book based perception of the library service persists. On the other hand the data also suggested changing perceptions and higher expectations in terms of the provision of new technology.' A complicated balance between expectations and provision, and one that acknowledges levels of user expertise with ICT, needs to be achieved.

Fears

Charging for services is an issue for users, particularly those of the public library. Will attitudes to this change? Perhaps a younger generation used to paying for the application of technology, for example their use of the mobile phone, will be more open to charges. 'Mixed views were expressed regarding the acceptability of charges. Young people were more prepared to pay for services generally. Many felt that it would be acceptable to charge for some services, and compared this to the charges now made for ordering a book, while others felt quite strongly that all services should be free' (Library and Information Commission, 1997, 2.31). This will be an ongoing issue for managers.

There have been public library closures in some communities, with a focus on fewer service points to balance costs. What are the implications for local communities of this? And what of electronic delivery of services via outlets other than libraries? There will be more competition for provision of information and leisure services; can some of this be channelled into collaboration?

Awareness

A factor reiterated in the literature as significant to judging users' perspectives is their awareness or unawareness of services. 'User needs are elusive. The central question that characterizes the analysis of user needs is "how do you know what you need when you don't know what you don't know?"' (Bailey et al., 2000, 21) LIS need to continue to strive to promote themselves and their services in a positive manner. What is the use of trying to ascertain users' perspectives if users are not aware of the full range of LIS services? This applies within the host authority or organization as well as to users:

In both authorities, it was felt that the potential of the library service was reduced because of a lack of integration with the wider organization . . . there was the potential for library services to have a higher profile within the authority.

(Linley and Usherwood, 1998, 83)

This relates to a need to get across an up-to-date and bullish image of the LIS and those who work in them.

Methodologies

Investment

The tone of this chapter is generally upbeat, reflecting the enthusiasm of those discussing or researching user perspectives, but: 'There is of course a down side, and it is of course, costs. To do something properly does require an investment in time and energy. . . . What surveys produce is knowledge and some extra understanding' (Hayden, 1998, 41). This is reinforced by Hicks (1998, 10–11):

Consultation requires a significant investment, sometimes staff time, sometimes financial provision, sometimes both. To justify this outlay you must be confident of the outcome. Be aware of what can go wrong. Be even more aware of what you are going to do with the end result of the consultation process. Don't go gathering facts in May that you can't use until next April. One survey doesn't make a consultation process. A rolling programme gathers a lot of information.

Research

Surveys alone will not provide a comprehensive picture. A balance of different methods of identifying user perspectives in LIS and innovative academic research are needed. In the UK there is an encouraging development in the use of new or applied and developed methodologies by academics and researchers in projects relating to users and LIS (see Black and Crann, 2000; Muddiman et al., 2000; Linley and Usherwood, 1998, for example, in public libraries). These projects are fostering debate among academics and practitioners relating to use and non-use of LIS and methods for investigating and measuring these. In academic and public libraries, academic research continues to be encouraged in partnership with practitioners, and much useful research into many aspects of the development of the digital library has been practitioner driven.

Research and studies in LIS are influenced by economic, political and technological factors. Attention in recent years has turned to the social and economic impact of public libraries, for example, while research into the development of the hybrid library has been popular in academic libraries. Research into electronic services in public libraries also takes place (see, for example, Eve and Brophy, 2001); and academic libraries also are interested in impact. A growing area of interest here is the effectiveness of electronic services for teaching and learning (see, for example, eVALUEd – an evaluation model for e-library developments, a HEFCE-funded project, conducted by the Centre for Information Research (CIRT) at the University of Central England (eVALUEd, 2002). Despite financial constraints, research continues to be dynamic in certain key areas. Such is the pace of ICT-led developments in particular that there is perhaps a need to check the focus of research and work-based studies so that a balance between effective insight into users' perspectives at the micro- and the macro-level are achieved. Cullen (2000), discussing perspectives on user satisfaction surveys in academic libraries, draws attention to this:

> The expectations of users are likely to change in the electronic environment, and these will impact at both the macro and micro level on service quality and overall satisfaction ratings. . . . Research that throws more light on the complex relationship between service quality and satisfaction at the macro and micro level is also much needed.

She also identifies a need to explore 'the gap between user expectations and perceptions . . . as well as the gap between user expectations and managers' perceptions of these'.

Feedback and use of software

In this age of user feedback and survey fatigue ('Oh no! Not another questionnaire!'), how can managers continue to enlist users' co-operation in attempts to get their views? 'A persistent theme from pilot institutions was that staff, students and librarians all suffered from questionnaire fatigue: the longer the questionnaire, the lower response rate' (West, 2001, 6). Don't forget other institutional/authority departments will also be targeting students and the public, for their views and satisfaction ratings.

Once data has been gathered, it is vital that all involved are made aware of the findings and consequent actions. One of the features of Libra software felt to be attractive by the SCONUL Advisory Committee on Performance Indicators was its 'attractive graphical outputs. It was felt that the latter was particularly important in terms of the rapid dissemination of satisfaction surveys to customers and to the senior management of institutions. Libra software was also recognised as having strengths in drawing out the separate agendas of sub-groups: differing faculties, sites, &c' (West, 2001, 6).

The use of survey software will become more widespread:

For the university as a whole and not just for the library it is clear that the future lies with electronic methods of surveying. The university has just purchased snap survey software, which will allow the electronic design and administration of questionnaires via the Web, or e-mail which will in turn make it possible to survey more precisely targeted groups such as distance learners who have little physical contact with the university. It was notable that comments on the electronic questionnaire tended to be longer and more forthright than those on the paper returns and suggest that electronic methods of qualitative data collection may be a rich source of data in future.

(Crawford, 2001, 42)

But, be careful. As LaFleur (2002, 5) points out, with specific regard to monitoring the use of online resources:

There are many good reasons for libraries to use Web traffic analysis software. However, there are a number of important factors to keep in mind. Usage data does not provide rich qualitative information, such as a user's overall satisfaction with resources, and it certainly won't explain why people are searching for particular information. In this regard Web traffic analysis is not a substitute for more qualitative studies (focus groups, surveys, etc.) that the library should also be conducting.

Feedback mechanisms must cater for managers as well as users. Survey findings and performance measurement data are useful in making cases to senior management and politicians. They can be used to influence bodies who govern and/or fund the LIS. Proven (evidence-based) customer-oriented service not only benefits users directly but also convinces them and those responsible for its provision of its significance.

National versus local

The usefulness of comparative data on a national basis needs to be re-considered.

Although much of the motivation for satisfaction surveys in higher education has come from a desire for comparative data, this is on reflection, the wrong standpoint. The methodological and political difficulty of comparative data was one of the strongest messages from an analysis of the pilot survey. However, a more important consideration is why do we carry out surveys of this sort? The answer has to be to find out what our own users think of our services, and then to improve our services as a response.

(West, 2001, 11)

So, in the midst of seeking comparative methods for national analysis, it is important that sight of primary aims is not lost.

Management

Staff

Given the emphasis on the user, it is important not to overlook the views and experience of LIS staff as Hicks (1998, 11) points out: 'Make sure your staff don't feel they've been supplanted and their local knowledge ignored'. Corrall (2000, 237-8) rightly reminds us that there are other perspectives as well as those of the user. Balancing user perspectives against other perspectives, managers need to view the organization from different perspectives at the same time. She draws attention to the 'balanced scorecard' developed by Kaplan and Norton (1992), which 'claims to give a balanced presentation of measures which permit this'. She notes that Kaplan and Norton recommend a limit of 16–20 'key measures' reflecting four perspectives: Shareholder/financial perspective; Customer/service perspective; Internal/process perspective; and Innovation/learning perspective, and suggests goals and measures adapted from Kaplan and Norton.

In an increasingly user-oriented environment, staff training and development is particularly important, too. Its significance ranges from increasing awareness of services and user relations at all levels of staff to specific developmental activities such as training managers in the use of survey software or familiarization with new methods, and analysing user survey data and applying it effectively to strategy and forward planning and resource management. Morris and Barron (1998, 414) make the point that 'front-line staff need to be adequately trained in customer care in order to facilitate effective verbal communication, and the necessary internal consultation channels open for feedback to reach library management'.

LIS should look outside the sector, to the private sector, too, for examples of transferable practice:

> P&O European Ferries policy for customer feedback on board is to keep it relatively low key . . . For this policy to work it is important that staff are trained and involved in recognizing the value of feedback and of obtaining it informally in their contact with customers. P&O European Ferries regards its staff as the 'eyes and ears of the company' – they are the direct interface between customers' views and policy making.

> (Crawford, Cannon and Misra, 1997, 38)

Brophy (2001, 166) states that 'detailed knowledge and understanding of the needs, preferences and reactions of users is utterly fundamental to the future library'. Looking outside the sector should help LIS find new methods of finding out user perceptions and anticipating them. As well as staff training, attention should be paid to staff selection. In a user-centred environment, staff should have a customer-oriented attitude with skills that can be developed.

Customization of services

A move towards personalization of services facilitated by ICT has already begun and seems likely to continue.

> The ability to personalise an interface is common in commercial web services. . . . It is expected that future portal development will include facilities to allow users to configure their own personalized Information Landscape which takes account of their chosen academic discipline and area of study. . . . It has been argued (Brophy, 2001) that in the future libraries will have to pay as much attention to maintaining complex and accurate data about their users as they do about information resources. For example, in order to personalise services libraries will need information on each user's display preferences, course of study or area of research, subject interests, recent reading and even personal contacts. Libraries may use this data to deliver proactive services, including alerting services which draw attention to new information or new services.
>
> (Wynne, 2000, Personalised interfaces)

Hylife's findings echo the need for user-centred developments and underline the significance of the growing diversity of users: 'The hybrid library aims to make it easier for users to locate and obtain the most appropriate information resources for their needs. They should therefore be the central focus of new service developments. In doing so, however, developers must remain aware of the increasing diversity of information users within higher education' (Wynne, 2000, Users. Introduction). (See Deegan and Tanner (2002, 174–7) for further discussion and examples of personalization.)

Conclusion

During the course of writing this chapter, Resource: The Council for Museums, Archives and Libraries published (January 2002) invitations to tender for research projects investigating the impact of museums, archives and libraries. One, *Impact evaluation of museums, archives and libraries: available evidence*, seeks, inter alia, to 'identify what impact evaluation evidence for museums, archives and libraries already exists' and to 'synthesise at a general level the available evidence to present a coherent picture of the impact museums, archives and libraries have had'; this is to include 'all types of library (e.g. public, academic [school, FE and HE], workplace'; a critical review of evaluation should be produced and this should cover different methodologies employed (Resource, 2002a)). The other, *Impact evaluation of museums, archives and libraries: quantitative time series data*, seeks, inter alia, to 'identify all existing quantitative data that is being collected on a regular basis that relates to UK museums, archives and libraries', with particular reference to data of relevance to social and economic impact evaluation (Resource, 2002b). Both projects will inevitably identify and review various sources, which will provide qualitative and quantitative information, including user perspectives. But these projects will also identify gaps and are to provide the basis for more comprehensive surveys and studies. They, hopefully, point the way forward – one that will allow the voices and opinions of users and non-users to be expressed and listened to, in traditional and innovative ways that encourage the participation of all within the diverse range of users and potential users of LIS, and that can be undertaken effectively and economically by LIS or with their co-operation. This approach is vital for LIS at a time of dynamic change and growing competition in the 24x7 information society. The balance between services and resources seems likely to become more sophisticated and more user interactive.

References

Armstrong, C. et al. (2001) A study of the use of electronic information systems by higher education students in the UK, *Program*, **35** (3), 241–62.

Bailey, P. et al. (2000) Information needs analysis to inform the development of a library and information service at the Marie Curie Centre, Newcastle upon Tyne, England, *Health Libraries Review*, **17** (2), 71–6.

Black, A. and Crann, M. (2000) *A mass observation of the public library*, Library and Information Research Report 69, Library and Information Commission.

Black, A. and Muddiman, D. (1997) *Understanding community librarianship*, Avebury.

Bohme, S. and Spiller, D. (1999) *Perspectives of public library use 2. A compendium of survey information*, British Library Research and Innovation Report 166, Library and Information Statistics Unit and Book Marketing Ltd.

Bremner, A. (1999) OU students and libraries project 1999, *Library and Information Research News*, **24** (76), 26–38.

Brockman, J. (ed.) (1997) *Quality management and benchmarking in the information sector. Results of recent research*, Bowker-Saur.

Brooks, P., Revill, D. and Shelton, T. (1997) The development of a scale to measure the quality of an academic library from the perspective of its users. In Brockman,

J. (ed.), *Quality management and benchmarking in the information sector. Results of recent research*, Bowker-Saur, 263–304.

Brophy, P. (2000) *The academic library*, Library Association Publishing. (NB Ch. 4, Users of the academic library, 55–69.)

Brophy, P. (2001) *The library in the twenty-first century: new services for the information age*, Library Association Publishing.

Corrall, S. (2000) *Strategic management of information services: a planning handbook*, Aslib/IMI.

Courtney, N. (2001) Barbarians at the gate: a half-century of unaffiliated users in academic libraries, *Journal of Academic Librarianship*, **27** (6), 473–80.

Crawford, J., Cannon, H. J. and Misra, A. (1997) *Customer feedback: a good practice guide*, National Housing Federation.

Crawford, J. C. (2000) A survey of the use of electronic services at Glasgow Caledonian University Library, *Electronic Library*, **18** (4), 255–65.

Crawford, J.C. (2001) Report on the General Satisfaction Survey conducted at Glasgow Caledonian University Library, February/March 2001: executive summary, *SCONUL Newsletter*, (23), 42–3.

Cullen, R. (2000) Perspectives on user satisfaction surveys, [paper presented at] ARL Measuring Service Quality Symposium Washington, D.C. October 20-21, 2000, available at www.arl.org/libqual/events/Oct2000msq/papers/Cullen/cullen.html

Deegan, M. and Tanner, S. (2002) *Digital futures. Strategies for the information age*, Library Association Publishing.

Dugdale, C. (2000) User expectation and reality in higher education libraries, paper presented at BOBCATSSS Symposium, *Access 2000, Intellectual Property vs the Right to Knowledge, 24–26 January 2000, Krakow, Poland*, available at http://ix.db.dk/bobcatsss/access2000/symposium/abstracts/christine_dugdale.htm

Dutch, M. and Muddiman, D. (2001) The public library, social exclusion and the information society in the United Kingdom, *Libri*, **51** (4), 183–94.

England, L. and Sumsion, J. (1995) *Perspectives of public library use. A compendium of survey information*, Library and Information Statistics Unit and Book Marketing Ltd.

eVALUEd – an evaluation model for e-library developments (2002) [a HEFCE-funded project conducted by CIRT at the University of Central England], available at www.cie.uce.ac.uk/evalued/

Eve, J. and Brophy, P. (2001) *The value and impact of end-user IT services in public libraries*, Library and Information Commission Research Report 102, CERLIM, Manchester Metropolitan University, available at www.mmu.ac.uk/h-ss/cerlim/projects/vital.htm

Ford, G and Revill, D (1996) *User satisfaction: standard survey forms for academic libraries*, SCONUL.

Garrod, P. (1998) User needs and interface design: issues from the HyLIFE project, *New Review of Information and Library Research*, **4**, 67–74.

Great Britain. Department for Culture, Media and Sport (2001) *Comprehensive, efficient and modern public libraries – standards and assessment*, DCMS.

Hayden, M. (1998) Satisfaction surveys using Libra software and focus groups. In Spiller, D. (ed.) *Academic library surveys and statistics in practice. Proceedings of a seminar held at Loughborough University 2–3 June 1997*, LISU Occasional Paper 16, Library and Information Statistics Unit, Department of Information and Library Studies, Loughborough University, 33–42.

Heap, E. (2001) *Distance learners: information resource issues for policymakers. Briefing Paper*, SCONUL.

Hicks, J. (1998) Why consult with library users? In Sugg, A. (ed.) *Consulting the customer: using market research in libraries: proceedings of a seminar held at Stamford, Lincolnshire on 13th October 1998*, Capital Planning Information, 5–11.

Hull, B. (2000) Identifying the barriers to libraries as agents of lifelong learning, *Library and Information Research News*, **24** (77), 16-22.

Kaplan, R. S. and Norton, D. P. (1992) The balanced scorecard – measures that drive performance, *Harvard Business Review*, **70** (1), 71–9.

LaFleur, L. (2002) FAQ. My institution is interested in monitoring the use of our online resources. Is web log analysis an effective means of doing this?, *RLG DigiNews*, **6** (1), available at www.rlg.ac.uk/preserv/diginews/v6_n1_faq.html

Lancaster University Library. Library Users' Forum, available at http://libweb.lancs.ac.uk/luf.htm

Lancaster University Library (2002) *What's new, results of our User Satisfaction Survey*, available at http://libweb.lancs.ac.uk/survres.htm

Library and Information Commission (1997) *New Library: the People's Network*, Library and Information Commission, available at www.lic.gov.uk/publications/policyreports/newlibrary/

Library and Information Commission (2000) *Mass observation of the public library by Alistair Black and Melvyn Crann*, Library and Information Commission Research Report 69, Executive Summary available at www.lic.gov/publications/executivesummaries/rr069.html

Lilley, E. and Usherwood, B. (2000) Wanting it all: the relationship between expectations and the public's perceptions of public library services, *Library Management*, **21** (1/2), 13–24.

Line, M. B. (1988) Ignoring the user: how, when and why. In Anthony, L. J. (ed.) *Lines of thought: selected papers of Maurice B. Line*, Clive Bingley, 68–76. (Originally published in Hyams, M. (ed.) *The nationwide provision and use of information, Aslib–IIS–LA Joint Conference*, 15-19 September 1980, Library Association, 1981.)

Linley, R. and Usherwood, B. (1998) *New measures for the new library: a social audit of public libraries*, British Library Research and Innovation Report 89, The British Library Board.

Lock, D. and Nordon, J. (1998) Designing DiLIS: a distance learners' information service, *Journal of Librarianship and Information Science*, **30** (4), 241–48.

Maher, M. (2001) Financial planning. In Scammell, A. (ed.), *Handbook of information management*, 8th edn [formerly *Handbook of special librarianship and information work*], Aslib-IMI, 307–21.

Millson-Martula, C. and Menon, V. (1995) Customer expectations: concepts and reality for academic library services, *College & Research Libraries*, **56** (1), 33-47.

Morris, A. and Barron, E. (1998) User consultation in public library services, *Library Management*, **19** (7), 404–15.

Muddiman, D. (2000) Images of exclusion: user and community perceptions of the public library. In Muddiman, D. et al., *Open to all? The public library and social exclusion*, vol. 3, Working papers, Library and Information Commission Research Report 86, Resource, 179–88.

Muddiman, D. et al. (2000) *Open to all? The public library and social exclusion*, 3 vols, Library and Information Commission Research Report 86, Resource.

Newcastle University Library (2001) *How to tell us what you think about the Library*, available at www.ncl.ac.uk/library/tellus.html

Nicholas, D. et al. (2002) The digital information consumer, *Library & Information Update*, **1** (1), 32–4.

Palmer, D. and Robinson. B. (2001) Agora: the hybrid library from a user's perspective, *Ariadne*, (26), available at www.ariadne.ac.uk/issue26/case-studies/intro.htm

Resource (2002a) *Impact evaluation of museums, archives and libraries: available evidence*, available at www.resource.gov.uk/information/tenders/impevalavev.asp

Resource (2002b) *Impact evaluation of museums, archives and libraries: quantitative time series data*, available at www.resource.gov.uk/information/tenders/impevalqt.asp

Rowley, J. (2001) *JISC User Behaviour Monitoring and Evaluation Framework incorporating JUBILEE (JISC User Behaviour in Information Seeking: Longitudinal Evaluation of EIS) and JUSTEIS (JISC Usage Surveys: Trends in Electronic Information Services)*. *Second annual report*, JISC, available at www.jisc.ac.uk/pub01/m&e_rep2.html

Rowley, J. (2002) eCRM [e-customer relationship management] through your website, *Library & Information Update*, **1** (1), 44–5.

SCONUL (2001) *SCONUL vision: academic information services in the year 2005*, SCONUL, available at www.sconul.ac.uk/vision2005.htm

Spiller, D. (ed.) (2000) *Performance measurement in further education libraries. Proceedings of a seminar held at Loughborough University 9–10 March 1999*, Library and Information Commission Research Report 41, Library and Information Statistics Unit (LISU), Loughborough University.

Thebridge, S., Nankivell, C. and Matthews, G. (1999) *Developing research in public libraries*, Library and Information Commission Research Report 24, Library and Information Commission.

UNESCO in cooperation with the International Federation of Library Associations and Institutions (IFLA) (1994) *UNESCO public library manifesto*, available at www.ifla.org/documents/libraries/policies/unesco.htm

University of Bath Library and Learning Centre (2001) *Library Survey 2001*, available at www.bath.ac.uk/library/about/general/surveys/2001-lib/

University of Birmingham Information Services Distance & Part-Time Gateway *Distance Learning Survey*, available at www.is.bham.ac.uk/dlsurvey/

University of Nottingham Information Services Directorate, Library Services *Special projects and developments*, available at www.nottingham.ac.uk/library/services/about/projects.html

University of Nottingham Information Services Directorate (2001) *User survey report, Update 2: November 2001*, available at www.nottingham.ac.uk/library/news/survey2.html

University of Sunderland Information Services (2001) *Information Services annual performance report 2000/2001*, available at www.library.sunderland.ac.uk:8080/is/zfeedback/annual_performance_report_2000-2001?zfeedback

West, C. on behalf of the SCONUL Advisory Committee on Performance Indicators (2001) *Measuring user satisfaction: a practical guide for academic libraries*, SCONUL Briefing Paper, SCONUL.

What users really want (2002) *Library & Information Update*, **1** (1), 8.

Williams, T. (2000) The Law Society Library: users' views, *Law Librarian*, **31** (2), 108–11.

Winkworth, I. (2001) Innovative United Kingdom approaches to measuring service quality, *Library Trends*, **49** (4), 718–31.

Wynne, P. M. (comp. and ed.) (2000) *Hylife. The Hybrid Library of the Future. Hylife project final report, December 2000. An eLib project funded by the JISC*. (Web version, created by A. Hutton, available at http://hylife.unn.ac.uk

2

Planning and policy making

Sheila Corrall

Introduction

Customer service is a strategic issue for library and information managers. It is at the heart of what we do and why we exist – our purpose and mission – and it is the means by which we move our organizations forward. Customer service must drive library and information policy and planning. This cannot be an afterthought, seen just as a supporting/subsidiary strategy or an operational matter. It is a fundamental enabler of effective library and information services and therefore a primary concern for senior managers and team leaders.

Library and information managers have responded to the customer service imperative in various ways, including interpersonal skills training for frontline staff; formal suggestions schemes for staff and users; customer surveys and focus groups to identify needs; customer charters and service definitions or standards. However, many customer care initiatives have not delivered the benefits expected, because they have concentrated on training for frontline staff and not pursued customer focus at a strategic level. In contrast, significant improvements in customer service have been achieved through Total Quality Management programmes which emphasize both standardized systems and cultural change throughout the organization.

Customer service is thus as much about purpose and culture as it is about service and delivery. The key to building a successful customer service culture is strategic management which brings together corporate values, planning capabilities, organizational responsibilities, strategic thinking and operational decisions at *all levels* and *across all functions* of an organization (Gluck, Kaufman and Walleck, 1980). This chapter discusses the concepts and processes of strategic management and shows how library and information managers can manage customer service strategically by putting customer focus into their planning systems. It uses contemporary examples from university, public and national libraries, but the principles identified and practices illustrated apply to all library and information services.

Concepts and terms

Strategic management is essentially about deciding and refining organizational objectives and working consistently and persistently to translate those objectives into actions and outcomes. It requires an understanding of the business arena, assessment of your resource base and the creation of a shared view of the future. This can be expressed as a series of questions:

- Why do we exist? What business are we in? (mission)
- Where are we now? How did we get here? (situation audit)
- What factors will impact our future? (environmental appraisal)
- What do we want to be? Where do we want to go? (vision and goals)
- How can we get there? What are the implications? (strategic options)
- What needs to be done? Who will do it? When? (action plans)
- How will we track progress? (performance indicators)

Strategy

The word 'strategy' is used at one level to denote overall direction, as shown by Johnson and Scholes (1999): 'Strategy is the *direction* and *scope* of an organisation over the *long term*: which achieves *advantage* for the organisation through its configuration of *resources* within a changing *environment*, to meet the needs of *markets* and to fulfil *stakeholder* expectations.'

However, as well as representing the overall objective for an organization or *what* it aims to do, 'strategy' is also used to describe *how* an organization will achieve its objective or aim. At this level, strategies are defined sets or emerging patterns (not necessarily articulated) of actions and tasks taking the organization towards its goals and targets. Drucker (1988) accordingly defines strategy as 'a company's basic approach to achieving its overall objectives' and describes *strategic planning* as 'the planning for a company's long-term future that includes the setting of major overall objectives, the determination of the basic approaches to be used in pursuing these objectives, and the means to be used in obtaining the necessary resources to be employed'.

The terminology of strategy and planning is confusing as there is no standard usage: people use the same terms in different ways, and the terms can also have different meanings according to context. People often confuse 'policy' and 'strategy' and find it difficult to distinguish between 'mission' and 'vision'. Writers often conceptualize aims, directions, goals, objectives, strategies and targets as a hierarchy of objectives (using 'objective' as a generic term) but may place these terms in different orders; the choice of term at successive levels in the hierarchy is not significant, but it is important to have consistency of usage within an organization to aid communication and avoid confusion.

Policy

The term 'policy' is sometimes used interchangeably with 'strategy' and also has connotations of long-term high-level decisions. However, 'policy' is more often seen as a statement of *principles*, intended to provide a framework for decisions on a continuing basis. This contrasts with the time-limited nature of strategy statements which guide action over a given period. McKee (1989) draws a useful distinction between *strategic plans*, which encapsulate decisions converting the basic goals and objectives of an organization into actions, and *standing plans* (in effect policy statements), which enable an element of 'programmed' decision-making on matters of agreed policy that arise in a recurring pattern or cycle.

Examples of issues that libraries have traditionally dealt with in policy statements include the scope of their collections, the borrowing entitlements of customers and any limits or charges imposed for enquiries. An indicative contemporary example is the University of Sydney Library (2001) *Policy on networked electronic access – preference over print*, which sets out the rationale for the policy and five guidelines for its implementation, as well as outlining the consultation with customers that preceded its development. The policies website of the British Library (2001a) includes statements on specific areas of its activities (for example, on collections and digitisation) as well as statements in support of wider concerns, such as freedom of information and equal opportunities.

This differentiation of ongoing (standing) policies from time-specific strategies is evident in the guidance on annual library plans issued to public library authorities in England by the Department of Culture, Media and Sport (DCMS). This guidance explicitly links delivery *policies* with service *philosophies*, but relates three-year *strategies* to planned *changes* – improving or varying services in line with identified strengths, areas for development, opportunities and threats. The areas expected to be covered by policies include the location of libraries and their opening times; stock selection, deployment and withdrawal; study facilities; reservation services, including any limitations; and the use of library premises by community groups (Great Britain. DCMS, 2001; 2002).

Despite differences in terminology and presentation, literature and practice point to general consensus about what constitutes 'strategic management' – the term generally preferred now to emphasize the iterative nature and comprehensive scope of the policy and strategy process. There are four main aspects, which can be seen as a set of interlocking components:

- *environmental/situation analysis* – which involves gathering information about external factors and internal concerns, using tools such as competitive benchmarking, stakeholder mapping, customer surveys and SWOT (see below)
- *strategic profiling* – which requires discussion of fundamental issues (such as the scope, purpose, functions and principles of your organization) and decisions about high-level objectives, future aspirations and goals
- *strategy development* – which determines the forward path to the destination identified, by evaluating alternative options, considering supporting strategies, specifying performance indicators and developing action plans
- *programme management* – which includes both strategy implementation via projects and operational control of services: taking actions, monitoring progress and balancing service development with 'business as usual'.

Planning processes

Both planning horizons (timespans covered by plans) and planning timelines (time taken for the process) have shortened significantly in recent years. In past decades long-range plans covered five, ten or even 20 years, but today organizations generally opt for no more than five years – often only three, as required by DCMS – and the same pattern is evident in information services. Irrespective of the period covered, strategic plans are usually reviewed annually to inform yearly budgets and operational plans and sometimes 'rolled forward' by dropping the first year and adding another at the end; a more fundamental reappraisal is usually required every three or four years.

In the 1980s, when many libraries first embarked on strategic planning, it was quite common for the process to be conducted over a year or more. Today the period of any formally defined process is more likely to be six months or less as the pace of change is so fast that a longer gestation period makes no sense. This streamlined approach is exemplified by the latest planning model promoted by the US Public Library Association, which recommends a timeline of four to five months, compared with the eight to ten previously suggested (Nelson, 2001).

Models for operationalizing the strategic planning process vary and need to be considered in relation to the size and type of organization and the scope and purpose of the plan. Library and information managers have learned over the years that planning processes (whatever their scale) need to be properly managed and carefully planned. The key activities are as follows:

- defining the project
- assessing your position
- setting strategic objectives
- identifying different strategies
- evaluating the alternatives
- preparing budget estimates
- formulating the plan
- initiating action programmes
- monitoring service developments
- reviewing the strategy.

These tasks can be interpreted at various levels: for example, 'setting strategic objectives' could include a full review of organizational values, purpose and functions and the development of a strategic vision, or it might be confined to determining strategic directions and goals for the next year or two. Apart from the crucial first step of defining the task – 'planning to plan' – the ordering of activities is largely a matter of individual choice, as some people like to start with strategic objectives (including mission and vision) whereas others prefer to begin with situation analysis. The last three tasks move beyond planning to implementation, but often information obtained and insights gained here will prompt revision and rethinking of earlier work, demonstrating that the process needs to be seen as iterative – and interactive – rather than linear.

Interactive planning

Ackoff (1981) introduced the concept of 'interactive planning' more than two decades ago but the principles of his approach are particularly relevant today, namely that planning should be

- *participative* – to build understanding and help implementation
- *continuous* – to monitor the environment and evaluate any changes
- *holistic* – to co-ordinate and integrate multiple units and different levels.

One of the trends evident in both library planning and business strategy is the progressive move to a more participative and inclusive style with more extensive involvement of staff, customers and other stakeholders. Hamel (1996) makes the case for involving 'new voices' in the strategy process, complementing the 'hierarchy of experience' with a 'hierarchy of imagination'. He particularly advocates inclusion of staff with a youthful perspective, those who are new recruits and people on the geographical periphery (distant sites). In the public library context, Nelson (2001) identifies several categories of participants, such as people with specialist skills and knowledge, community representatives – users and non-users – and decision-makers. She also argues that the respective levels of participation for community representatives and library staff should shift during the process, with the community having more influence on the vision, needs and priorities, but less involvement in discussing goals, activities and resources.

Ackoff's (1981) principle of continuity is reflected in growing acknowledgement by managers of 'real-time strategy' as a continuous process rather than a 'one-off' exercise or part of an annual ritual. The compression of the formal strategic planning process into only a few months makes the requirement for library and information managers to engage staff continuously in less formal strategic thinking and environmental scanning even more important. The formal or organized planning process then becomes more concerned with capturing and documenting information and decisions rather than initiating and undertaking scans, benchmarking and surveys as the latter become ongoing activities.

The holistic principle is evident in the need for library and information planning to be co-ordinated and integrated with the objectives and plans of the parent organization and wider community. The DCMS (2001, 2002) guidelines require public libraries to show how their objectives and plans fit their authority's corporate objectives and plans requested by other government departments, such as local and regional cultural strategies, plans for lifelong learning and e-government as well as the corporate ICT plan. Academic libraries should similarly demonstrate linkage between their strategic plans and the strategies and policies of their institutions. Many UK higher education institutions now have not only a strategic/corporate plan, but also strategies for research, enterprise, learning and teaching, recruitment, widening participation, regional collaboration, internationalization, external relations, human resources, estates and information, as well as strategic plans for their different academic, administrative and service units.

The planning context has thus become much more complex and fluid with continuous identification of policy issues by government and others. This requires a more sophisticated and flexible approach to policy and strategy, which is best seen as a *network* or *web* of strategies, rather than the traditional conception as a hierarchy of plans. Fortunately, this coincides with the establishment of the World Wide Web as a universal communication medium which provides the ability – literally and technically – to make links between related documents and demonstrate relationships between different activities.

Practical examples

Library and information services use a variety of planning models and methods but some common themes are evident from their websites and documents, such as the use of steering committees, management retreats, facilitated workshops, focus groups, customer surveys and public consultation. New Mexico State University Library (1998) designed a planning process around five special committees responsible for environmental scanning, values scan and mission formulation, strategic business modelling, performance audit and gap analysis, and contingency planning and implementation. The University of Memphis Libraries (1999) worked through a strategic plan team and five goal teams, with objective teams to oversee implementation. Waterford Public Library (2001) used a planning consultant to lead its research phase and then brought in trustees and managers for decision-making about the future.

Several textbooks and many case studies describe and detail the pitfalls of planning exercises. Common mistakes include: allowing some managers to opt out; assigning responsibilities to committees rather than individuals; confusing strategic planning with operational planning; constructing over-elaborate systems and procedures; generating long lists of unprioritized initiatives; ignoring resource implications and funding issues; and not following through from strategy to action. Less well documented, but obviously a critical success factor for service organizations, is the incorporation of customer focus in every step of the process. This can be achieved either directly, by involving customers in person, or indirectly, by involving frontline staff, who are close to customers and understand their wants and needs. Experience suggests that a mix of these methods is likely to produce the best results.

Environmental appraisal

Information about your current situation and likely future developments can be analysed and synthesized using various strategy tools.

Stakeholder mapping

A 'stakeholder' can be seen as any individual or group with an involvement or interest in an organization in the past, present or future. The stakeholders of a library or information service obviously include its customers, subdivided into various categories, but also include service staff, top management, funding authorities, other regulators, suppliers, partners, competitors and the local community. A *stakeholder analysis* can be used to identify people who could or should be informed about or involved in the planning process. For example, Merton Library & Heritage

Service consulted staff, managers, users, non-users and suppliers as 'key stake-holders' in the development of its strategy (Pateman, 2002).

There are several different ways of categorizing individuals and groups, for example by their perceived importance to or influence on the service. A common method of representing this diagrammatically is to draw a *stakeholder map* with the service at the centre of the page and to position stakeholders in boxes or circles whose closeness or distance from the service reflects their perceived influence. Conducting this type of exercise with various groups of service staff often exposes different views of stakeholders and their importance and can thus be used to stimulate debate on the priority to be given to these groups and their needs.

Customer surveys

Regular surveys of actual and potential customers are now standard practice for most library and information services and the findings of such exercises obviously should inform strategy and policy development. Thus the DCMS (2002) guidelines formally require public libraries to include in their annual plans the outcome of user surveys, public consultation exercises and market research carried out in the last two years, as well as a review of comments and suggestions received in the previous year. Similarly, the strategic planning team at the University of Arizona Library (n.d.) included the following questions about customers and the environment to focus initial input from library teams to its current situation analysis:

1   If you have conducted customer surveys or collected other customer data over the last 12 months, either formally or informally, summarize the key findings.
2   Based on the feedback, what are you doing to meet customers' needs (e.g. projects created, process improvement undertaken)?
3   What products and services have been requested that you have not been able to provide (e.g. access to *all* full-text journals online)?
4   What would need to change to be able to provide these products or services?
5   Looking to the environment beyond the library, list forces that will change the way we serve our customers (e.g. electronic publishing, copyright laws).

However, as well as drawing on the results of past surveys, it is desirable to consult customers (and other stakeholders) as an explicit part of any strategic planning process. This enables managers to confirm and update previous findings, to focus questions on emerging strategic issues and to raise awareness of planning activities among stakeholders. DCMS does not require local authorities to consult the public on the preparation of their library plans, but the guidelines for 2002 (in contrast to 2001) state that 'this would be welcomed'.

Various methods can be used to identify the perceptions and preferences of individuals and groups. Methods commonly used for library planning include general surveys, open forums, focus groups and personal interviews. For example, Tacoma Public Library (n.d.) used small group discussions and a random sample telephone survey; Waterford Public Library (2001) gathered opinions from about 1000 people through a user survey, focus groups (with town department heads, school teachers, community organizations and library users) and personal interviews with community leaders (business people, philanthropists and government officials) in addition to feeding in results of a previous user survey conducted via touch-screen computers. Redwood City Public Library (1998) conducted focus group discussions with young people, civic leaders and multicultural representatives, using the following questions:

1   What words come to mind when you hear the phrase 'public library'?
2   If you were talking to a person from another city, what would you tell him/her about Redwood City Libraries?
3   Many people see the library as a support for formal learning. How do you see it?
4   What do you see as the 2 or 3 weaknesses or shortcomings of the library?
5   Why do you think people don't use the library?
6   What do you see as the 2 or 3 key opportunities which the library could take advantage of in the future?

Redwood also included summaries of the focus group discussions in the public version of its strategic plan, providing visible evidence of the importance and influence of community input to the strategic planning process.

Another method of surveying opinion is to produce a *consultation paper* setting out ideas about the future of the service and inviting responses on specific points. For example, the National Library of Wales (1999a) published a paper, *Choosing the future*, which was launched at five briefing meetings around the country, distributed to 1700 organizations and individuals, and mounted on its website. The paper invited general comments and responses to six questions:

1   Are there ways in which you think we should perform the core functions differently or better? (The functions were collecting, preserving, giving access and information, publicizing and interpreting, and professional collaboration.)
2   Do you agree that the Library should seek to develop in the five new directions described? (The directions were encouraging more use of the building, a bet-

ter service to higher education, a service to all learners, bringing the Library
to the world, digitization, and building partnerships with others.)

3 If so, which do you think are the most important? Have you any particular
suggestions about the way they should be developed?

4 Are there other 'new directions' you think the Library should take?

5 Are you interested in discussing the opportunity of a partnership with the
Library on any issue? If so, what might you be looking for from such a partnership?

6 Have you any views on how the Library should seek the substantial resources
needed to implement new initiatives?

The Library then published a summary of the responses, which then informed
the development of a new strategy, which was presented in the form of a corporate plan (National Library of Wales, 1999b).

SWOT analysis

The tool often used to gather together information about external forces and internal capabilities is SWOT analysis, which involves capturing the Strengths and
Weaknesses of an organization or service and the Opportunities and Threats represented by environmental trends. Although widely used by library and information
managers, SWOTs are often conducted with insufficient thought and focus,
resulting in long unstructured lists, unclear and ambiguous wording, no prioritization or weighting of factors and apparently conflicting statements (e.g. the
same point listed as a strength and a weakness).

Contradictory statements can be dealt with by asking what particular aspects
of the attributes identified are a strength or weakness. Focus can be achieved by
asking those involved to think about particular areas; for example, the DCMS
(2002) guidelines specify the following:

Analyse the strengths, areas for development, opportunities and threats for your
library service in a tabular form against *at least the following key areas*:

- stock provision and deployment, including the quality of the stock
- reader and audience development
- meeting the public library standards
- social inclusion
- lifelong learners
- customer response
- resource issues.

Significantly, the areas specified by DCMS vary slightly from year to year. More to the point, in carrying out SWOT analysis, it is essential to ask whether *customers* see the attributes identified as strengths and weaknesses in the same way that staff do. Managers thus need to ensure that a customer perspective is injected into every step in the planning process by asking for evidence of customer behaviour and opinions in relation to statements made by staff. This perspective can be provided either indirectly (by drawing on user surveys, etc.) or directly, by involving customer representatives in the analysis (e.g. via focus groups).

Strategic profile

Decisions about your long-term objectives, desired future situation and medium-term goals should be captured in a series of cohesive statements.

Information missions

Most library and information services include a formal statement of their fundamental purpose or mission in their strategy documents. The length and format of such statements varies from a few lines to several paragraphs or a full page. A common model is to begin with a sentence or paragraph summarizing the overall role and then supplement this with a set of bullet points or sentences, highlighting key functions or activities.

While the purpose of libraries has not changed fundamentally, the shifts of emphasis from holdings to access, from print to electronic and from mediation to self-service have led to changes in the phrasing of mission statements to reflect more accurately the customer focus and networked service of the contemporary environment. Thus the University of Queensland Library (2001) purports to 'link people with information' and the Mission of the University of Washington Libraries (2001) refers to 'connecting people with knowledge'. Maintaining currency in the language used is one of the prime motives for reviewing mission statements periodically; another is the desire to differentiate a service from its peers, by highlighting distinctive aspects, illustrated by the Birkbeck College Library (2001) aim to 'develop and maintain services which especially suit the needs of students who are in employment'.

The motivational dimension of a mission statement is often overlooked: this is not just an intellectual exercise, it is an important communication task. If customer service is your *raison d'être*, this must be reflected in the content, style and tone of your statement. The following examples illustrate this point.

The Redwood City Public Library is the learning center of our community and the place people turn to for the discovery of ideas, the joy of reading and the power of information. Community needs drive our services and we take a personal interest in ensuring that they are delivered in a welcoming, convenient and responsive manner.

> (Redwood City Public Library)

The University of Arizona Library is dedicated to meeting the diverse information, curricular and research needs of students, faculty, staff and other customers.

> (University of Arizona Library)

The Library's aim is to deliver information in the form, at the place and at the time of most benefit to the user, within the requirements of the University. . . . To fulfil this mission it is important that the Library gives absolute priority to the needs of its user community.

> (Edinburgh University Library, 2000)

Syracuse University Library (2000) distinguishes its *purpose* statement as a timeless expression of its 'reason for being' from its *mission*, which is defined as 'a bold, audacious statement . . . connecting [our] values and purpose with concrete, time-specific goals and initiatives'. On that basis, cultural change centred on the user is an essential plank of its mission:

> By 2005, we will transform the Library into the University's primary gateway for scholarly information. To accomplish this mission we must:
>
> • develop and sustain a highly user-centered culture
> • secure staff, facilities, technology, and funding that support and promote this new culture
> • deliver information literacy programs that enable effective use of our services, collections, and resources.

Service values

The production of formal statements of the beliefs or principles that underpin organizational or professional philosophies has become more common recently and this is reflected in the prominence now given to values in many library strategic plans. Values statements can be seen as a part of the framework that guides discretionary decision-making along with policy, vision and direction statements. Statements of service values can be particularly useful at times of rapid change in reassuring people that underlying values remain constant even though the service around them is changing radically. Such statements can also be used to support cultural change by asserting new values seen as critical to success in the future, such as customer service or user focus.

Values statements in library plans typically take the form of five to seven words or phrases as 'headlines' which are then elaborated in a longer phrase or sentence. Libraries have traditionally concentrated on values associated with our professional mission, such as the preservation of our cultural heritage, service to the community, promotion of information literacy and support for intellectual freedom, but they have often also incorporated into their statements references to more general humanistic values, such as democracy, diversity, equity, integrity, literacy and privacy. Contemporary examples still reflect these important concerns but tend to give more prominence to modes of working and styles of delivery felt necessary for success in the changing environment around us, notably collaboration and partnership, flexibility and responsiveness, initiative and innovation.

Redwood City Public Library (1998) echoes the sentiments of its mission statement in the first element of its statement of core values – 'The Library is driven by community needs' – and reinforces its commitment to customer service in two more of the ten points. The values of the Waterford Public Library (2001) extend over a whole page and cover collaboration with community groups and sensitivity to community values as well as an explicit commitment to customer service: 'Quality customer service is our hallmark. We value courtesy, helpful and friendly service, patience, and the display of interest and enthusiasm for all patrons' needs. We value our role as information providers, helping patrons discern the quality and accuracy of information.'

The University of Queensland Library (2001) lists eight shared values – commitment to excellence, teamwork and personal responsibility, flexibility and innovation, open communication, staff development, accountability, equity and integrity – and specifically mentions customers in five of the eight points. The University of Arizona Library (n.d.) expresses its values in the form of *Principles* and places *Customer Focus* as the first of five concepts that are elaborated in a series of statements:

I. CUSTOMER FOCUS

We actively seek to identify, meet, and exceed customer wants and needs.

We welcome, guide, and support customers, both internal and external, with attention and respect.

We create and sustain partnerships.

We provide access to information in its most useful form.

In contrast to their American and Australian counterparts, few British libraries include values statements in their strategy documents.

Strategic visioning

Visioning is now a much more frequent activity in all types of organizations, as an integral part of strategic planning and management, particularly associated with rapid and radical organizational change. Visioning exercises and vision statements are used to capture insights and ideas about the future and to communicate to stakeholders the scope and scale of the transformation envisaged. The content and length of statements vary, but most commentators agree that visions need to be both aspirational and inspirational, which means that style and tone are critical to their success. Managers can add power and immediacy by using striking imagery and writing in the present tense.

Library vision statements are most often around one to two pages long, but published examples range from a few paragraphs to several pages. A few libraries have chosen to present their visions much more succinctly in a short paragraph or even just a single sentence. Short statements run the risk of blandness and require careful drafting to ensure that they have real meaning and sufficient focus to distinguish the service from its peers.

The Waterford Public Library (2001) Vision for the Future runs to almost three pages and also sets out a list of 20 *planning assumptions* which underpin the vision and other aspects of the strategic plan. The vision restates and elaborates the commitment to quality customer service given in the values statement, as shown by the following extracts:

> Serving the community involves both responsiveness and leadership: the Library must not only respond to patron demand but also anticipate patron needs for new materials, resources, and services. It regularly monitors patron satisfaction and analyses community needs through data provided by the computer system, surveys, and conversations with focus groups.
>
> Our Library of the future means a building that is comfortable, with amenities that welcome patrons of all ages. This could include seating that invites relaxation, a café, quiet areas, group work areas, a teen lounge, and more. It requires materials, services, programs, policies, and dedicated, dynamic staff members. It means more personalized customer services that consider individual needs.

The British Library (2001b) offers a more succinct vision which effectively brings together its main strategies for collections and access with its three 'enabling strategies' of *user focus*, partnership working and web delivery – 'Making accessible the world's intellectual, scientific and cultural heritage. The collections of the British Library and other great collections will be accessible on everyone's virtual bookshelf – at work, at school, at college, at home.'

This top-level vision statement is elaborated by five short paragraphs explaining in more detail what is envisaged and how these strategies will work together, for example:

> We will work closely with our major users and other stakeholders to support their objectives and develop services in line with their changing needs. We will reach out to schools and lifelong learners in collaboration with public libraries and education agencies who share this commitment. We want the British Library to make a difference to the broadest possible range of people and for them to be able to engage with us wherever they happen to be and whenever they choose.

The University of Arizona Library (n.d.) Vision 2010 is similarly presented in six paragraphs but is approximately twice the length, running to almost a full page. The following extract reinforces the messages about *customer focus* and partnership working already conveyed:

> Students are at the center of our work. We are full partners with faculty collaborating in the development of courses that provide learning experiences matching students' needs. We create an environment of exchange among students, scholars, researchers and ourselves. We help students graduate as self-sufficient, free-thinking, and productive members of society who continue to learn and grow.

The Syracuse University Library (2000) Vision is much shorter, a single sentence providing 'a snapshot of the Library transformed', but it places similar emphasis on meeting user needs: 'Our vision of Syracuse University Library – its people, services, collections, and facilities – is of a nationally significant research library that understands the needs of its users and has actively developed the resources and methods to meet those needs now and in the future.'

Some organizations have developed more personalized 'mini-visions' as illustrative material for plans or reports, to show how the future might look from different stakeholder/customer perspectives. For example, the Follett report on UK academic libraries offered three 'sketches' to illustrate some of the possibilities opened up by the technology of the 'virtual library', written from the perspectives of an undergraduate, an academic and a 'virtual librarian' (HEFCE, 1993). Similarly, Rutgers University Libraries (1999) included five 'scenarios of the future' in their plan proposing a digital library initiative (DLI). Under the headings 'Undergraduate teaching and learning' and 'Advanced research', these scenarios explained how a professor, an undergraduate, a graduate student and researchers might find and locate information resources if the DLI became a reality. Providing customers with personalized visions of this type is an effective and powerful way of engaging individuals and demonstrating concern for their needs.

Goal statements

Strategic goals or objectives are statements that indicate the movement or improvement needed to achieve the desired future state (presented in the vision). Effective goals are expressed in action-oriented terms that are capable of conversion into specific targets enabling managers to plan tasks and measure performance. Libraries often group their goals/objectives and targets under broad headings, variously described as 'strategic directions', 'strategic priorities', 'strategic thrusts', 'key action areas', 'key performance areas', 'key result areas', etc.

The Kitchener Public Library (2000) has put customer service as the first of six strategic directions in its strategic plan and set out six commitments under this heading:

CUSTOMER SERVICE
The Kitchener Public Library will improve access and excel in customer service. We will:

- consult with the community to understand and keep pace with your changing needs
- look for new ways to deliver traditional, valued services
- broaden electronic access and offer new services using technology
- provide customized information and self-service options to meet your priorities
- help you develop the skills that are critical to find and evaluate information in an increasingly technological world
- ensure that everyone has equitable access, regardless of financial situation.

The British Library (2001b) gives similar prominence to its enabling strategy of *user focus* by setting out the rationale, goal and two-pronged approach immediately after its vision and mission statements:

Enabling strategy: user focus
The Library provides a wide range of services to a great variety of user groups. We are now working with our users to establish their changing patterns of need. Our goal is to provide services that are relevant, easy to use and fulfil expectations. We will integrate related services and offer seamless access in ways which are appropriate to our different user groups.

Strategy for user focus
- To interact effectively with our users to maximise the fitness for purpose and value of what the Library provides
- To extend our user base by enhancing the relevance and accessibility of services.

Syracuse University Library (2000) sets out both a rationale and success indicators for its goal of a *user-centred* culture:

Goal: Develop a highly user-centered culture that guides the actions of Library staff and informs all Library policies, procedures, and decisions.

Rationale: To be a viable and responsive service organization, we must fully understand the needs of our users and deliver consistently excellent service in response.

Success indicators:
- user surveys/feedback tell us that we are consistently meeting their needs, providing excellent service, etc.
- reconfigured public service points focused on core user activities
- staffing schedule consistent with users' needs
- initiate innovative reference service delivery, e.g., Netmeeting, webcams, tele-reference, instant messenger, chat software
- self-service options (e.g., recall, hold, interlibrary loan (ILL), copy requests, checkout, email notification)
- improved output options: e-books, ILL/document delivery, faxing, email, photocopying, printing; delivery and return of materials (e.g., Paging/courier service)
- reduction in users' complaints about the Bird Library entrance and other services.

Continued development of a *user-centred culture* is the first goal of the New Mexico State University Library (1998), reflecting its top strategic thrust: 'User focus drives decisions'. This goal is followed by a list of seven action points and nine critical success indicators and then further supported by a separate paragraph on culture:

In order to accomplish our goals, all library personnel need a common understanding that the user is the reason we exist and that service to the user is the central focus of what we do. The ideas expressed in the mission and values statements must be translated into shared understandings, beliefs and behaviors in our organization. In turn, the Library recognizes contributions at all levels and provides encouragement and respect for creative dissent. A cooperative, risk-taking, collaborative, empowered staff will work together to make decisions that provide the most efficient and effective service to our users.

Identifying customer service, user focus or an equivalent issue as a key strategic direction or priority sends a strong message to both customers and staff about expected behaviours and attitudes. Explicit statements of this type are most often made in the context of a planned programme of major organizational and cultural change. However, such statements can – and arguably should – be used to strengthen or reinforce customer-service culture, even where already embedded. There are several arguments for doing this: first, you simply cannot over-emphasize the importance of customer service; secondly, it is easy for staff to become complacent and stop striving for improvement; and thirdly, the message needs to be effectively conveyed to new staff and new customers.

Strategy development

Goals specify the key directions for an organization or service over the planning period but they cannot be finally confirmed until strategies have been properly developed to the point where resource implications and organizational dependencies can be assessed.

The 'goal-translation process' – whereby each top-level 'goal', 'objective' or 'strategy' is converted from a general statement of what you want to achieve to a more specific description of how it will be done – is the key to successful strategy implementation. Thus, for each of its 17 goals, Syracuse University Library (2000) lists specific initiatives and details of the project managers, action team leaders and start dates.

Supporting strategies

The process of strategy development needs to extend beyond the selection of core/primary strategies associated with high-level goals, as these strategies may have policy and resource implications that necessitate changes to existing practice and funding. They may also have wider implications for areas such as service promotion and publicity, staff development and training, the ICT infrastructure and organizational structures.

A useful model for thinking about organizations and strategy development is the '7-S' framework developed at the McKinsey consulting firm and popularized by ex-McKinsey consultants, such as Peters and Waterman (1982) and Pascale (1990). This framework identifies seven inter-related factors that determine the effectiveness of an organization and its ability to change – Strategy, Structure, Systems, Style, Staff, Skills and Shared values. It makes the point that it is hard to make progress in any one of these critical areas without considering the others. For example, the commitments of Kitchener Public Library (2000) to broaden electronic access and help customers develop skills require *supporting strategies* for ICT systems and staff skills, which are picked up under two other themes – technology and organizational effectiveness. The British Library (2001b) lists seven 'key support activities' required to progress its strategy for user focus, for example

- Increase our investment in research into the needs of users and potential users
- Develop an integrated approach to service provision so that users can easily access the range of services which are of value to them
- Develop and promote the British Library brand in order to improve public understanding of what we provide.

Cultural change, such as the shift from a functional/product-based service to a mission/customer-led service, is frequently carried through with corresponding structural adjustments as giving people new roles, responsibilities and relationships often forces new behaviours and fosters different attitudes. Re-structuring a library into client-oriented teams as the main organizational unit sends a clear message to both staff and users about the importance of customer focus. Thus many university libraries have replaced 'subject librarians' with 'liaison librarians' supporting designated academic units, signalling a more outward-looking and proactive style with the focus on people rather than subjects. At Merton Library & Heritage Service, development of a new strategy required structural change to support the strategic objectives and espoused new culture: the split between professional staff and so-called customer service/non-professional staff was 'ditched' and three new posts of library and service managers were created, each with responsibility for one of the three new objectives – community development, economic regeneration and lifelong learning (Pateman, 2002).

Performance indicators

Performance measurement is an essential part of strategic management with a potential role at every point in the planning cycle, from the gathering of baseline data about your current situation, competitive position and customer perceptions, through the setting of performance targets in strategy development, to the monitoring and evaluation of progress in programme management. Traditional approaches to performance measurement in library and information services have tended to concentrate on operational and financial data, related to resource utilization (e.g. money and staff used to purchase and process materials) and service transactions (e.g. interactions between staff, materials and users) rather than strategic issues such as quality of service and outcomes for customers.

In the last decade there has been a conceptual breakthrough in performance measurement with the development by Kaplan and Norton (1992) of the balanced scorecard framework. As the label indicates, this framework aims to provide a *balanced* presentation of measures, offering several perspectives of organizational performance in a concise but comprehensive scorecard. An effective scorecard should enable instant recognition of an organization's strategic objectives. Kaplan and Norton recommend a limit of 16 to 20 'key measures' from four perspectives, balancing the traditional financial/funding and operational/process concerns with additional customer/service and innovation/learning measures. In this model, managers set goals and measures under these headings, reflecting the targets of their forward strategies. This ensures that customer service gets top management attention alongside financial performance. The goals (and measures) might include improvements in quality (satisfaction ratings), speed (turnaround times), access (opening hours) and support (training sessions).

Service budgets

The relationship between strategic planning and resource allocation is often problematic. Strategic objectives should inform budget allocations, which should in turn inform the phasing and refinement of strategic developments and service goals in an iterative process. However, in some organizations, planning and budgeting are not properly connected, with the result that planning and strategy-making are constrained by resource allocation decisions taken without reference to strategic priorities. Irrespective of organizational circumstances, it is essential for library and information managers to think strategically and imaginatively when preparing service plans and to consider the funding implications and options for achieving their strategic objectives. At a minimum, plans should distinguish between goals that can be met within existing resources and those that require additional funds. Preferably, they should include estimates of the amount of additional resource needed and indicate whether any internal reallocation or external funding might be possible.

The 'line-item' method of budgeting, which lists elements of expenditure in basic categories (such as salaries, materials, equipment, etc.), is not a very effective approach as this focus on inputs makes it difficult to relate expenditure to services or objectives. In contrast, *programme budgeting* organizes line-item budgets around service areas (typically reflecting management structures) and has the potential to support fuller understanding of the level of investment in different services. Service managers therefore need to consider whether their budgeting and accounting methods should be modified to reflect changes to organizational structures and culture, for example to provide information on the relative costs of serving different customer groups.

Strategy documents

Some people argue that it is not worth bothering with formal plans because they become out of date almost as soon as they are written. This assumes that strategy documents are static entities, but a sensible process makes provision for refining and updating both the plans of an organization and the assumptions on which they are based. Many libraries are formally required to submit some form of plan as part of an organizational planning cycle, but in any case there are sound reasons for documenting plans – in print or electronically.

1 The process of writing and editing forces people to think through their goals and objectives and serves as a double check on overall consistency, organizational capacity and other critical issues.
2 Written plans provide a visual medium of communication with both internal and external audiences and make it easier to convey a consistent message to staff, customers and other stakeholders in different places at different times.
3 A formal record of intended activities serves as a mechanism for control, enabling regular and ad hoc monitoring of whether specified actions have been carried out and underlying assumptions have proved correct.

The level of detail included will be influenced by formal requirements, personal preferences and specific decisions on whether to develop a hierarchy or family of plans presenting successively more detailed elaborations of strategies, actions and timetables. The plan needs to state what you intend to do and why, how you will do it and when, with enough information on background and resources to convince readers. It is essential to define the scope of the plan, particularly the period covered and the services included (for example, library services only, library and ICT services) and it is desirable to provide a contents list and an executive summary if the document runs to more than five pages.

Practical examples

Contemporary library planning statements vary significantly in length, content and format, with examples found of five, ten, 20 and 30 pages. Documents prepared in accordance with the DCMS guidelines tend to be around 100 pages, but the general trend is towards more concise documents, covering shorter timespans, with a sharper focus on intended results. Lengthy descriptions of service characteristics have been replaced with briefer summaries of strategic issues, proposed approaches and performance indicators. Vision statements have become more prominent, often forming the main narrative section of the plan and sometimes comprising a set of alternative scenarios representing different planning assumptions or particular customer perspectives. Many elements previously included (such as SWOT analyses and statistical data) are now relegated to appendices or excluded altogether.

The content of the final documentation usually has three elements:

- an introductory section, which sets the context of the document, covering both the external environment and internal issues
- the overall strategy, which states the ambitions of the service, expressed in its vision, mission, values and goals
- the forward plan, which lays out the intentions for the period, elaborated as strategies and actions with responsibilities and timescales.

The latter part may form a separate document and additional information may be included as appendices (for example, the remit and/or membership of the planning team, the results of customer surveys, risk analyses and contingency plans). The introduction may be prefaced by a foreword (from the library director or committee chair) and include acknowledgements of staff and community contributions.

Many libraries now make their plans available via their websites, often offering several formats (typically HTML and PDF or Word). The style of presentation is generally quite simple, but some libraries have been more creative in their use of layout and design: for example, the Kitchener Public Library (2000) plan is professionally designed, with sidebars and photographs on many pages; Houston Public Library (2001) uses sidebars to provide quotes from stakeholders, highlight facts and figures and reinforce key points; and Macquarie University Library (1999) makes creative use of blocks and columns of text in double-page spreads to convey 'where we want to be', 'desired outcomes' and 'how we will do it' in relation to teaching partnerships, research partnerships and community outreach.

More significantly, there is a trend towards using websites to make the planning process more transparent and participative. The Strategic Long Range Planning Team home page of the University of Arizona Library (n.d.) provides links to a wealth of documentation, such as the 'team charge' and other descriptions of the planning process, in addition to end-products from that process (including a 17-page current situation analysis). The University Libraries at Virginia Tech have a web page devoted to their strategic plan steps, which lists their steering committee and co-ordinators and then describes the process, with links to working papers, workshop outputs and draft plans (Virginia Polytechnic Institute, 2002). The website for the Syracuse University Library (2000) strategic plans has links to progress reports, invites questions about the plan and allows library staff to express their interest, suggest an initiative or submit a report. The introductory part of the plan provides an explanation of the process and a glossary of planning terminology; definitions of terms (such as 'mission statement' and 'planning themes') are then repeated at the relevant points in the text.

National and public libraries are also explaining their planning processes and inviting comments from customers via their websites: the British Library (2001b, 2001c) launched an online consultation survey when it published its *New strategic directions* and then published a report on the responses; Houston Public Library (n.d.) has a web form for comments on its plan, which promises a personal response to those who request it. The annual library plans provided for DCMS are not very customer-friendly documents, but some authorities, such as West Berkshire Council (2002) and Westminster City Council (n.d.), have added introductory overviews and/or produced special summaries to aid communication.

A significant weakness in current practice is that plans are often not very customer-friendly. Electronic communication offers opportunities to repackage material in imaginative and innovative ways for different audiences, but such facilities are not yet being widely exploited. Many stakeholder groups do not want or need the same amount of detail as funding bodies and formal committees and so managers should be giving more thought to reworking their plans for communication with service customers, special interest groups, community leaders, etc. In addition to the complete versions of their plans, strategy websites could include summaries, extracts and key points for particular groups, as well as background papers and PowerPoint slides from presentations to open meetings.

Conclusion

A successful customer-service culture is not something that can be designed and built in the way that you can plan and construct a new building or a computer system, but the tools and techniques of strategic management can be used to facilitate cultural change or to strengthen an established culture. Library and information managers need to ensure that their policies and strategies (as stated and enacted) reflect a culture of real customer service. The key to achieving this is to build customer perspectives into your planning processes, through a combination of direct personal engagement and indirect 'proxy' involvement via frontline staff, and to make your service responsive to changing needs by making strategic planning a continuous process that is also integrated with the wider internal and external policy context.

Customers are more likely to participate if they can see evidence of your commitment to listen to their views and act on their suggestions. Customer focus can be demonstrated in formal statements of your mission, values, vision and goals, but must also be reflected in performance measures, service budgets, organizational structures and management behaviour. Communication style is a critical issue: managers need to shift from the one-size-fits-all mindset and think carefully about their intended audiences; concise customized messages in clear everyday language will support and promote a customer-service strategy and culture.

References

Ackoff, R. L. (1981) *Creating the corporate future: plan or be planned for*, John Wiley.

Birkbeck College Library (2001) *Mission statement and strategic plan 2001–2004*, available at www.bbk.ac.uk/lib/STRATPLN.PDF.

British Library (2001a) *British Library policy statements*, available at www.bl.uk/about/policies.html.

British Library (2001b) *New strategic directions, 2001*, available at www.bl.uk/about/strategic/planfor.html.

British Library (2001c) *Report on the responses to the New Strategic Directions survey*, available at www.bl.uk/about/strategic/consultation.html.

Drucker, P. F. (1988) *Management*, rev. edn, Butterworth-Heinemann.

Edinburgh University Library (2000) *Library strategy 1999–2002*, available at www.lib.ed.ac.uk/lib/about/policy/strategy.shtml.

Gluck, F. W., Kaufman, S. P. and Walleck, A. S. (1980) Strategic management for competitive advantage, *Harvard Business Review*, **58** (5), 154–61.

Great Britain. Department for Culture, Media and Sport (2001) *Annual library plans: guidelines for the preparation of plans in 2001*, DCMS, available at www.libplans.ws/.

Great Britain. Department for Culture, Media and Sport (2002) *Annual library plans: guidelines for the preparation of plans in 2002*, DCMS, available at www.libplans.ws/.

Hamel, G. (1996) Strategy as revolution, *Harvard Business Review*, **74** (4), 69–82.

HEFCE (1993) *Joint Funding Councils' Libraries Review Group: A report for the Higher Education Funding Council for England, Scottish Higher Education Funding Council, Higher Education Funding Council for Wales and Department of Education for Northern Ireland, Higher Education Funding Council* (the Follett report), available at www.ukoln.ac.uk/services/papers/follett/report/.

Houston Public Library (2001) *Strategic master plan: standards for excellence*, available at www.hpl.lib.tx.us/hpl/press/smp_approved.html.

Houston Public Library (n.d.) *Comments regarding Library 2010: a strategic master plan*, available at www.hpl.lib.tx.us/cgi-bin/comments/smp_comments.

Johnson, G. and Scholes, K. (1999) *Exploring corporate strategy*, 5th edn, Prentice Hall.

Kaplan, R. S. and Norton, D. P. (1992) The balanced scorecard – measures that drive performance, *Harvard Business Review*, **70** (1), 71–9.

Kitchener Public Library (2000) *Strategic plan 2000–2002: connecting tradition with technology*, available at www.kpl.org/.

McKee, B. (1989) *Planning library service*, Clive Bingley.

Macquarie University Library (1999) *Strategic plan 1999*, available at www.lib.mq.edu.au/resources/staffpublications/strategic/index.html.

National Library of Wales (1999a) *Choosing the future*, available at www.llgc.org.uk/adrodd/adrodd_s_papymg.pdf.

National Library of Wales (1999b) *Choosing the future: a summary of responses*, available at www.llgc.org.uk/adrodd/adrodd_s_dewis.pdf

Nelson, S. (2001) *The new planning for results: a streamlined approach*, American Library Association.

New Mexico State University Library (1998) *Strategic plan 1997–2002*, available at http://lib.nmsu.edu/aboutlib/straplan.html.

Pascale, R. (1990) *Managing on the edge*, Penguin (see also *Famous models: 7S framework*, available at http://www.chimaeraconsulting.com/7s_model.htm).

Pateman, J. (2002) Cultural revolution, *Library & Information Update*, **1** (1), 42–3.

Peters, T. and Waterman, R. H. (1982) *In search of excellence*, Harper & Row.

Redwood City Public Library (1998) *1998–2001 strategic plan*, available at www.redwoodcity.org/library/reference/strategic.html.

Rutgers University Libraries (1999) *A bridge to the future: the Rutgers digital library initiative*, available at www.libraries.rutgers.edu/rul/about/long_range_plan.shtml.

Syracuse University Library (2000) *Targets for transformation: a strategic plan for the Syracuse University Library 2000–2005*, available at http://libwww.syr.edu/information/strategicplan/index.html.

Tacoma Public Library (n.d.) *About the Tacoma Public Library's strategic plan*, available at www.tpl.lib.wa.us/v2/ABOUT/Plan.htm.

University of Arizona Library (n.d.) Strategic Long Range Planning Team home page, available at http://dizzy.library.Arizona.edu/library/teams/slrp/frameref.html.

University of Memphis Libraries (1999) *Strategic plan 1998–2003*, available at www.lib.memphis.edu/stratgic.htm.

University of Queensland Library (2001) *Profile and operational plan 2001–2004*, available at www.library.uq.edu.au/about/.

University of Sydney Library (2001) *Policy on networked access – preference over print*, available at www.library.usyd.edu.au/about/policies/networked.html.

University of Washington University Libraries (2001) *2001 strategic plan*, available at www.lib.washington.edu/about/StrategicPlan2001.html.

Virginia Polytechnic Institute and State University (2002) *Library strategic plan steps 2000-2001*, available at www.lib.vt.edu/info/stratplan/overview.html.

Waterford Public Library (2001) *Strategic plan, summer 2001–June 2006*, available at www.waterfordpubliclibary.org/contents.html.

West Berkshire Council (2002) *Libraries – annual library plan*, available at www.west-berks.gov.uk/westberkshire/Leisure.nsf/pages/AnnualLi141656.html.

Westminster City Council (n.d.) *Annual library plan*, available at www.Westminster.gov.uk/libraries/about/alp.cfm.

3
Leadership and management

Robert Gent and Grace Kempster

Introduction

In this chapter, we will explore the most talked-about aspect of building a customer service culture: the leadership. There is no doubt that all activity towards
change and transformation of services always refers to the importance of good
and strong leadership. It is the most blamed and the most pivotal aspect of the
organization. However, as we will show in the following sections, this is not a
matter that is the preserve of the 'formal' leaders of the customer-centred service – it is a matter for everyone in the organization who is concerned with the
leadership aspects of their role.

We will explore the changing nature – some say fashions – of leadership
styles and explore pragmatically and theoretically the process of creating a culture for modern leadership. We will look at the characteristics of a leader and
the demands on his or her creativity, skill and judgement, and explore how
the development of leadership throughout the organization is the only way
to succeed.

In exploring accountability for leadership in the public service context we will
look at the ways in which leaders can use techniques and tools to demonstrate
progress and have this externally validated in the wider context.

We finally look at the way in which leadership is a role to be played as
much with our customers as with other internal stakeholders and how the
wider standing of the library leader in the community context can and should
be developed and explored.

In general terms the state of library leadership in the UK is considered to
be a mixed one. In the workplace environment TFPL (2001) have observed the
characteristics of Chief Knowledge Officers and interestingly have highlight-

ed the need for vision to drive the agenda for knowledge management development as a key emphasis at a time of recession. In contrast, the study by Bob Usherwood on recruitment and retention (2002) points to a crisis of leadership in the public sector, arguably the result of years of decline in investment in these services. This is a debatable point as the holding of master classes in leadership by the Society of Chief Librarians in 2001 points to a more optimistic picture, given that they are over-subscribed with 'wannabe' leaders in this sector. It is clear that some success is evident – the first appointment of a librarian to the role of Chief Executive of the British Library heralds an acknowledgement of leadership skills among library and information professionals. On an international dimension, the Bertelsmann Foundation (www.stiftung.bertelsmann.de/ english/netz/publib/) brings together entrepreneurial leaders from public library services around the world to forge new and innovative futures and the UK has had no difficulty in fielding its share of leading leaders.

Leadership styles

It is not the purpose of this chapter to offer an in-depth analysis of leadership styles: the literature on the topic is enormous and easily accessible. Nevertheless, it is appropriate to make some comments on the development of leadership theory.

Until the fairly recent past, the most commonly accepted model of leadership was characterized by the charismatic leader, the individual who stood out through the force of ideas, personality and ability to articulate. Many people working in organizations would have had first-hand experience of this type of leader: one who led from the front, who set the agenda for the organization, set the targets for achievement and acted as the figurehead. This phenomenon has also been referred to as 'the chairman as hero'.

The driven leader, standing head and shoulders above his or her peers, may also, however, have been an autocratic individual, results-oriented and intolerant of disagreement. The organization led by the autocratic style of leader might have retained a very clear focus on the task, but could also hold within it a great deal of unexploited talent and creativity.

This style of leadership may have been suited to, or may have been born of, bureaucratic, task-based organizations with clear hierarchies. It was far less well adapted to respond to the challenges of a rapidly changing environment, one in which anticipation, responsiveness and flexibility to customer needs are the key.

At the other end of the spectrum there is the democratic style of leader, one who works hard to ensure that decisions are based on consensus, that everyone has an opportunity to participate in discussions, and that there is widespread acceptance of the way forward. This style of leadership may also involve a considerable degree of delegation, based on recognition that scope needs to be given for individuals to develop and to make their own contribution to clearly agreed goals. It is coupled, too, with recognition that some degree of control may need to be relinquished if the energy and creativity, which exists at different levels of the organization, is to be released. The great disadvantage of the democratic style of leadership is that it may take an unacceptably long time for decisions to be reached. The leader who is by nature a democrat may find it difficult to assert himself or herself, and to give a clear sense of direction and to act quickly when this is required in the interests of the organization and its customers.

At the far reaches of the leadership galaxy there is the laissez-faire, or 'delegate and disappear' leader. This is the individual described by Blake and Mouton (1985) as 'the impoverished leader', who is committed neither to achieving the task nor to maintaining and developing the team, preferring to allow the team to do whatever it wishes and to remain detached from the process.

'Transactional' and 'transformational' leadership

In recent years, the literature around leadership has tended to focus on the distinction between 'transactional' and 'transformational' leadership. Each of these models envisages a very different type of leader.

Put very simply, the transactional leadership style is characterized by emphasis on the task, and on the achievement of organizational goals by means of the reinforcement that the leader offers to subordinates. This reinforcement may take the form of promises, rewards or threats, depending on whether the subordinate has achieved what he or she has contracted to do. The leader will allocate tasks and responsibilities, possibly after consultation or negotiation, and will monitor performance and take corrective action as necessary. This may be either proactively or by waiting for problems to arise and responding accordingly.

What is distinctive about transformational leadership? It implies a contract between leader and led of quite a different nature. Bass (1985) identifies four key characteristics of transformational leadership. These are:

1   *Idealized influence*: characterized by high moral or ethical standards. In some respects, this function of the transformational leader is similar to the best of the charismatic style of leadership, enabling him or her to create a vision to which others want to subscribe.

2   *Inspirational motivation*: the leader communicates in an exciting way the goal and the shared journey towards its achievement; he or she sets out challenges and gives subordinates meaning and a reason for embarking on the journey.

3   *Intellectual stimulation*: the leader encourages constructive questioning, challenges assumptions and enables more creative approaches to problem solving, releasing creativity and ideas wherever they are to be found in the organization.

4   *Individual consideration*: individuals are valued and their development is seen as important. The organization may be committed to coaching, mentoring and other tools to identify and develop the talent of its members.

What transformational leadership presupposes is a move away from the hierarchical, task-based approach to organizations, which has been so prevalent in the public sector. It demands a flatter, more flexible, more responsive organization, and leaders who are prepared to allow space for their staff to grow and develop. It is better geared to the uncertain world in which all organizations operate in the 21st century.

Transformational leadership could be seen as embodying the best of both charismatic and democratic styles, while avoiding the dangers of rigidity and slowness to adapt to which both of these traditional models were prone. It requires a leader to display a number of fundamental traits if people are to follow willingly. These include honesty, integrity, competence, intelligence, fair-mindedness, courage, decisiveness, imagination and forward thinking. Above all, the leader must have credibility – with followers, with peers and with those, such as politicians, who need to be influenced.

This is an impressive set of attributes, but it is clear that they are not only to be found among the fortunate few who are successful in rising to the top of organizations. They can be honed by practice, experience and learning, but they are not a set of techniques and skills, but personal qualities to which all can aspire.

Basic principles

Covey (2001) comments:

> When all the fashionable management hype and buzz words have been stripped away, what is left at the core are the basic, universal principles such as integrity, trust, respect, fairness and compassion. Managers today must retain and inspire valuable knowledge workers; reduce cynicism and improve morale; forge a co-operative culture to reach new levels of performance; and generally 'do more with less'. All of this

is only possible if the principle of trust is well established. So how can managers build trust? In fact the methods are simple, but take time and effort, and it is not a quick fix. Managers need to genuinely listen to people, seek to understand them and mentor them. They need to demonstrate respect, and communicate people's worth and potential so clearly that they come to see it themselves – which is the true essence of leadership. Principle centred leadership is the surest way for managers to effectively lead. Regardless of position, rank or status, everyone in an organisation can begin to see themselves as a leader in their own right.

Creating the culture

It is self-evident that the demands upon managers and leaders are greater than they have ever been before. The acceleration of change and in particular the endemic changes in the knowledge industries as we move in the hybrid times of virtual and physical services provide unique stresses for the contemporary leader. One could argue that the demands and needs of our customers are becoming more sophisticated and also more demanding. Cleveland Ohio (www.cpl.org) gives us a pertinent example of this trend. This public library service has 6 million 'virtual' users each year. One would perhaps have predicted that the convenience of virtual visits and the library service coming into the home would have diminished actual visits to premises. In fact, over a five-year period, they were able to show that the visits actually increased. This indicates that the demand does not migrate in the electronic services age, but actually stimulates new demands and other services. In a wider context, the closure of local branches by a well-known banking chain in the UK created a public outcry and led to the company reversing the policy. The public clearly want virtual *and* physical services and libraries would be wise not to forget this legacy of presence.

The development of the e-university with pilot courses from September 2002 and other distance learning initiatives do not lessen the requirement for more traditional learning or for the validation of courses through the presence of and contact with a tutor as part of a blended learning package.

Such ambivalent and demanding times, where the diversity and intensity of customer demand is so marked, require the power of good leadership to pick a path through this new territory and accent three leadership characteristics:

- holding ambivalence
- holding the vision
- integrity.

Holding ambivalence

The People's Network development for the UK public library network (www.peoplesnetwork/) has been heralded and acknowledged globally as among the most advanced programmes to actually deliver the widest possible access to the benefits and opportunities of the knowledge age. It is clearly a most welcome development, which, by the end of 2002, enables public libraries to catch up with academic colleagues in terms of connectivity. However, as the recent Audit Commission report pointed out (2002), the use of libraries for the borrowing of leisure reading has markedly declined and this report points to a reduction of spending on the books and other traditional and infrastructure costs to the service. Indeed, Resource, the Council for Museums, Archives and Libraries, is seeking ways with government to sustain this one-off investment in the People's Network.

From this apparent tension can and should come the creativity of the sort of leadership that holds such contrasting situations and finds innovative and creative responses. For example, Essex Public Libraries (www.essex.gov.uk) plan to offset the ongoing costs of the network through added-value services such as specific training courses run in the library and the hiring of connected venues to third parties, in particular as satellite locations for a range of learning.

Leaders will also take the contrasting and divergent demands of customers and find new and often surprising solutions to them. The much-lauded Millennium Library in Norwich has combinations of service that cater for diverse needs and seek innovatively to be both the present and future 'living room' for the communities.

Holding the vision

These are tough times for leaders and sticking to the vision of the future despite opposition is especially relevant today. For example, despite the logistical challenges of varying institutional policies and approaches, the City of Sunderland drove the agenda for the learner to have the right of access to any resources wherever located. The patient insistence on behalf of user need was essential to glean real and lasting benefit for the citizens. Now this is much emulated as an obvious way to support learners and to generate new and wider markets for formal learning. At the time, one recalls it was considered unproven and pioneering. We shall return to this theme of making partnerships work in 'Community' leadership at the end of this chapter.

Integrity

This may appear a less than central characteristic for a leader in uncertain times. However, the ability to be trusted and trustworthy could not be more relevant for staff and customers in times of change and uncertainty. The pressures for shortcuts, quick fixes and perhaps the veneer of service that looks OK or advances political ambition are the daily diet of leaders. The skill and strength of a good leader are knowing when to bend and when to stand firm about issues. In talking about their experiences of getting to the top, women leaders (Burrington, 1993) spoke most about the desire for fairness and equity that had driven their pathways, and the comments about leaders and managers they had experienced are drawn up as a kind of recommended dos and don'ts of library leadership.

All the above are enduring characteristics despite rapid change and tumult. They are especially important today when leading in a context of constant change where challenge is the norm.

Leading by example

There are literally hundreds of books and articles on the importance of a walking-the-talk style of leadership. This counsel of perfection which began with John Adair's action centred leadership (1997) has been through some refinements. Stephen Covey's *Seven habits of highly effective people* (1992) usefully points to the fact that all leaders have weaknesses and are human – the big difference is good self-knowledge and the ability to select teams and colleagues who can really counterpoise their own strengths. *The fifth dimension* (Sengi, 1990) takes this further and articulates the art of leadership in terms of creating environments and climates in which others can thrive, orchestrating rather than playing oneself but able to take command at chosen times.

What do you say about leaders you know? There is no doubt that you will comment on what they say and do – how the talk matches the walk. Being a leader means being observed and commented on, not often being understood.

For example, how you talk to customers and treat them, how much you talk about the customer perspective and how you value customers – for example if you call staff meetings at really busy times for the service – will be observed and commented on.

Asda as a leading retailer has produced some extremely innovative customer-focused practices. At busy times of the year, everyone from headquarters will go into stores and help out in the rush.

In the context of libraries, leadership is very much about living the values and walking the talk. People who focus on self and personal power will never make it because they will not be emulated and inspire customer focus in others.

Enjoyment and self-motivation are clearly the features of good leaders as their passion and interest shine through. Anecdotal stories of leaders do centre around their actions and deeds rather than their words.

Developing leaders

Public library leaders in the UK agree that the profession is facing a crisis of leadership. Research carried out by the University of Sheffield in 2001 and published under the title *Recruit, retain and lead* (Usherwood, 2002) for example, revealed that 50% of chief librarians in the UK were not sure where their successor would be found.

The discussion of transformational leadership and the qualities it demands of the leader have made it plain that leaders are born, and not made. However, the qualities are those to which many can aspire: they are not the sole preserve of a small elite; and there are supporting skills that can be acquired and that make the exercise of leadership more effective. It is clear, therefore, that in all organizations individuals with leadership potential will be found at many levels, and not merely at the level of senior management. The challenge for leaders of library and information services in all sectors, not just public libraries, is to harness and develop this potential for the present and future good of the organization and its customers. This section looks briefly at what the organization can do to identify, nurture, support and reward its natural leaders, wherever they are to be found.

Management structure

Recent years have seen a move towards flatter management structures in libraries, with fewer steps in the chain from front line to top management. This has been prompted partly by the experience in other sectors and partly by expediency, as organizations attempt to respond to a constantly changing agenda with relatively static, or reducing, staffing and managerial resources. This has inevitably led to an increased reliance on delegation, as senior managers' time becomes ever more constrained, and to a spectacular growth in short- and medium-term, project-led working. Challenge funding and other short-term funding opportunities have contributed to the growth in opportunity for members of staff at all levels to participate in service development. This has resulted, in many organizations, in the creation of a pool of staff with some expertise in, and experience of, the management of change.

Ironically, another effect of flatter management structures has been to limit the potential for career development, as individuals have fewer opportunities to progress to more senior posts in a planned and gradual way. Improvement in communications throughout the organization may also have failed to keep pace with other managerial and service developments, as the small core of senior managers becomes more and more hard pressed and unable to devote adequate time to this essential task.

Identifying potential leaders

It is all the more essential, therefore, that the leadership talent that undoubtedly exists is encouraged and used effectively. Modern leaders need a range of skills: charisma on its own is no longer adequate. The good leader will also be a good manager, but most importantly he or she will be able to inspire and enable others to sign up to the vision. How does this impact on the quality of service that the customer receives?

At the top of the organization, the leadership role is to articulate clearly its aspirations in relation to its customers and to ensure that every member of staff understands what customers are entitled to expect. Managers at other levels in the organization, including front-line supervisors, have a role in making this vision real to the people they lead. Good customer service is not achieved only as a result of what happens at headquarters, but depends on the enthusiasm and engagement of staff on the front line of service, day after day. To support front-line staff, the organization needs to be able to highlight areas where excellent customer service is the norm, and enable the rest of the organization to learn from these.

This will also mean taking steps to identify high-performing individuals and use their skills and enthusiasm for the benefit of the wider organization and its customers. Initiatives such as the Investors in People programme now offer a means of combining individual performance review with staff development. Clearly, it is important to retain the principle of confidentiality in any appraisal discussions that take place between the employee and the line manager; but it is vitally important also that the organization has a consistent strategy to facilitate communication from the front line to senior management. This will help ensure that performance review becomes a learning exercise for the organization as a whole. Senior managers should be looking, not merely to identify training and development needs that will feed into strategic planning, but also to capture information about those members of staff who show particular evidence of leadership potential. A more strategic approach to the planning of training and development, one that is linked firmly to the objectives of the business, implies a more inclusive approach. Participants in development activities are no longer a self-selecting minority, but can be selected on the basis of their potential contribution.

Formal performance appraisal mechanisms are only one way of identifying potential. The leader should always be seeking to identify potential in others, through observation, through discussion and through the comments of other colleagues and service users. Some employees will have creative ideas and be prepared to articulate them; they will show that they are willing to take calculated risks in the interests of improving service; and they will be willing to put themselves forward for tasks that the majority would prefer to leave to someone else.

Development programmes

Having identified potential leaders, the organization will need to use a variety of means to ensure their continued development. This might involve attendance at training and development events, participation in a mentoring scheme, taking responsibility for planning a project or event, or solving a problem facing the organization. It will almost certainly entail taking the individual out of their normal place of work and exposing them to new ideas and opportunities. Traditional hierarchies are broken down, as the organization benefits from the contribution of staff at all levels. The introduction of ICT in UK public libraries has been one example of this move to more flexible working, as ICT 'champions' have emerged from staff at all levels.

The prevalence of flatter management structures may mean that leaders from within the organization cannot be rewarded in traditional ways. Personal development, the acquisition of new skills, the challenge of a new environment and the opportunity to become involved in exciting new initiatives may have to take the place of financial reward.

Eye on the ball: the role of performance management

The fundamental role of the leader is to articulate the vision for the organization and to inspire everyone with the desire to undertake the journey. It is equally important, however, to provide a clear focus, day to day, so that the organization and its employees know how well they are doing, how the journey is going, and how much remains to be done. Creating a performance culture does not imply simply number crunching, but an emphasis on communication, quality and responsiveness that permeates the whole organization. How is this to be achieved?

Planning frameworks

Public libraries have been fortunate in recent years, as the introduction of national performance frameworks has helped provide the necessary focus. For public libraries in the UK, within the local authority as a whole, planning and evaluation have taken centre stage, with community plans and best value performance plans increasingly driving the corporate planning and development process. These centrally inspired mechanisms not only provide a framework for the process and format of plans, but also determine to some extent what direction the local authority will take. Electronic government, for example, is a broad government policy with a very explicit objective: to make all national and local government services in the UK available electronically by 2005. This target has focused the thinking of local authorities and its achievement has become central to their planning, but the means by which the target is to be achieved have not been prescribed by central government. There is scope for flexibility at local level, and this offers a great opportunity for the public library network, with its presence in every community and its increasingly sophisticated ICT provision, to play a leading role in delivering this corporate imperative.

Comprehensive performance assessments

Government engagement with local service delivery goes even further, as the number of inspection regimes continues to grow. As well as Best Value and the service-specific regimes, such as Ofsted, the latest development (Great Britain. Audit Commission, 2002) is the comprehensive performance assessment. This entails a thorough investigation of all aspects of a local authority's service planning and delivery, and it results in a published assessment of the authority's performance, categorizing it as 'high performing', 'striving', 'coasting' or 'poorly performing'. For most local authorities, a designation as anything worse then 'striving' will be a stinging criticism, while a favourable verdict will be valuable recognition of achievement, and spur the organization on to further effort. It carries with it also a number of financial and operational freedoms from which the local authority can benefit in improving the responsiveness and flexibility of local services. The fact that it is a judgement delivered publicly means that its impact on the perceptions of service users and citizens may be considerable. The inspection process, with its linking of corporate with service-specific factors, offers an unprecedented opportunity for the leadership of the library service to demonstrate its contribution to the local authority's performance, through excellence in service delivery and high levels of public satisfaction, and through its contribution to the achievement of corporate objectives. Library service managers can look forward to exercising considerable influence at a corporate level.

Annual library plans and public library standards

Looking more specifically at the local authority library service itself, there have been two developments in recent years that have put performance management high on the agenda in the UK. These are annual library plans and public library standards, both of which initiatives have been introduced at the behest of the Department for Culture, Media and Sport.

Annual library plans require the library service to set out clearly its proposals for the medium term (i.e. the next three years) and for the shorter term (18 months). It is a specific requirement that the plan should show clearly the linkages between the library service's objectives and the overall council plan priorities. This plan is a document that is the basis of performance management throughout the service. In the best authorities, staff at all levels have an opportunity to contribute to the formulation of the plan, through their local area responsibilities and by virtue of any specific functional or strategic responsibility they may hold. The annual library plan provides a readily accessible summary of the service's priorities, plans and performance, and an indication of where remedial action needs to be taken.

Similarly, public library standards have acted as a catalyst for library leaders, politicians and front-line staff by listing targets for 19 areas of public library activity. All local authority library services are required to demonstrate that they have realistic plans in place for achieving the targets within three years. Penalties for failure to achieve the standards may include intervention by the Secretary of State in the running of the service.

The leader's role

Effective leaders will use external mechanisms such as these to help them communicate the vision, set the targets and secure the resources for future service development. They will ensure first of all that the planning process is embedded in the organization, and is not viewed merely as a task that has to be completed to satisfy an external agency. This will mean creating opportunities for staff at all levels to contribute to the formulation of the plan, and ensuring that the overall plan is only the top level of a planning process that permeates all levels of the service. This will enable service-wide objectives and priorities to be translated into targets that can be delivered by geographical and functional teams; it will also enable staff lower down the organization to influence the plan by feeding in their ideas.

Most importantly, the plan must be a working document, and the leader must ensure that performance against the plan is reviewed regularly and that remedial action is taken in the light of failure to achieve targets, or evidence of changing needs and priorities. Without this continued focus, the plan will indeed become a file document, and the process itself will be seen as having little relevance to those delivering the service to customers. It is too late, when the plan is dusted off for next year's revision, to discover that a majority of the targets have not been met.

If the organization is to be driven by its customers, this can come only from the top. The leader must communicate the message that listening to customers, stakeholders and potential users is the only way to ensure that the organization remains relevant, responsive and effective. If there is a comments, complaints or suggestions procedure, for example, the leader must demonstrate through his or her interest and involvement that this is a genuine learning exercise for the organization. Of course, many comments received will require nothing more than an explanation and will need no further action. Nor would it be appropriate for every comment to find its way to the top of the organization. The principle of resolving an issue as close to the point of service as possible can only serve to empower managers lower down the organization, provided that they are able to act in the interests of the customer and in the knowledge that they will have the support of senior management. The role of the leader is to be aware of trends and themes, so that the organization as a whole can respond to significant shifts in customer need, or to major customer concerns.

Consultation

There are other means of enabling the organization to demonstrate its willingness to listen to customers and stakeholders and for them to have an influential voice. Best Value has encouraged libraries to look again at the problem, formerly considered intractable, of consulting with non-users of services, and there have been some notable examples of work with other agencies – for example, to look at the role of the public library in reaching those who have not been well served by formal education (Procter, 2001). The establishment of citizens' forums, friends' groups and similar offer opportunities to tap into the experience and the views of users and non-users and, of course, the Public Library User Survey (PLUS) has been enormously influential in UK public libraries in identifying issues and priorities for individual library authorities, as well as highlighting national trends. PLUS was originally conceived as a voluntary activity, designed and co-ordinated by public library authorities and assisted by the Institute of Public Finance (IPF), but has proved its worth and is now embedded in annual library plans, and indeed the goverment's Public Library Standards.

If organizational leadership has moved away from the concept of the all-powerful, all-knowing leader to a more collegiate approach, the initiatives described above have brought about a similar shift away from the notion of the service provider as expert. This does not imply a dumbing down of professional library and information services, but a growing recognition that customers are the lifeblood of the organization and that they have a legitimate voice in its future development. What is crucial is that library leadership demonstrates to staff and users alike that their evidence is being used 'to change the way we do things'. Too often in the past the evidence from user surveys, for example, has failed to go beyond the stage of analysis into influencing planning and service delivery.

Performance appraisal

Hand in hand with organizational performance monitoring must go the evaluation of individual performance. A critical success factor for the leader is ensuring that the right balance of skills, experience and expertise is available to meet all present and foreseeable future needs. Individual members of staff and teams should be encouraged to reflect on their performance and to take responsibility for their individual and collective development. This can be supported by a variety of formal mechanisms, such as individual performance appraisal or personal development reviews. Whatever name is given to such reviews, their focus should be forward looking, identifying future development needs and planning how these will be met, so that the organization will be in a position to anticipate changing demands.

Perhaps the most crucial element in all of this is the leader's own development needs, yet these are often overlooked. This may be because of a sense of having 'arrived', or because the day-to-day pressures of the job make it difficult to stand back and take a look at longer-term personal development needs. Yet if the leader cannot demonstrate through his or her own practice that continuous development is a critical success factor for the organization, how can employees at other levels be expected to take this seriously?

There are opportunities in abundance for those who wish to take advantage of them. One such is the leadership programme at the University of Leeds, which prepares local authority staff for chief officer and even chief executive responsibilities. Less formally, the Society of Chief Librarians has inaugurated a series of leadership master classes for public library managers who show real potential. The aim of these events is to enable managers to share ideas and to learn from leading practitioners.

Participation in a mentoring scheme can be an effective antidote to the pressures of the day job. The ability to talk through performance, personal development and other issues with an experienced but objective colleague is one that many leaders have found invaluable, and that can help overcome the sense of isolation that many new leaders experience.

Many heads of service will already be subject to some form of performance appraisal, perhaps even linked to a performance-related reward system. It is only the brave, however, who voluntarily subject themselves to 360-degree appraisal, from their peers and subordinates as well as their superiors. Yet this can be a vital source of high-quality feedback, coming as it does from those who are most affected by the leader's performance. It requires commitment from all concerned: to prepare thoughtfully and to feed back honestly. It requires courage from the appraisers, to criticize openly and constructively, and from the leader to accept feedback in an open-minded way. With good will on all sides it can be a positive empowering experience for both the leader and his or her staff.

Validation

Increasingly services are required to benchmark themselves against others in order to compare and improve. One can see clearly from the previous section that openness to public scrutiny is inexorable for all publicly funded services. The league table trends in education and health in the UK are setting the pace for all of us. As we have seen, Best Value in the public sector is a key focus that seeks to measure services from the customer perspective. It give a key role to stakeholders, to consultation with users and to impact as well as outcome and cost–benefit indicators.

In general terms there is a fusion of these soft measures for all kinds of organizations. Social accounting as well as environmental, social and ethical measures are growing in importance in the private sector and there are developments to measure the impact of knowledge management, for example at TFPL (www.tfpl.com). The balanced scorecard approach combines the hard data of statistical performance with the storyboard approach for the softer side.

In the late 1980s US libraries looked at sets of indicators and performance measures for like institutions (Zweizig, 1984). This useful means of comparison of organizations that had similar sets of aspiration could usefully be revised and brought into use since we often reflect on the inappropriateness of comparing organizations with differing purpose and focus. Voluntary benchmarking and informal comparisons have long been features of collaboratively minded services.

Compulsory validation is a result of growing customer demand for transparency and evidence of relative impact.

Business Excellence Model

A significant trend is the regime of continuous improvement that underpins the Business Excellence Model (BEM) used by many blue-chip companies and with a public sector version (www.efqm.org); it also underlies the performance indicators for Best Value. The idea that improvement and world-class service achievement are not endpoints but a continuous process is driven by escalating customer expectation. Today's innovative service is tomorrow's norm.

BEM is especially useful to indicate for organizations the role and performance of leadership and management and is an effective tool for indirect processes. The mapping of inter-dependencies can lead to improved workflow and the focus on hotspots in an organization. The model is based on a periodic self-assessment process and there have been documented applications of it in academic contexts (www.efqm.org).

Gaining a 360-degree view of one's organization is important as the number and variety of stakeholders increase (especially partners). Getting more detail as to the workings can lead to at least a comparative view on the impact of leadership on organizational performance.

Charter Mark

In customer terms, the awarding of Charter Marks to service organizations is widespread and the need for renewal validates ongoing standards in relation to customer service.

Investors in People

In looking to the future and the need to invest in the human capital of any organization, Investors in People (IiP) is widely seen as an indicator toward a learning organization, indicating one that has the capacity to embrace change, adjust and learn and learn again new and improved skills. It is an indicator of flexibility and also of the valuing of people both inside and outside the organization.

It is interesting to note that such moves to validate are context driven and are neutral tools. They can validate and evidence an improving service and be an affirmation and a motivator. However, they can equally de-motivate or be seen as superficial and done 'for the badge' rather than reflecting any intrinsic value or quality. Leaders will use such validation with care and judgement as a spur and a celebration of milestones achieved. It is as important to look at improvement over time and to track the internal performance against the shared vision. In this context, external comparison is less meaningful for the organization that seeks to exceed boundaries and be truly world class.

Customers and leaders

It is clear that the customers of services expect a higher degree of engagement and more understanding and anticipation of their requirements than ever before.

Much has been written in the context of health services. At one time the professional knowledge of the expert doctor went unchallenged and unquestioned. Today with access to evidence-based medicine and the communities of interest around medical conditions, there is more expectation of explanation and justification.

This trend, which we shall term the democratization of knowledge, affects all areas of public service. The burgeoning of focus groups, referenda and consultation are all attempts to engage and involve the customer in increasingly transparent businesses. Naomi Klein in *No logo* (2000) argues the sophistication of the young consumer generation who expect to know about the ethics of companies and are not content to receive a well-hyped product.

There is evidence that libraries of all kinds are ahead in embracing this movement. While consultation and engagement in, for example, new library design is quite common, there are examples of deeper engagement. Hertfordshire Libraries consulted on a range of spending options with its residents, asking them to help prioritize quite complex packages of services.

Many services have groups of advocates from boards of advisers in corporate environments to academic and student bodies to friends groups in public libraries. Hounslow Leisure Services includes members of the public on its Board of Trustees. Managing such stakeholder groups requires political and diplomatic skills, especially when these groups co-exist with more formal bodies – for example the cabinet of elected members in a local authority.

Self-service

Library services are ahead in the engagement of service users to help themselves to products and services. Understanding and anticipating customer behaviour is a vital skill for all leaders in the organization. Paco Underhill's *Why we buy; the science of shopping* (1999) is a seminal read on the psychology and observation of consumer behaviour in a retail context and in the UK such thinking is being applied as part of the reader development movement (www.openingthebook.com).

Library services are constantly seeking to increase this kind of use in order to deliver more service for the same or less cost. Leadership skills to reassure staff are crucial but also the integrity to state clearly increasing demands for staff to work outside of their comfort zones and even to reinvent and re-shape their roles. The freedom to transform services with concomitant skills development and a chance to take risks through practice and experimentation all require the loyalty of leadership. Derbyshire County Libraries (Bruwell, 2002) is a strong example of allowing staff the freedom to grow and develop new skills through the training for the People's Network and seeing those skills used to effect service improvement in a continuous and empowering way.

The development of portal and increasingly sophisticated web use with the use of agents and other AI (artificial intelligence) tools will further challenge the leaders of library service to do what they uniquely do well and innovate new and relevant services.

Segmented services

Increasing focus of services is a noticeable trend in this era of customization. The award-winning Cable Book Library in Helsinki (aimed at young people with adventurous lifestyles) and the focus of Singapore Libraries to the young next generation of users (www.nlb.sg) are stunning examples. However, while we see increasing zoning of services in the UK (including study areas, areas for young people, for children, for performance and events), the concept of stopping some services that make up the value of providing 'comprehensive' services is resisted. At one time the diversity of a public library service 'for everyone' was seen as an unfocused weakness and today it is an acknowledged strength. Despite falling use for lending, the uses of libraries cross all socio-economic and age boundaries. There is innovation where cross-generational and family work is undertaken.

Managing the disappointment caused by stopping some service and by implication ceasing to serve some users or serving them differently is a complex and skilled matter for leaders to handle.

One can see and touch physical spaces – but the virtual service is less easy to value as highly. The ability of leaders to tell stories and paint vivid pictures of services is crucial. In the same way that people in the film industry need to sell a script to financial backers, so too do leaders need to articulate the vision through scenarios, stories and the creation of clear pictures. It is worthy of note that the scenarios for the People's Network were significant in drawing a picture of the difference and impact on lives the investment would make.

Increasing personalization

Customer relationship marketing (CRM) gurus talk of the power of one and the trend of highly individualized servicing needs. Customers want you to know about their needs, they want to tell you once about their details and position and for you to remember. This significant trend will require the library leader to make good judgements about resources and to be adept at prioritization of services. The ability to think clearly and to manage disappointment as well as delight through support for staff innovation and excellent customer communications will be essential.

In conclusion, involving customers can be a two-edged sword and needs skill to handle well. As a leader, one always needs to understand and engage with customers but while they are always at the centre, they are not always right. Strong user criticism surrounded the long and controversial building of the British Library at St Pancras. Today, it is universally admired as a truly great and worthy building, generating pride, identity and huge levels of use. If strong leadership and determination over many years had not prevailed, the project would have faltered.

Sometimes our customers are wrong, sometimes they change their mind, but they are always at the centre.

Community leadership

More and more leaders of library and information services are also leaders of wider knowledge, culture or learning services. In workplace environments, Chief Knowledge Officers may also be accountable for leading records management and internal communications as well as IT-based services; in academic contexts, the leader will also have a role in bringing together all services and resources to support learners, and in the public sphere leadership posts are increasingly responsible for other community-based services, particularly the arts and heritage as well as leisure. Internationally, trends are less discernible and distinct.

Even without this widening of leadership role across a spectrum of service areas, there is an evident and accelerating trend to find partners, work in collaboration and to connect services. While these may be financially driven as in the public sector, there are other drivers too. We opened this chapter with a view that customers are becoming more demanding and sophisticated. Wider trends of globalization and the awareness of options that the mass media no doubt brings heighten the demands of customers for personalized and seamless services.

In the UK, the development of UKonline (www.ukonline.gov.uk) is a clear symbol of the need to place the customer and their life episodes or experiences at the heart of developments, and the requirements of leadership are clearly to see things from this perspective. *Libraries for all: public libraries and social inclusion* (Great Britain. DCMS, 1999) highlights many good examples of the ways in which entrepreneurial libraries have sought innovative services to engage with all sections of communities under the banner of social inclusion. Trends for this community leadership emphasis are most marked in Scandinavian countries and the 1999 Finland Library Act places a new duty on these well developed libraries to be the heart and hub of community life (www.publiclibraries.fi).

This requires of the new leader a real holistic view and an ability to develop and sustain partnerships to all degrees with a range of other agencies. In effect this requires a network of leaders working together to a common purpose. The requirement of UK local authorities to develop community strategies in equal partnership with other agencies is a test of this strength of purpose. In terms of customer-centredness, the pilot local cultural strategy from the London Borough of Newham *Reasons to be cheerful* (2000), demonstrates strong collective leadership focused on celebration of diversity and strength in this inner city borough.

In North America, there is a clear and wider acknowledgement of the civic pride generated by a strong library service and it is clearly seen as an asset to the sense of community identity. The part New York Public Libraries played in response to September 11 together with their proactive marketing of libraries shows what a significant feature the service is in the daily lives of citizens. National libraries have the same unifying role, often celebrating the past heritage of knowledge to symbolize and power the future. A leading example is the Digital Scotland initiative (www.scotland.gov.uk/digitalscotland).

Therefore the current and future role of leaders as entrepreneurs of community development leads to a question. What will be the role of library leaders as global communities develop? In Australia, one territory has the maxim 'From anywhere in the world to anywhere in the state'.

Certainly in terms of civic life, community life and the shaping of multiple identities and new virtual communities, future leaders will need both strong vision and tenacity to make global citizenship a reality out of a dream.

To use a contemporary acronym familiar to mobile phone texters, TOTB (thinking outside of the box) is not an option but a norm.

References

Adair, John (1997) *Effective communication*, Trans-Atlantic Publications.

Bass, B. M. (1985) *Leadership and performance beyond expectations*, New York Free Press.

Bertelsmann Foundation International Network of Public Libraries
www.stiftung.bertelsmann.de/english/netz/publib/

Blake, R. R. and Mouton, J. S. (1985) *The managerial grid III: the key to leadership excellence*, Gulf Publishing Company.

Bruwell, J. (2002) Conference paper at the PLG Weekend School, unpublished.

Burrington, G. (ed.) (1993) *Equally good: women in British librarianship*, AAL.

Business Excellence Model, public sector version www.efqm.org

Cleveland Public Libraries current performance www.cpl.org

Covey, S. R. (2001) *Seven habits of highly effective people*, Simon & Schuster.

Covey, S. (2001) Principles hold key to leadership success, *Professional Manager*, (September), 41.

Digital Scotland www.scotland.gov.uk/digitalscotland

Essex Public Libraries (n.d.) Strategy documents, unpublished.

Finland Library Act, available at www.publiclibraries.fi

Great Britain. Audit Commission (2002) *Building better library services*, Audit Commission.

Great Britain. Audit Commission (2002) *Delivering comprehensive performance assessment*, HMSO.

Great Britain. Department for Culture, Media and Sport (1999) *Libraries for all: public libraries and social inclusion*, DCMS

Klein, N. (2000) *No logo*, Flamingo.

London Borough of Newham (2000) *Reasons to be cheerful* (local cultural strategy), available at www.newham.gov.uk/leisure

Opening the Book www.openingthe book.com

The People's Network www.peoplesnetwork.gov.uk

Procter, R. (2001) *Low achievers, lifelong learners*, University of Sheffield, unpublished.

Sengi, P. (1990) *The fifth dimension; the art and practice of the learning organization*, Doubleday.

Singapore Libraries www.nlb.sg

TFPL current research, www.tfpl.com

TFPL (2001) *Knowledge strategies – corporate strategies, TFPL's fourth international summit held October 2001*, TFPL.

UKonline, www.ukonline.gov.uk

Underhill, P. (1999) *Why we buy; the science of shopping*, Simon & Schuster.

Usherwood, R. (2002) *Recruit, retain and lead*, University of Sheffield.

Zweizig, Douglas (1984) *Public library user studies; applications and issues*, Ablex.

4

Human resource planning

John M. Pluse and Alix Craven

Introduction

If we take the definition of a customer-focused organization as one which has 'a total organisational approach making quality of service – as perceived by the customer – the principal driving force of the organisation' (Albrecht, 1988) then clearly this is people focused: people serving and supporting people. This therefore has strong implications for human resource management (HRM). Much of what is needed to successfully foster this approach to service is 'merely' good, standard HRM but a customer-focused approach has some particular requirements. This is to ensure that the workforce have the skills needed and are enabled to use them to deliver exemplary service. We aim to deal with both the general and the special requirements in this chapter. Some of the points we make will be in areas dealt with by other authors in this book: we deal with them here merely for completeness of the context in which we write.

From mission statement to service strategy

To achieve effective customer service all those involved with its design and – especially – its delivery must have the same clear concept of that service and of its purposes for the customer. These should be clear from the mission statement and/or service strategy, but these documents often leave staff unclear about their roles and ill equipped to think creatively about ways of doing their jobs better.

A mission statement should be brief: the most effective we have ever seen was that of British Airways in its heyday: 'To fly. To serve.' Four words summing up everything the airline should do. A service strategy is normally longer, but if it is too long, few – staff *or* customers – will bother to read and understand it. Both should be relevant to the organization, capable of practical delivery, clear and specific, motivating to staff and clearly indicative to customers as to what they may expect from the organization. They should reflect the service philosophy of the organization and aim to inspire staff, help to set personal goals and give a unifying context to all parts of the organization. They must meet the workforce's need to know, as members of the organization, what it is about, what it is doing and what it stands for.

People need to be assured that someone is in control of the organization's direction and knows how to get there. The ever-present danger here is of empty slogans, all of which are soon, if not instantly, seen through by staff and customers alike. Empty slogans seem to be a particularly strong temptation in the area of customer service. For example: 'The customer is always right' is an old favourite but 'As all customer contact employees soon find out, not all customers *are* right, and some are even abusive and out of control' (Bitner, Booms and Tetreault, 1990). The net result of too much of this sort of empty slogan is customer reluctance to believe any statement from that organization and de-motivation among the workforce. We should always remember that merely asserting that our service is high quality does not make it so, and that 'the quality of any product or service is what the customer says it is' (Albrecht, 1988).

An additional complication can arise where a library and information service aspires to a high level of customer service but its parent organization doesn't see this as such a high priority. This can easily be the case, for example, in a local authority or a university. It is no accident that polls of public opinion on the quality of local authority services almost invariably put the public library service at the head of the list of appreciation. To get the library service there can require determined leadership from the head of the service.

Implementing the mission statement

'Our staff are our greatest asset.' This statement has become a cliché, but that doesn't mean it is not true. Problems arise where an organization uses this as an empty slogan and fails to build its policies and practices in recognition of it. Translating this belief realistically into an effective service requires focused planning and positive action to succeed. It is no longer enough (if indeed it ever was) for the top management of an organization to set out the mission, service strategy or any other behavioural statement as an edict for others. Top managers, and where appropriate *any* managers, must be seen to support it by their own actions. If this is not the case then the staff at large will pay little heed to it, and the service users are likely to see a growing mismatch between what is promised and what is actually delivered. In particular, the head of the organization has a key responsibility to preach, live and breathe the chosen mission. There are two great dangers here: that the organization's top management loses credibility with the workforce in general because it manifestly fails to practise what it preaches; and that the service loses credibility with its customers because gaps between service promises and service delivery become increasingly obvious. We see constant examples of these service gaps in the world around us as consumers, and inevitably have suffered service failure ourselves. Furthermore, in HRM terms, we have all seen such examples as not the fault of the staff member serving us but as flaws in the organization itself.

What we are building here is a chain from mission statement to everyday service delivery. The next link is a statement – a 'menu' if you will – of exactly what service the customer can expect to be available, how, when, where and – particularly importantly – to what standard. This is a particularly significant element in a customer-focused organization. The importance of this building block, in HRM terms, is that it is a foundation for designing individual jobs and for setting individual objectives.

Recruitment and selection

The organization's attitude to customers must be a prominent factor throughout the selection process. This is an opportunity, through all material used, to ensure that all candidates are left in no doubt as to the organization's standpoint on customer service. Also, the written material used and all verbal messages given should build up into the clearest picture possible of the job in question and the environment in which it sits. For all concerned, this is a golden opportunity to enhance the reputation of the organization.

The main tools used to give a clear picture of the duties, relationships, skills and competence levels, attributes and behaviours required in a particular job are:

- job analysis
- job description
- person specification.

The customer focus of the organization will be reflected in these instruments, as a basis for service delivery.'

Job analysis

Before creating any post it is essential to ensure that it is both necessary and viable within the organization's structure. This process is job analysis and consists of collecting data on the tasks, role and responsibilities of a job and the skills needed to do it effectively. Pearn and Kandola (1993) define the process as 'any systematic procedure for obtaining detailed and objective information about a job, task or role that will be performed or is currently being performed'. Job analysis has a range of techniques, notably observation, diaries/logs, self-description, interviews and critical incident analysis – all fairly straightforward and manageable by the non-specialist.

Job description

When the purpose and content of a job are established, it is time to produce a job description. It has become *à la mode* in some circles to belittle job descriptions as being inflexible relics of outmoded bureaucracy; however, their flexibility or otherwise is not inherent, but a factor of how they are used. Even in today's volatile working world, some relatively stable reference points are necessary: productive flexibility is the alternative to dysfunctional chaos. The areas covered by a job description include:

- *job title* – this should be clear and simple; over-grand titles should be avoided
- *pay level* – this should be fair in relation to comparable jobs in the organization and, if appropriate, beyond it
- *location(s)* – this should build in appropriate flexibility, without being unfair
- *who the postholder reports to* – these two statements should be clear
- *who the postholder is responsible for* – and unambiguous
- *purpose of the job* – this should be a short and simple statement
- *broad statement of duties and responsibilities* – this should be succinct
- *any special circumstances attached to the post* – such as 'unsocial hours' and mobility required within the job.

A job description should be written with flexibility in mind, to avoid having to re-write it every few months in the light of change.

Person specification

Having thus set out what the job is, the next step is to identify the qualities needed to do it effectively. This is the person specification and it must have sufficient clarity and detail to help a selection team, for example, to make an informed and confident choice from candidates before them. Of the several frameworks for person specifications produced over time, the classic Rodger (1952) remains the most helpful. It classifies the features of the ideal postholder by seven headings:

- *Physical make-up* – important for many manual situations.
- *Attainments* – including educational and professional qualifications and experience. How will an employer assess these? Are certificates sufficient, or should specific selection tests be carried out? This may well depend upon past satisfaction with recruits' paper claims and upon the nature and clarity of skill requirements.
- *General intelligence* – if important, sometimes assessed by standard tests.
- *Special aptitudes* – particular skills, attributes or competences needed for the job in question; again, sometimes assessed by testing.
- *Interests* – both work-related and leisure, provided they are demonstrably relevant to the job in question.
- *Disposition* – personal attributes related to working with others and attitudes to work; structured personality testing is sometimes used here.
- *Circumstances* – for example, availability to work unusual hours or patterns; great care is needed in this area: items specified must be demonstrably and strictly relevant to doing the job in question and all candidates must be identically and fairly assessed.

Each of these groups of skills should be classified as either 'essential' or 'desirable'. It is fundamentally important to a fair selection process that 'essential' only includes those requirements so crucial to effectiveness in the job that lack of them disqualifies any candidate. Essential must mean essential: there must be no fudging of this at any stage of selection otherwise a serious breach of fair and objective practice occurs. It is also necessary for the person specification to indicate how each required item is to be assessed. Some will be readily discernible from an application form or curriculum vitae, others from references, some may require a practical exercise of some sort and many will only become clear at interview.

An important element in the selection process discussed above will be consideration of educational qualifications: what is required for the job and what a candidate has already achieved. As part of an individual's development within the job as well as for future jobs, it may well be necessary for further educational qualifications to be pursued. This is not the easiest area for employers, since they have little if any control over educational providers and can only choose from the menu of their provision. This may well change over time, but one course of action open to employers in the meantime is to 'mix and match' appropriate parts of a wide variety of qualifications, where the whole qualification is not relevant. This is already widely practised in the area of customer service, management and ICT skills and knowledge. A structured system for doing this – the Information Services Skills Passport – is under development (ISNTO, 2002a).

Advertisement

There are many ways – formal and informal – to build a list of candidates for a job, but current practice, especially in the public sector, holds that fairness and openness require jobs to be publicly advertised. However, there have to be circumstances where this is not the best option. For example, where a major re-structuring is in progress – and indeed the job in question may well have arisen from such re-structuring – fairness to existing and displaced staff should override public accountability. There is also a dilemma here for managers between openness of procedure and allowing proper opportunity for existing staff to have their loyalty and good work rewarded by progression within the organization. At the other end of the scale, too much internal promotion, at the expense of bringing in new blood, can result over time in an inbred and stale organization. The answer lies in striking a sensible balance between the two approaches. A job advertisement, wherever it is placed, should be clear, specific and concise. It should be attractive to its target audience without being gimmicky, which often misfires. It is customary to offer additional details to potential applicants and these should include job description, person specification and background information on the job, the organization and – often – on the place in which it is located. The overall package must be attractive as well as informative: it is not just an aid to recruitment but also an advertisement for the style and quality of the whole organization.

Curriculum vitae

The question arises at this point as to whether applications should be on a standard form or candidates should be allowed the creative licence of the curriculum vitae. The selection process is made easier, and probably fairer, if the essential information required from each candidate is presented in a uniform and readily comparable format. This does not preclude opportunity for creative and persuasive expression within the application form – description of career history and reasons for wanting this particular job, for example.

Shortlisting

When all applications are in, the process of elimination that results in the shortlist begins. As a start, all applications must be set against the person specification and any that fail to meet any of the 'essential' criteria satisfactorily *must* be eliminated – hard though this may be. Further scrutiny, this time against the 'desirable' criteria, will identify those candidates who best match the person specification as a whole: this is the shortlist and should ideally number somewhere between four and eight, depending of course on the quality of the whole range of applications.

Interview

Imperfect though it is, the interview remains an indispensable part of the selection process. It is important that the process is focused on the prime tasks: to select the best person from those applying, to make the successful candidate feel that they are joining a thoroughly competent and attractive organization and to leave unsuccessful candidates feeling they have been fairly treated by an organization they would not hesitate to apply to again to join. We believe the optimum number of interviewers is three or four: one is unacceptable, two is difficult and five or more run the risk of tripping over each other. It is difficult to see clear and necessary roles for a large panel of interviewers. For very senior jobs, there may be a case for a large number to be involved in some way with the selection process (councillors in the case of a head of a public library service, for instance) but the final selection interview should still be conducted by a small panel. It must always be borne in mind that a purpose of the interview is to allow each candidate to appear in their best light: questions aimed at tripping up a candidate serve no purpose other than to massage the ego of the interviewer! Remember the value of situational questions of the 'what would you do if . . .' nature. If it is thought necessary to bring practical tests (often useful for clerical or technical jobs), group discussions (most usual for senior and managerial posts) or psychometric testing (Toplis, Dulewicz and Fletcher 1997) into the selection process then these must have a clear and stated purpose and be closely managed to ensure they fulfil that purpose. Candidates must not be left puzzled as to why they happened. Finally, it is important that the selection processes seek to identify candidates' potential to develop in the job in question: off-the-peg readiness is tempting, but can prove static and of diminishing value. Suitable reading for those wanting to go into recruitment and selection in more depth includes the well-established Plumbley (1991), Roberts (1997) and the more technical Smith and Robertson (1993).

Training and development

If an organization has set clear and focused skill requirements at the recruitment stage and has selected successfully against them, subsequent training and development will be based upon what skills and knowledge need adding and/or updating from time to time. The concepts of the learning organization (Pedler, Burgoyne and Boydell, 1996) and the customer-focused organization (Albrecht and Zemke, 1985) and the idea of the Investors in People award (IiP) (Taylor, 2001) as a yardstick of commitment to effective training and development for the whole workforce, are the backcloth against which the effectiveness of this activity in an organization should be considered.

The learning organization

Organizational learning is crucial to the success of a customer-focused service. A learning organization has been defined as 'one that learns continuously and transforms itself' (Watkins and Marsick, 1993). Such learning is not, of course, merely a matter of training members of the organization. Marsick and Watkins (1999) identify seven 'action imperatives' for organizations aspiring to continuous learning and transformation. These are:

- Provide strategic leadership for learning.
- Connect the organization to its environment.
- Empower people in pursuit of a collective vision.
- Create systems to capture and share learning.
- Encourage collaboration and team learning.
- Encourage a climate of enquiry and dialogue.
- Create continuous learning opportunities.

This approach emphasizes system-level, continuous learning in order to create and manage knowledge outcomes, leading to improvement in the organization's performance and finally to enhanced value in terms of both financial and intellectual assets. 'Learning helps people to create and manage knowledge that builds . . . intellectual capital' (Marsick and Watkins, 1999). In a learning organization we see the twin aspirations of working towards a skilled and learning workforce and continually updating the organization in service terms come together in a successful focus on effective service delivery.

Investors in People (IiP)

We would strongly commend IiP as an invaluable quality award in the area of HRM and particularly as regards training and development. The aim of the award is to improve an organization's performance by a planned approach to setting and communicating business or service goals and by developing people to meet these goals, so that what people can do and are motivated to do clearly match what the organization needs them to do. The award is based on a number of clear and basic measures. The four criteria are:

1   Commitment – an Investor in People is fully committed to developing its people in order to achieve its aims and objectives.
2   Planning – an Investor in People is clear about its aims and objectives and what its people need to do to achieve them.
3   Action – an Investor in People develops its people effectively in order to improve its performance.
4   Evaluation – an Investor in People understands the impact of its investment in people on its performance.

Each of these criteria has a number of sub-criteria, termed 'indicators', giving more detail as to what is required to satisfy the assessment process. For each indicator, examples of acceptable evidence are given in the documentation. Judgement as to whether an applicant organization meets the criteria is made by an assessor on behalf of IiP UK (www.investorsinpeople.co.uk). If approved, the organization holds the award for three years – after which it must be re-accredited. IiP stands alongside the learning organization concept as an invaluable methodology for judging and improving readiness to deliver exemplary service to customers. The great benefit of IiP lies not in achieving the award but in the analysis, planning and improvement necessary in preparing to be assessed for it.

The training cycle

Effective training and development of a workforce is continuous and cyclic, in these stages:

1   identification of training needs
2   planning of appropriate responses
3   carrying out training
4   evaluation of outcomes and transfer of learning to the workplace.

This classic training cycle can appear static and it is therefore important to realize that the loop of activity never ends: Stage 4 always leads back to Stage 1 of the next cycle and therefore constant development can be achieved over time. This structured approach, which actually mirrors other learning-related cycles and also the criteria for the Investors in People award, appears to be in marked contrast with the reality of many organizations. This reality is characterized by large elements of chance, based upon 'what comes up' in the way of training opportunities within the parent organization and externally, and hurried consideration of 'who shall we send on this?' The net result is that the funds available for training, usually already overstretched, are expended with little or no perceivable benefit to either the organization's service performance or its individual members.

Where an organization's mission is to deliver exemplary service to its customers, training and development of the workforce takes on an enhanced importance – both in establishing the service structure and in maintaining it. Good service does not come without effective training of the workforce: effective training of the workforce does not come cheaply, either in terms of cash outlay or staff time involved. Where a new service is being set up on customer-focused principles, or an existing service is being re-launched on customer-focused lines what is required is a widespread, sustained and consistent training effort: wall-to-wall training, in effect. Widespread, because every member of the workforce is likely to require some exposure to training; sustained, because not only will the initial training effort take some time but other training and development needs are likely to emerge in the process; consistent, because all of this effort must point in one direction only – the achievement of the mission and agreed service standards – and there is no room for mixed messages. Some organizations continue to approach this training on a simplistic 'customer care' basis, which will only bring superficial and short-lived improvement. To succeed, the whole culture of the organization must be focused on good customer service, and all training and development must be geared to support and reinforce that way of life. Again, this is an area where leaders must *lead* by example and close involvement, not just preach good practice from on high.

Identification of training needs

The message here is that all training and development activity in an organization must be in response to identified need, and must be monitored and evaluated to ensure that it has met that identified need. There is, of course, the view that *all* training and personal development activity is inherently good and should be supported – in particular financially – by the employer. Such an altruistic view is very noble but, realistically, probably has little place in today's economics. The example of the long and expensive higher education course, for which there can emerge a widespread demand, is one that is likely to bring agonized debate to the most well-intentioned of employers.

In general terms the training and development of the workforce must support the objectives, targets and activities of the organization and the first stage in any properly considered and value-for-money programme is a systematic and ongoing analysis of what training and development is actually required to achieve this. A range of questions need to be dealt with, including:

- What knowledge and skills are needed by individuals to function effectively in their allotted roles – and in interaction with colleagues?
- In particular, what are the challenges to staff from a customer focus culture?
- What, of the required knowledge and skills, does each member of staff possess, at what level of competence?
- What knowledge and skills does each member of staff need to acquire?
- What is our action plan for bringing this about?

We make the assumption here that the staff selection process discussed above has succeeded in recruiting people with the skills and knowledge called for in the relevant person specification.

A range of tools can help both the organization and the individual with this analysis, for example, the Personal Skills Analysis Toolkit, Record Book and Guide now being developed by the Information Services NTO (Craven, 2002) or training needs analysis criteria (Bartram & Gibson, 1997). A system of individual performance review, which we deal with below, also feeds into this ongoing analysis as an essential element. The regular, routine communication that should occur between managers and their staff members is another essential building block in ensuring the appropriateness – and effectiveness in organizational improvement – of training and development expenditure, and is pivotal throughout the training and development cycle described here.

There are regularly occurring situations that are usually indicators of training need, including:

- new recruits
- job change
- below par performance
- new services, processes or equipment.

New recruits

A customer-focused organization can only be sustained if everyone in the workforce knows what is expected of them, and how they are doing, at all times. It is therefore important that an individual new to any job – whether they come from inside or outwith the organization – has a structured induction and orientation period in which to properly absorb their new environment and expectations. Although this is quite normal for outside appointments, it is still common for someone promoted or moved internally to be left to sink or swim in their new job. Everyone needs help at this stage and if they don't get it they may take an undue time to become effective in their new job – in extreme cases they will never reach effectiveness. This is especially the case, we suggest, for someone in their first managerial role and absence of this support may go some way to explaining why managerial skills are not generally regarded as the strong suite among information workers. Now is the time for personal targets to be initially set: they will develop over time through the individual performance review process, which we discuss below.

Induction can be described as the 'survival kit' for new recruits: who's who and what's where in the immediate work environment. This is the opportunity for the manager to explain – almost in coaching mode – the job in greater detail, and it is a good idea to keep a particularly supportive eye on the new recruit for the first few weeks. It can also be helpful, in many circumstances, for someone at or near the new recruit's level to be asked to act as guide and mentor for a while. A balance needs to be struck here between imparting enough guidance to the new recruit, without subjecting them to information overload. They can't be expected to take in everything about a job and workplace in a short space of time, nor is it necessary that they should.

Orientation complements induction and is about the wider organization. Induction should take place over the first two or three weeks; orientation is a longer-term process. It can usefully be spread over several months. Its aim must be to introduce the newcomer to a broad view of what the whole organization is and does. Examples could include visits to related work sites, to other departments, to departments in other parts of a parent organization and to senior staff – including if appropriate the head of the organization. The whole process needs to be structured to be fresh and interesting, and needs to be regularly reviewed to keep it so and to prevent it becoming a mechanical chore.

Job change

An internal change of job almost always brings with it some training needs, in addition to the induction process outlined above. These should be identified at the time of agreeing the job change and a timetable drawn up for their implementation. As we said earlier, this is an area of training that is often overlooked but there can be no excuse for this. To throw someone in at the deep end in a new job is not the way to ensure optimum performance from them. This seems to be a particular problem in the case of someone appointed to their first managerial job. Despite the fact that their preceding training and development should surely have given them some preparation for this move, it is difficult to see how they can perform at all effectively without further support. This may be from conventional training programmes but much more useful may be close support from this new manager's manager, in coaching mode. An organization with a proactive, well organized approach to development of its workforce is, of course, likely to find their people better prepared for job changes and progression up the ladder of the organization – but there is still the probability of some training needs arising on these occasions.

Below par performance

What to do with the under-performer is a perennial and thorny problem for every organization at some time or other. The main counter to it must be an effective system of individual performance review, as outlined below. This, together with effective management, should diagnose problems and those with a training and development solution can have action planned and taken. In cases of performance deficit, of course, training may well not be the solution and the problem may even eventually require disciplinary action – also dealt with below – or a change of job within the organization.

New services, processes or equipment

It seems obvious that the introduction of new services, processes or equipment signals a need for staff training, but this is not necessarily fully recognized in organizations. We always recommend that an organization makes it a rule in preparing service/business plans, or project planning generally, that the training implications of each item be identified and planned in detail. This means answering the questions: what are the training needs? How will they be met? Who takes responsibility? What are the resource implications? Even planning to maintain the status quo – not a frequently encountered option these days! – has training and development implications.

Skills foresight

Every organization – if it seeks long-term survival – needs to look ahead and attempt to foresee developments and changes likely to affect the services it offers and/or their manner of delivery. From this process it will become clear what skills and knowledge the organization will need within its workforce in order to meet these challenges and it can then plan accordingly. For example, to what extent will it train and develop its existing workforce to meet these needs; to what extent will it seek to cover the need by recruiting appropriately skilled staff at that time? The latter option, of course, runs the risk that everyone will be chasing similar staff at the same time – with a resultant skills shortage. This process is known as skills foresight and the Information Skills Organisation has taken a UK-wide strategic overview of it up to 2007 (ISNTO, 2001a) and facilitated for individual organizations the carrying out of foresight exercises related to their own circumstances by providing a toolkit (ISNTO, 2001b).

Succession planning

A related concept is succession planning, which tends to be concentrated on key and senior positions rather than the skills of the whole workforce. The aim is to ensure that the organization has enough people with the right combination of skills, knowledge and ability to promote into important senior jobs as they become vacant. In some instances a named individual is groomed over time for a specific job – probably the top job. In publicly funded organizations such a practice could be seen as directly conflicting with openness and accountability in recruitment policies, as mentioned above. In any case, this seems a somewhat hazardous business: the favoured candidate could die, leave the organization or be shown to have feet of clay as the moment of succession approaches. Even in its broader form, succession planning seems vulnerable to charges of favouritism as the chosen few are selected and specially treated.

Planning of appropriate responses

Just as the identification of individual training and development needs has been carried out systematically, so the response to it must be equally methodical. We believe that ensuring appropriate training and development of staff is a prime responsibility of every manager, though there are tasks within this process that can usefully be co-ordinated by one person within the organization: a good example is in pulling together all of the identified training and development needs across the organization and planning responses. This responsibility must rest at the highest level but in medium or large organizations there is a case for a full- or part-time training officer – reporting to the highest level – to carry out the practical day-to-day work.

The various processes, described above, by which the specific training needs of individuals and the overall skills needs of the organization are identified and collated, will produce a substantial body of data. Taken together, these will form a 'wish list' that will almost certainly outstrip the resources that the organization has available to meet it. This will make it inevitable that some prioritization must take place. Such prioritization will not be easy given the origins of this overall list:

- individual training and development needs – identified during performance review and tied to that system
- skills needs of the organization – made necessary by service development or innovation and central to its success, or identified as a result of a skills foresight exercise

- the unquestionable need to support staff new in post by induction and orientation, and staff with performance difficulties.

Prioritization for the organization overall should be the responsibility of a senior
management group; prioritization in relation to individual needs should be
resolved by the individual and his or her relevant manager, in the context of
resources available.

This problem is exacerbated by the low level of investment in training across
library and information services. Work recently carried out by our organization
underlines this (ISNTO, 2002c; ISNTO, 2002b). These studies show financial
investment in training and development of the workforce in those services to be
fractions of 1% of total payroll costs, whereas moderately adequate practice today
would be around 2% of those costs – and good practice much higher. Moreover,
some library and information services do not know what funds are actually
invested in this area and many are unable to put a figure on total training costs
including staff time involved. Those aspiring to the Investors in People award will
certainly need to be able to show a reasonably accurate figure for those overall costs
as part of their evidence. While recognizing that it is difficult to protect any particular budget head in times of financial pressure, it is clear that not enough is
being done to ensure that adequate resources are available for training and
development of the workforce. It must be stressed at this point that an organization
aspiring to good and customer-focused service stands little chance of sustaining
such a level of service where investment in workforce development of all kinds
is inadequate. This is one of the greatest challenges facing library and information service leaders today.

Carrying out training

While it is important for adequate financial resources to be available for training and development of the workforce, it is a fact that a great deal can be done
in this area by use of internal, non-financial, resources. Where training and
development is an inbuilt high priority in an organization, we find widespread
use being made of its staff at a variety of levels as a training resource. To make
this possible, it is wise for organizations to train key members of staff to act
effectively as occasional trainers. Development of staff is particularly amenable
to this use of internal resources, and a number of techniques in this area are worthy of specific mention.

It is something of a paradox that good customer service, which is helped by
flair and initiative from individual service personnel, also needs some rules and
procedures to ensure a basic high standard of service. These procedures should
be gathered together in a *staff manual*. This manual must be concise, clear,

immediately accessible in all workplaces, rigorously kept up to date and comprehensive. Its maintenance should be the responsibility of a single, named individual. The staff manual can then be the basis for a range of necessary training on procedural matters, as well as a ready reference guide as needed.

Coaching by line managers can be a particularly powerful one-to-one support, particularly where an individual is new to a job or where such close support will help improve performance. The organization should ensure that managers at all levels are properly equipped with this skill.

Counselling is often bracketed with coaching, but in reality they are very different techniques and for different purposes. Counselling is a one-to-one problem-solving undertaking, where one individual – usually more senior – helps another to find their own acceptable solution to a work or personal problem or difficult situation. This work must not be attempted by untrained individuals, or more harm than good can result. It is not necessary to have all managers trained as counsellors: what we suggest is that a suitable number of named and known individuals are trained and act across the organization – rather in the way nominated first aiders are designated.

Development of individuals can be helped by *mentoring*. This is similar to coaching, but less concentrated on the immediate workplace and usually undertaken by a senior manager other than the individual's line manager. These relationships must be openly acknowledged and operate in a climate of trust to avoid line management difficulties. Many readers will recall how they have been helped in their personal development by such a relationship, official or unofficial. Some organizations have formal and procedurally regulated schemes of mentoring which, in the right climate, can work very well. The only pitfall to avoid here is that, because the scheme is in a sense compulsory, it can become a mechanical routine without real commitment from the people involved.

Another powerful developmental tool is *action learning*. Action learning groups – known as 'sets' – tend to be cross-organizational, mixed-level groups charged with a particular short-term project. They choose their own leader and working methods and find solutions in their own way, within a defined period of time. This technique has been shown to be effectively developmental, as well as being an innovative and fruitful way of conducting project work.

Other tried and tested methods to aid staff development are adding new elements to an individual's job, known as *job enrichment*, and giving individuals opportunities to spend time on *secondment* to different jobs. Both of these methods successfully broaden the experience of an individual member of the workforce and therefore benefit the organization. This constant refreshment aids commitment and motivation among the workforce and is particularly supportive of good and focused customer service. Readers wanting to know more on these and other developmental techniques will find Landale (1999) and Reid and Barrington (1999) helpful.

Internal or external?

What elements of training and development to provide internally and what to provide from external resources is a fine balance. It will, of course, be significantly influenced by the level of financial resources available for training purposes. That apart, it is undesirable for a preponderance of this activity to come from either within or outside the organization. Too much from outside will be overly expensive and tends to draw due responsibility for training and development away from the managers on whom it should rest. Too much from inside will tend to overstretch internal resources, including people with already demanding roles in the organization apart from training, and will over time create an inward-looking culture. An outside view is always refreshing. For library and information services that are part of a larger organization there is often a middle way: training and development opportunities offered by the parent organization. These can often be particularly useful in exposing staff to the overall policies and environment which also govern the service-providing unit, as well as giving opportunities for useful contacts. They can also prove very cost-effective.

Whether internal or external, however, the quality of training delivered is of paramount importance: therefore, as we have already mentioned, it is sensible to train a wide range of appropriate staff in basic training techniques so that they are both confident and effective in this role. For external training, it is essential if buying in bespoke programmes to ensure that what is delivered is exactly what is wanted: this pre-supposes that the organization is clear about what it wants and has been firm and totally clear with the provider in this respect. In the case of external off-the-peg programmes, these should only be used where they clearly meet an identified need, rather than someone being sent on them because they are there! This is all bound in with an effective training evaluation system, discussed below.

Evaluation of outcomes

The most neglected and poorly carried out part of the training cycle is without doubt evaluation. Those who take our earlier advice and compute the total of their training and development costs will know that this activity is not cheap. It is therefore very important to ensure not only value for money but also value for the staff time and effort expended. Also, bearing in mind that most of this training and development will have arisen from high-priority needs, as described above, it is surely important to know to what extent these needs have been met – or, indeed, if the objectives of the training have been met at all.

Like the training identification process, this evaluation process must be equally systematic. Too much training and development activity is wasted because it is neither evaluated nor effectively absorbed into the workplace. Like most elements of the training cycle, proper outcomes depend on managers taking their natural responsibility in this area. We are all familiar with the scepticism, hostility or indifference from colleagues which too often greets individuals returning from a training programme. If this is matched by lack of support from the manager then the likelihood of either the individual or the workplace properly benefiting in terms of the transfer of learning from the event into the organization is minimal. Training evaluation is not of itself the remedy for this, but as part of a closely followed training cycle it can help significantly.

Evaluation of training as a process begins at the point where the decision is made that an individual will participate in a particular programme or event. At this stage clear and specific expectations must be agreed and recorded as to the outcome sought, in terms of identified individual or organizational need.

Evaluation can be used to assess the value of training relative to the objectives and targets of the organization, to assess the effectiveness of training systems and procedures in that organization and to gather feedback for training organisers and providers. There are also a range of changes in the trainee that evaluation may seek to measure:

- *reactions to the training*, although this is too often restricted to immediate reactions at the end of the event – characteristically, 'happiness sheets'; a much more valuable measure would be reactions four to six weeks after the event, when any immediate afterglow has dissipated
- *improvements in relevant skills and knowledge*, particularly if measured against expectations identified and recorded when this particular training was agreed and planned; several months must be allowed to elapse before this can be properly judged
- *changes in attitudes and behaviours* – also measured against pre-agreed expectations and on the same timescale.

By cumulating evaluations across a number of trainees it is possible to track the impact of training programmes on achievement of the organization's objectives and targets. What needs to be established is how the individual and the organization have benefited from a particular training or development activity, and how this compares with the benefits sought when the training was agreed. Dialogue between managers and their staff is the key to accurate evaluation.

Like individual performance review, discussed below, all aspects of the evaluation process must be recorded for reference and to build up a long-term picture of trends and achievements. A training evaluation system is easily applied by an informed manager and those requiring further detail will find Bramley (1992) useful.

Individual performance review

We have already referred to the need for people in any organization to know how they're doing in their jobs. Leaving aside any question of human rights, this is a matter of maintaining motivation, identifying training and development needs, and helping to ensure good service delivery. It can also head off the growth of disciplinary issues before they become major problems.

The instrument for this is individual performance review, otherwise known as appraisal or performance management. Whatever title is used there are several requirements for the process to be effective:

- The appraiser must normally be the immediate line manager.
- The process must be a partnership of appraiser and appraisee throughout, balancing the needs of each.
- It must be rooted in clear, jointly agreed and attainable targets.
- The review of performance must be in terms of those targets.
- Both the process and the targets associated with it must have firm and consistent managerial support, including opportunities for appropriate training and development related to agreed needs and work targets.
- The process must be based only upon objective and contemporary data – not, for example, hearsay nor raking up three-year-old incidents!
- The entire process must be open, honest and confidential as between appraiser and appraisee, with the appraiser's manager peripherally involved as moderator and court of appeal in case of dispute.
- Memories are unreliable; therefore proper, agreed records must be kept by both parties.
- Agreed notes of review meetings should be seen (but not filed) by the appraiser's manager in the interests of overview; both parties must have equal access to this manager in cases of disagreement.
- Notes of meetings should not be seen or filed by any other party (for example, personnel officers) although agreed consequential notes (requests for training, for instance) may be.
- The agenda of review meetings must include all items either party wish to discuss, be as wide-ranging as necessary and be agreed far enough in advance for both parties to think over what they want to say.

- As well as an annual performance review meeting, there must be intermediate review meetings at a frequency agreed by both parties as useful and effective – typically this works out at not less then two and not more than four per annum. The frequency should be sufficient for workplace issues and incidents to be raised and discussed within reasonable time of their occurrence.
- In addition there must be a climate of regular, routine dialogue and feedback in the workplace which will tend towards critical incidents and problems being dealt with on the spot as they arise; they must not consciously be stored away by either party until the next review meeting.

In short, review meetings should contain no nasty surprises, from either party – these would tend to poison the process. The whole process is intended to be developmental for the appraisee and not an opportunity for confrontation or other manifestations of macho management styles. The whole process must have full and ongoing commitment from all parties involved; the time when it is seen by anyone in the organization as having become an empty mechanical process to which only lip-service is being paid is the time either to refresh the process – or to abandon it altogether!

The outcomes of the process should be:

- continuously updated and realistic work targets
- specified support from managers and colleagues to attain those targets
- appropriate training and development to support meeting the current targets and to prepare the appraisee for foreseeable future tasks and targets – including, where appropriate, the appraisee's next likely job in the organization.

The spirit of the process of individual performance review must be one of support to the appraisee to help them achieve optimum performance, including a strong focus on identifying and reviewing training and development needs. For more detail on performance review principles and systems readers may turn to Fletcher (1997) or the classic text on the subject, but still useful, Randell (Randell et al., 1984).

Disciplinary and grievance procedures

In even the happiest and best-managed organizations situations will arise when disciplinary action is necessary against a member of the workforce, or an individual or collective grievance will develop and need to be effectively dealt with. Either of these situations, if not promptly defused, will all too soon spill over and be visible to customers in the shape of deterioration of service. A set of standard procedures is essential for both these situations to ensure fairness and consistency in handling them. Moreover, these are areas fraught with difficulties and legal pitfalls, where access to expert advice and guidance is needed – whether from within, if available, or outwith the organization.

The UK Advisory, Conciliation and Arbitration Service (ACAS) has for some time offered a code of practice for disciplinary procedures (Great Britain. ACAS, 1985). The key points are that the procedural framework should be in writing, specify to whom it applies, provide for matters to be dealt with quickly, and specify who does what and what disciplinary actions may be taken. It is important that disciplinary procedures should apply equally to all employees – regardless of length of service, seniority or any other factor. Meticulous records must be kept of all disciplinary procedures. Managers untrained in HRM will find Marchington and Wilkinson (2000) has useful information on these and many other HRM matters, including a sample disciplinary procedure framework.

Individual grievances and collective disputes must also be subject to a written procedural framework, and full records of cases must be kept. As with disciplinary matters, it is important that grievances and disputes be dealt with promptly and fairly within the agreed procedure: such matters tend to fester and assume an exaggerated importance otherwise.

In both these areas it is important that all parties, but particularly managers, follow not only the letter but also the spirit of the agreed procedures. The spirit must surely always be to seek an outcome satisfactory to both parties. It is certainly not an area where 'macho' management will bring anything but trouble and resentment.

Conclusion

The underpinning message of this chapter is that a customer-focused service aspiring to excellence can only be created and sustained if the workforce as a whole are skilled, empowered and supported to enable them to deliver such a service.

References

Albrecht, K. (1988) *At America's service*, Dow-Jones-Irwin.

Albrecht, K. and Zemke, R. (1985) *Service America!*, Dow-Jones-Irwin.

Bartram, S. and Gibson, B. (1997) *Training needs analysis*, Gower.

Bitner, M. J., Booms, B. H. and Tetreault, M. S. (1990) The service encounter, *Journal of Marketing*, **54**, 71–84

Bramley, P. (1992) *Evaluating training effectiveness*, 2nd edn, McGraw-Hill.

Craven, A. E. (2002) *Fostering a skilled and learning workforce in Wales*, ISNTO.

Fletcher, C. (1997) *Appraisal*, 2nd edn, IPD.

Great Britain. ACAS (1985) *Disciplinary practice and procedure*, HMSO.

ISNTO (2001a) *Skills foresight in the Information Services sector, 2000–2007*, ISNTO.

ISNTO (2001b) *Skills foresight toolkit supporting note*, ISNTO.

ISNTO (2002a) *Information Services Skills Passport*, unpublished.

ISNTO (2002b) *In-house skills benchmarking toolkit and supporting notes*, ISNTO.

ISNTO (2002c) *Skills benchmarking in the Information Service sector*, ISNTO.

Landale, A. (ed.) (1999) *Gower handbook of training and development*, Gower.

Marchington, M. J. and Wilkinson, A. (2000) *Core personnel and development*, 2nd rev. edn, IPD.

Marsick, V. J. and Watkins, K. E. (1999) *Facilitating learning organizations*, Gower.

Pearn, M. and Kandola, R. (1993) *Job analysis*, 2nd edn, IPD.

Pedler, M., Burgoyne, J. and Boydell, T. (1996) *The learning company*, 2nd edn, McGraw-Hill.

Plumbley, P. R.(1991) *Recruitment and selection*, rev. edn, IPD.

Randell, G. A. et al. (1984) *Staff appraisal*, 3rd edn, IPD.

Reid, M. A. and Barrington, H. (1999) *Training interventions*, 6th edn, IPD.

Roberts, G. (1997) *Recruitment and selection – a competency approach*, IPD.

Rodger, A. (1952) *The seven point plan*, National Institute for Industrial Psychology.

Smith, M. and Robertson, I. T. (1993) *The theory and practice of systematic staff selection*, 2nd edn, Macmillan.

Taylor, P. (2001) *Managing for Investors in People*, Kogan Page.

Toplis, J., Dulewicz, V. and Fletcher, C. (1997) *Psychological testing*, 3rd edn, IPD.

Watkins, K. E. and Marsick, V. J. (1993) *Sculpting the learning organization*, Jossey-Bass.

5

Keeping focused on our customers

MARKETING AS A TOOL FOR LIBRARY AND INFORMATION MANAGERS

Christopher West

Introduction

This chapter will relate some key marketing concepts to managing libraries from a practitioner's, rather than a theoretical point of view. In particular, it will relate these concepts to the centrality of a customer-oriented service, along with their relevance to hybrid libraries, providing a mix of print and digital information services. Perhaps inevitably, most of the examples given are from my own sector and relate to UK academic libraries. However, the basic concepts that underlie the marketing process can be easily translated to all sectors of the profession.

Marketing concepts

If you work in an academic library, most of you will have a rather daunting array of marketing textbooks on your shelves, stretching to several linear metres. Recently, I was in the marketing section of our stock, along with one of my more cynical colleagues. 'Look at this', he said. *'Marketing. An introduction to marketing. An introduction to strategic marketing. Strategic marketing: an introduction.* Shelves and shelves of statements of the obvious.'

A first impression of marketing can suggest that it is a rather facile discipline, which has little practical benefit for library and information managers. Much of the general literature on marketing seems to be based on memorable but unverifiable concepts, which are aphoristic rather than scientific. Many of these aphorisms appear to have more to do with the self-help books for business people that seem to clutter up airport bookshops ('Seven successful habits of highly effective superheroes') than academic disciplines.

One of the most pervasive of these concepts is the four Ps of marketing: product, price, place and promotion. The first two of these, product and price, sit rather uneasily with a non-profit service. Quite apart from definitions (what exactly are our products, particularly in a digital environment? Does price just refer to our costs?), libraries have a strong service tradition and an even longer customer perception as a free service. Interestingly, the free use at the point of access tradition has been maintained, and even extended, for most electronic information. Virtuous circles in marketing based on the four Ps, where effective marketing leads to increased product sales, allowing profits to pay for further market domination (Davies, 1998, 7) seem rather removed from the parameters of most libraries. Library and information managers have also probably regarded marketing as one of their intuitive skills, arising from their customer experience and attitudes, which doesn't require any formalization. Like many other aspects of human relations, we may do it every day without labelling what we do.

Marketing also suffers from many misconceptions. Popularly, it is often seen purely as the process of promoting and selling products and services. Related to this is the concept that this process of promotion is an optional add-on. 'Two commonly-held, but mistaken, views of marketing [are] marketing is selling . . . [and] marketing is mainly a department' (Kotler, 1999, 19). This rather limited view of marketing is also often shared by customers. Rather predictably, in two large-scale customer surveys, improved marketing and publicity for library services comes low down in lists of customer priorities. At Leicester University Library (1994, 60), better promotion of library services came 35th out of 38 customer priorities. A survey carried out by Library and Learning Resources at University of Wales College, Newport in 1998 saw 'improve LLR publicity about its services' come ninth out of 14 priorities (University of Wales College, Newport, 1998, 7).

We also may not like to admit it, but the traditional view of the library/information world as a 'given', fixed resource is still a pervasive influence. Our customers just need to grasp how easy it is to circumnavigate the internet or to find their way around the eight floors of our building and everything will be fine. This may, still, be related to the fact that many of our professional skills don't have the immediate results, or feedback, of those in other professions. Much of what we do has a delayed and intangible impact. How many of the books we diligently catalogue are borrowed immediately and have a major intellectual impact on our customers? This long-term, intangible use of professional skills sits uneasily with marketing's emphasis on a direct impact on customer needs and a measurable quantification of this.

Despite these initial qualms, marketing concepts can be effective and practical tools in managing libraries. One of the many attractive features of library and information work is its inclusiveness. Unlike many other professions, we rarely limit our activities: 'What? Touch a computer? Not me, mate, nothing to do with my job.' At various times, we are happy to add an eclectic mix of skills, ranging from architecture to personnel management, to our core skills of organizing and communicating information. Marketing based on effective two-way communication with our customers can undoubtedly improve our quality of service. Libraries form a crucial element in the communication process, as gateways to physical and digital information. Communicating effectively with our customers is of key importance: we don't want to create any barriers between them and the information they need. Equally, we need to be aware of the often sophisticated levels of media literacy of our customers and their intuitive knowledge and expectations of media genres.

Definitions

Conceptually, marketing suffers from popular misconceptions. It is a much broader concept than simply an enabling mechanism for selling (promotion, advertising and public relations) and it is far more than a function at the end of a production process (a sales or marketing department). Marketing has also moved away from an emphasis on products to a concentration on customer needs as part of a process of exchange. This reflects changes in the world economy away from manufacturing to a service-led situation. Once again, library and information managers will be very empathetic to an emphasis on the primacy of customer needs and services.

Davies (1998, 336) offers a succinct definition: 'Satisfying and maintaining customer needs profitably'. If one substituted 'effectively' for 'profitably', then most libraries could relate to this. Kotler and others have emphasized the need for marketing to be regarded as a managerial and strategic tool. The Chartered Institute of Marketing's definition reflects this: 'Marketing is the management process which identifies, anticipates and supplies customer requirements efficiently and profitably' (Cannon, 1992, 3). A recent definition by Kotler further stresses the managerial and exchange characteristics of marketing: 'a social and managerial process by which individuals and groups obtain what they need and want through creating and exchanging products and value with others' (Kotler et al., 1999, 10). Kotler and Andreasen (1995, 36) have further developed these concepts for public sector and non-profit organizations:

> [Marketing] means developing a philosophy . . . that puts the customer at the centre of everything one does. . . . Marketing is not intimidation or coercion. It is not 'hard selling' and deceptive advertising. It is a sound, effective technology for cre-

ating exchanges and influencing behaviour that, when properly applied, must be socially beneficent because its major premise is responding to customer needs and wants.

A helpful, and surprisingly readable, summary of marketing concepts and trends can be found in *Kotler on marketing* (Kotler, 1999). Among others, two brief introductions to marketing from a libraries perspective can be found in Coote (1994) and in Elliott de Sáez (2002). In addition, the impressive work of the Colorado Library Marketing Council at **www.clmc.org/background.htm** provides an excellent resource for marketing library services.

A marketing model based on an exchange process, with customer needs and service delivery having primacy, has close correspondence to a parallel model based on a professional relationship between the library and information practitioner and their client. Just like the caring and teaching professions, library and information professionals seek to provide the best possible service to promote the intellectual and recreational development of their clients. This will not be impeded by any direct financial transactions, within the broader financial constraints of a public service. Kotler's increasing emphasis on marketing as an exchange process also has relevance for libraries' role as gateways between information providers and information seekers. In line with this, Kotler and others now suggest a more customer-oriented model than the four Ps of marketing, even where product is service and price equals efficiency:

Marketers see the marketing management process as five basic steps which can be represented as:

$$R \rightarrow STP \rightarrow MM \rightarrow I \rightarrow C$$

Where:

R   = Research (ie, market research)
STP = Segmentation, targeting and positioning
MM = Marketing mix
I   = Implementation
C   = Control (getting feedback, evaluating results and revising or improving STP strategy and MM tactics).

(Kotler, 1999, 30)

Research

Customer surveys

It seems axiomatic that a service which has customer needs at its heart should give the highest priority to finding out what those needs are. Discovering and understanding customer wishes is a key starting point in the marketing process. Libraries have made significant progress over the last decade in measuring and evaluating the needs of their users. Some of this has been in response to external pressures. Winkworth (2001, 718–31) provides a thoughtful and concise summary of this process in the UK. Public libraries have been measured against a standard set of performance measures, as well as separate, more qualitative Best Value reports. In UK higher education, the Follett Report (HEFCE, 1993, 31–2) emphasized the need for academic libraries to widen their quantitative and qualitative feedback from their users.

As well as external pressure, much of this trend towards improved measurement of customer needs has come from within the profession. The original motivation for this was not derived from the marketing process. Much of it was a well-intentioned attempt to produce a workable set of comparative performance indicators. The Joint Funding Councils' *Effective academic library* report in 1995 was, perhaps, the most ambitious attempt in this area. For academic libraries at least, two main trends in providing tools to measure customer needs can be picked out. Firstly, relatively simple and cost-effective toolkits have been developed to allow libraries to create regular measures of customer satisfaction and needs. The work of Nancy Van House and colleagues for the American Library Association (Van House, Neil and McClure, 1990) was very influential, and was continued in a UK academic library context by Ford and Revill (1996). More recently, SCONUL has further developed this toolkits approach, in the areas of user satisfaction surveys (West, 2001) and in the use of a standardized approach to the benchmarking of services (Town, 2000). In a more specialist area, the EQUINOX project (Brophy, 2000) has sought to develop performance measures for the electronic library. All of these projects seek to provide libraries with a relatively simple and adaptable set of tools (often based on specific software applications) to enable them to measure customer needs and perceptions of the services they offer.

The second trend has been to focus more on the qualitative aspects of customer perceptions. Techniques have been adapted from other sectors to gauge this. One of the more interesting current developments is the adaptation of the SERVQUAL methodology from the business community to American academic libraries, using the LibQUAL+ tool (Measuring service quality, 2001). Although still under development, this has the potential to provide a sophisticated methodology for gauging customer needs and their perceptions of the quality of service on offer (Cook and Heath, 2001). In the UK, the Libra software was developed by Priority Research from other areas of the public sector for libraries. It provides a user-friendly and adaptable method for establishing customer priorities, as well as an effective tool for more quantitative surveys (Hayden, 1997).

Essentially, regular surveys of customer needs should to be carried out to provide a current and longitudinal view of their:

- satisfaction with the current range of services and resources provided
- view of the relative importance of these services
- other, more qualitative, opinions and ideas on additional services needed, and their prioritization of these.

It is also crucial to include the whole customer base in the research process. This means including the views of constituencies like irregular and non-users of libraries. Patterns of use can be discovered by including questions on the frequency of use in surveys and then relating these to other demographic responses like travel distance to the library and the age of the respondent (West, 2001, 23). However, the Van House methodology, as developed by Ford and Revill (1996) and the SCONUL user satisfaction questionnaire, is explicitly aimed at active users of libraries. Many of the questions are based on customer activities in, and perceptions of, a library and information service on a specific day. We also need to develop tools that will easily allow us to investigate low and non-use, and the reasons for these.

Surveys that explore the reasons for non-use are particularly important for libraries where standard measures show a clear trend towards a decline in usage. Public libraries in the UK have seen a continuing trend over the last decade towards a lower level of use. There has been a 24% decline in the total number of books issued over the last ten years, with a 16% drop in library visits over the last five years (Creaser, Maynard and White, 2001, 15 and 79). There are several complex reasons for this, but a survey of non-users and, in particular, segments of customers with high non-usage rates like teenagers, must be one of the starting points for any marketing campaigns to promote use.

Other methods of customer feedback

Surveys of current and potential customers are not the only method of marketing research. Often, the simplest methods can be a starting point for improved marketing of services. Observation of customer behaviour within buildings is often under-valued, although the retail sector places great importance on the most effective design of buildings to maximize throughput and transactions. Libraries have tended to disregard this, despite its importance. One notable exception to this is the University of Northumbria at Newcastle Library, which redesigned its layout after an exercise on patterns of customer activity.

Suggestion forms (electronic and paper) should also not be disregarded as a source of customer feedback. These will give a qualitative overview, to reinforce quantitative responses from surveys. By the time you get 20 suggestion forms all telling you that your building is too warm then this more than reinforces the need to turn down the heating as quickly as possible. Suggestion forms can also provide valuable input on a plethora of small actions, all of which add up to a major improvement in customer satisfaction particularly in the area of the physical environment of our services (uncomfortable chairs, creaking doors, poor lighting, need for better signage, and so on).

Finding mechanisms to listen to our customers on an individual, or a small group basis, is a key element in market research. Allowing our customers to articulate views on aspects of services, or to develop their thoughts on the whole suite of services on offer, can be a stimulating and/or chastening experience. Customers, and non-customers, can often be extremely perceptive and articulate. The interviews carried out by Cook and Heath at Texas A&M Libraries for a pilot LibQUAL+ project were illuminating:

> He kept saying that what he wanted was 'ubiquity of access', a concept which resonated with me the first time he said it and became more meaningful to me each time he used it. Would it be too much, he asked, for the modern research library to ensure that he could obtain access to the information he required at any time of the night or day, without regard to its format?
>
> (Cook and Heath, 2001, 549)

Focus groups

As an extension of qualitative input from individuals and groups of customers, focus groups can be a cost-effective and valuable activity. They can either be held as free-standing starting points for marketing, or can form the basis of surveys to prioritize customer needs (Hayden, 1997, 38–9). Recently, focus groups have been derided in a political context: they represent the views of eight people in Kettering drinking wine, in Derek Draper's memorable phrase. Despite their obvious drawbacks in terms of short-termism and a lack of strategic coherence, focus groups can be a stimulating starting point for new service developments. Kotler (1999, 39) lists several services that have arisen from the free-thinking, idealized agendas of focus groups, including no-frills, low-cost airlines and multiplex cinemas. It is often the interplay between the inarticulate but valid demands of customers and our professional skills and knowledge as library and information providers that can produce leaps forward in service provision and the marketing of this. If we allow our customers to articulate their ideal library and information service then we may have the technical skills and vision to deliver this to all.

All of these processes of gauging current and future customer needs should be continuous. This will allow a longitudinal record of service improvement, as well as highlighting the more intractable problems of service provision and, most importantly, changing customer needs. An allied process in marketing research is testing market problems, by testing particular marketing hypotheses, or a cluster of related service options (Davies, 1998, 63–4). A good example of this from a libraries context is surveying customers' preferences for extended service hours (West, 2001, 22). A related activity is piloting a service, or product testing. In the context of new digital services offered on trial periods by CHEST and JISC, this is now a fairly common situation for academic libraries in the UK. One wonders how many of us take active measures to fully gauge customer responses and preferences on these trials.

Professional research

There are also important areas of market-based research that are not so closely related to a service's immediate customer base. Knowledge of innovation and service delivery elsewhere within the profession is crucial, particularly in a cross-sectoral context. In general, libraries have well-developed mechanisms for this, as well as our well-known natural disposition towards co-operation. However, it may be increasingly important to look at developments completely outside of our sector. The retail industry has transformed itself over the last 20 years. Libraries could learn much from their techniques in several areas of activity, including store design, unified marketing, stock control and building ambience. Another obvious area we can learn from is digital services. Web design techniques, and innovative methods of delivering information, are being led by the new media. We need to pick up ideas from these areas, as these are what our customers will judge us by.

We also need to look to ourselves for innovative services to market. Kotler (1999, 23–4) distinguishes between three types of marketing:

- *responsive marketing:* which finds and fills needs, using many of the techniques described above
- *anticipative marketing:* which recognizes emergent and latent needs (Kotler suggests the growth in demand for quality bottled drinking water as an example of this)

- *need-shaping marketing:* which introduces products and services that 'nobody asked for and often could not even conceive of' (Kotler, 1999, 23). This is the most difficult and risky of all. Kotler's well known examples include the work of the founder of Sony, Akio Morita, inventor of the Walkman and other innovative products.

Our responsive marketing in libraries has, undoubtedly, improved over the last decade, but how much time do we devote to anticipative and need-shaping marketing?

Segmentation, targeting and positioning

A continuous procedure of researching our customers' current and future needs is the first stage in the marketing process. Using Kotler's schema, the next step is the three inter-related areas of segmentation, targeting and positioning. Market segmentation divides up a market into differing groups of users. These specific groups will have specific needs and will tend to respond distinctively to services and products. These segments of the market are then targeted as part of a planned marketing campaign which attempts to meet their distinct needs and empathizes with and reinforces their specific lifestyles and aspirations. To reinforce this process, products, services and brands are positioned to appeal to these targeted groups. This is done in terms of brand image, lifestyle identity and, most importantly, in terms of 'value position': the range of benefits the product or service can offer that particular market segment.

Market segmentation and targeting

How can libraries use this process to ensure that they meet the needs of the variety of customers they serve? Segmentation is a potentially difficult concept for a mass market service like a public library, which has a commitment to meet a huge variation in customer needs within a locality. Even in academic libraries, with their clearly defined broad customer groups (academic staff, undergraduates, postgraduates), the process of market segmentation can be potentially complex. With the greatly increased participation in higher education in the UK, undergraduates have become a far less homogeneous group. They can be full-time or part-time students (with many full-time students behaving like part-timers because of the demands of termtime employment); ages can vary considerably with far more mature students; needs and attitudes can vary considerably across academic subjects.

To have an informed approach to the segmentation of customers, care needs to be taken with research. Who are the potential customer groups and what are their distinct needs? Public libraries will need current information on the demographic, social and cultural mix of customers in their local authority areas. With their relatively smaller and more clearly defined clientele, academic libraries need to find out what the primary needs of their customer groups are: do their English students need a different mix of services from their engineering students?

Libraries are not alone in finding the process of segmentation and market definition an increasingly complex process. The previous certainties of occupationally based social classes A to E, with clearly defined social attitudes and expectations attached to these, are becoming much more fluid. This is partly the result of fundamental changes in the nature of occupations, but also of paradigm shifts in social attitudes and aspirations. Marketing has tended to move away from a rigid five social classes pattern to much more flexible definitions, based on lifestyle trends and coalitions of social attitude. As I feel the advancing tread of time, my favourite lifestyle group is Faith Popcorn's 'Down-aging group' (quoted in Kotler, 1999, 80):

Down-aging is a tendency to act and feel younger than one's age. . . . Older people are spending more on youthful clothes, hair colouring and facial plastic surgery. They are engaging in more playful behaviour, willing to act in ways not normally found in their age group. They buy adult toys, attend adult camps and sign up for adventurous vacations.

It can be argued that there is an increasing trend for people not to see themselves as part of broad social classes, but as part of much smaller social groups, based on lifestyles and a common set of social attitudes and aspirations.

This bifurcation of the market is a huge opportunity for providers of services and products, in that they can target these at very specific market segments. This has become increasingly possible since post-1945 manufacturing techniques broke away from the single, Fordist production unit to a multiplicity of units based on the same basic design. As the market has moved away from production to services, then this process has accelerated, supported by increasingly sophisticated brand images linked to lifestyle-based market segmentation. A lifestyle becomes a series of brand statements and, yes, I drive a VW, shop in Gap and drink my coffee in Starbucks.

Faced with the sophistication and sheer depth of resources behind this targeting process, much of what libraries have done in this area appears ineffectual or naïve. Clearly, most libraries need to adopt multi-segmented marketing which, in turn, means a careful balancing of sometimes conflicting customer needs. Great care has to be taken so that, when targeting a particular group of customers, other major groups of customers are not alienated. Targeting activity of this type is often most effective if it is part of a clearly defined campaign aimed at a specific group of customers. Brewerton's description (2001, 19–24) of a brief campaign by Oxford Brookes University Library aimed at new students during the first week of term is an excellent example of this. It has clear objectives, a definite target audience and uses techniques appropriate to them and their environment. It also does not impinge on the library's other customer groups.

Positioning

The final element in the segmentation and targeting process is positioning. The service or product's corporate and brand image is developed to match the needs and aspirations of the targeted customer group. The brand image is linked to its value positioning: the major benefit it provides to its market segment, which can be reinforced by a series of related value benefits. In the commercial world, this can be a rather artificial process. In the UK, Stella Artois lager is positioned as a high-quality, high-value product; in Belgium, it is positioned as an everyday drink.

Libraries will, hopefully, have a more tangible range of customer benefits to contribute to their positioning process, but they will need to show equal sophistication and sensitivity in doing this. This can be a potentially complex process. Many of the older public libraries in the UK face the same problems as our high-street banks. They are housed in inflexible and inappropriate buildings, often in the wrong part of town with no parking facilities. The social and cultural population of the area will have changed radically over the last century and, in many cities, may have declined in number. It could also be suggested that public libraries have lacked a clear value position in such areas recently. Were they primarily for recreation? If this was the case then they faced an increasing level of competition, both in the home and outside. If they were for learning then until recently, this was far from explicit. The rediscovery and reinvigoration of the lifelong learning agenda by public libraries over the last few years has been a very positive process (almost a return to their 19th-century roots). Supported by the introduction of new technology to support it via the People's Network, this has allowed public libraries to re-position themselves in a much more positive way. However, great care needs to be taken with this not to alienate other customer groups within the public libraries' customer base. As an example, the Idea Stores concept in Tower Hamlets, where low-use public libraries and adult education centres were closed down and replaced by joint learning centres/libraries met a somewhat mixed reception at first (Benjamin, 2001; Middleton, 2000). By contrast, the equally radical Peckham Library has shown the value of investing and branding a modern library and learning centre in a similar area.

On a much smaller scale, care also needs to be taken with positioning even very targeted campaigns like the one in Oxford Brookes. One is reminded of the Colin Whelan cartoon of many years ago, which showed a librarian wearing a t-shirt, which had something like the following printed on the front: 'Despite this ridiculous t-shirt I am a qualified librarian'. Positioning edges into the broader public relations agenda of constantly fostering a positive image. The first step in creating this is the avoidance of any negative images.

The marketing mix

The next stage in a customer-led marketing process is the marketing mix. This is our old friend, the four Ps again (product, price, place and promotion). Originally developed by McCarthy in the 1960s, this is still a valid series of concepts, but now just forms part of a broader view of marketing as an exchange process focused on customers. Interestingly, Kotler (1999, 96) has attempted an update of the four Ps concept to reflect this:

Four Ps	Four Cs
Product	Customer value
Price	Cost to the Customer
Place	Convenience
Promotion	Communication

At first glance, some of the concepts in the marketing mix, whether they start with a P or a C, are only applicable to a commercial environment. However, they can also be useful tools for a library service to meet the needs of its customers. Many libraries are already using these techniques in an intelligent and focused way.

Customer value

Even in the commercial world, products have increasingly been replaced by services (do we need the four Ss?). This removes some of the barriers to this concept for libraries. Like all services, libraries face the problem of intangibility. Information is a slippery, invisible commodity which, potentially, is difficult to market (Coote, 1994, 20–1). As the world becomes more service oriented, however, marketing a cohesive package of information exchanges that have strong customer value becomes a mainstream activity.

An interesting element in product and service marketing in the commercial world is positive differentiation. How does one attach brand value to, say, one car insurance service competing with dozens of others, all of which have very similar services and costs? The inclusive nature of libraries has, possibly, made them slow to differentiate their range of services. We sometimes lack clarity as to what our USP (unique selling point) or value position is to our targeted customer groups. Particularly with the development of competition in information gathering (Brophy, 2002, 4), we may need to think about the key features that differentiate our services. Among others, these could include free access to information, expert support for learning, along with professional information gathering skills, as starting points. Also, as hybrid libraries develop further, providing seamless access to information in a widening variety of formats, then there is a strong need for us to link the multiplicity of services now on offer into a cohesive and explicable continuum, with access to information as its central point.

Cost

Price, or cost to the customer, also needs consideration in the marketing mix for libraries. Kotler's new formulation is more helpful here: can we save time and opportunity costs for part-time, remote students by providing as much information as possible through the desktops of their PCs at home? For a long while, libraries have used marketing price techniques like differential pricing: we charge more for photocopying by library staff compared with self-service copying, and so on. This process may extend in future, particularly if increased mediation is required in the information-seeking process. However, outside of the special libraries sector, free customer access to information at the point of use remains a potent brand image and, equally importantly, a strong customer expectation. Interestingly, after some unsuccessful attempts with other models, free access at the point of use has become the norm for digital information, with libraries subscribing to bundles of e-journals and digital information services for a fixed fee over a set time period, which then allows unlimited access for their customer groups.

Convenience

In a library context, place, or convenience, can be seen as the method it uses to distribute its services to its customers. Two diverse, but powerful, trends have affected this aspect of the marketing mix for libraries over the last decade. The first of these is the impact of alternative models in the retail sector. The improved design and efficiency of modern retail outlets have been noted previously: most libraries struggle to compete with the new genres of retail layout. Interestingly, some of the newer academic libraries in the UK (Liverpool John Moores University, for example) have design features that parallel modern retail stores. Perhaps the retail situation that is of most interest to libraries in terms of ambience is the new type of bookshop, which started with companies like Barnes & Noble in the USA. Some of the features of these new bookshops parallel libraries: they are often large, with extensive and wide-ranging stocks; some stores even design their shelving along traditional library designs. However, they also have other features that make them attractive places to visit and to linger in. They have high-quality coffee outlets, very long opening hours (compared with traditional bookshops) and encourage customers to browse, read and, most importantly, use them as places for social interaction. As we already have some of these features, would it be an effective marketing ploy for libraries to return the compliment and to mimic the modern bookstores?

A related issue arising out of the physical location of libraries is opening hours. Again, this has its roots in social changes and major improvements in the retail sector. Once again following trends in North America, many supermarkets in the UK now open for very long hours, often providing 24-hour opening. Shopping at 3 a.m. still seems a more perverse activity than writing essays or doing academic research at this hour, but, with a few praiseworthy exceptions, British university libraries haven't followed this trend. This is despite the 24-hour availability of web-based resources and the huge increase in student PCs in most university libraries over the last few years. UK public libraries have seen some encouraging trends towards opening on Sundays, again following a major trend in the retail sector. However, financial problems have meant that opening hours have decreased in UK public libraries over the last decade. Service-point hours declined by 12% between 1990 and 2000, with service points open for 60 hours per week or longer showing an alarming 73% decrease (Creaser, Maynard and White, 2001, 17).

A second, contrary trend in terms of the library as a 'place' has been the accelerating increase in distributed information (Dowlin, 1995). In many cases, the library now sits on the desktop of the customer's PC. Internet information, bundles of e-journals and digital information services mean that many customers have less need to travel to their library (Brophy, 2002). Although difficult to quantify, one suspects that this is already the case for most university staff and research postgraduates in the UK and will rapidly spread to other sectors. As with other services that have adapted to digital information, this won't mean that the need for a physical location for a library will disappear. Rather, like other services, we will provide an even more 'clicks and bricks' hybrid service, to different types of customer using us for differing reasons. This has big implications for providing a unified, consistent and customer-friendly service, which transcends the boundaries of format.

Communication

Kotler's update of the final P ('promotion') to 'communication' is helpful. As well as an information-rich world, we also live in a world of sophisticated communications avidly consumed by media-literate customers. We need to be aware of this and, particularly, the media sophistication and expectations of our clientele in all of our promotional activities. Amateurish and old-fashioned promotion will create an increasingly negative set of images. Libraries will need to further advance their skills in promotion techniques like public relations, advertising and direct marketing to make themselves heard against sophisticated competition.

Many promotional techniques will be familiar and will already be carried out effectively by libraries. Coote (1994, 24–36) has a brief, helpful checklist. The best promotion is often based on other factors in the marketing process, leading to service improvement. As we have seen, extended opening hours can be a simple, but very effective tool. Bath University Library has, quite rightly, used its pioneering 24-hour opening in this way. A new building can be used both by the library and its parent institution as the basis of a major promotional and recruitment campaign (recent examples include successful new libraries in Coventry University and the London School of Economics). Other elements in the marketing process that do not need major investment, such as customer surveys, discussed above, can also be used as promotional tools. As we have seen, simply carrying out regular surveys of your customers' needs is an excellent public relations activity. It shows that you are listening to them and are responsive to their needs and this creates an immediately positive image of your service.

The rapid growth in digital information services has made their promotion a key issue for libraries. As mentioned previously, the vast majority of these services are paid for by fixed-cost subscriptions over a period of time. Libraries need to maximize the use of these services by their customers, to ensure that they represent value for money. Another area for examination is the marketing aspect of public relations. A large element of public relations is the fostering of positive images of a service and the careful avoidance of any negative images. This should be a key element in any customer relations training carried out in our services.

Another promotion technique to which libraries could give more consideration is the concept of a sales force. In an interesting article, Noon (1994, 9–25) suggests this as an alternative model for subject specialists in academic libraries.

They could be seen as the library's sales force, promoting a wide range of services to customers in academic departments.

Whatever elements of the marketing mix are used by libraries, it is crucial that these form part of an integrated campaign (Kotler, 1999, 116-20). Once an appropriate and effective mix of tools is chosen, these must combined to provide a consistent message to widen the use of our services. All of the contact points with our customers, whether these are planned (for example, printed publicity) or are part of our daily services, should always show a clear and customer-based cohesion.

Implementation

After all of the aspects of tactical marketing, the next stage is the implementation of the marketing plan. This is the difficult bit: I'm sure that we all have the experience of preparing thorough and extensive strategic plans, only for the unexpected or the obdurate to diminish their effectiveness. Even if the planning stage is adequate, Kotler emphasizes that implementation is often the most difficult stage of the marketing process (1999, 33–4). This often results from a failure to link brand value to customer value. Customers of all types of services will not associate them with customer value if they do not meet the service parameters implicit in their brand values. The British transport system gives innumerable examples of this over the last few years. It is also crucial for the marketing plan to be completely integrated with the service process. Are your front-of-house staff fully aware of your marketing campaign to your part-time students? Do the new digital services splashed all over your newsletter actually work yet? Is your web-based and printed material harmonized and, even better, created as a unified resource?

One obvious managerial tool for ensuring effective implementation is to make marketing the clearly designated responsibility of an individual member of staff. Several UK public library services have posts of this type, although they are rather less common in UK academic libraries. A notable exception to this is the British Library of Political and Economic Science at the LSE. In 2000, they created a new post of Communications Manager, with the remit to 'improve internal and external communication and raise the profile of the Library' (BLPES, 2001, 6). More usually, marketing and communications are part of a range of the duties of a relatively senior library manager. To support this and, more importantly, involve a cross-section of staff in this key activity, it is also worth establishing a marketing group to prepare and guide the process.

Oxford Brookes University Library adopted the approach of using a marketing group, made up of a cross-section of staff from various functions and sites. The marketing campaign to new students, although light-hearted, was successfully implemented and got across a variety of key messages about the range of services on offer:

> Rule 4: back up all of this nonsense with a serious message. For both Fairs we have focussed on specific services to market: Library tours, Subject Librarians and our Web site can all enable our customers to get the most out of the Library, become more effective and efficient in their research and make better use of electronic (and more traditional) sources. This is the message we are *really* trying to get across.
>
> (Brewerton, 2001, 23).

Another key element in ensuring the successful implementation of marketing campaigns is to embed them in staff development programmes and procedures, particularly those that focus on customer care and service provision. The Colorado Library Marketing Council (www.clmc.org/) has taken this an innovative step further by providing professional staff development opportunities in marketing techniques for library staff across the state. These are both generic programmes, based on formal teaching and a wealth of web-based materials, and programmes aimed at specific groups like school librarians.

Control

The final stage in the marketing process is control or, for those who do not like the Orwellian tone of this concept, evaluation. As with all other aspects of management, evaluating the effectiveness of strategies and their impact on customers is the essential final stage in a process of continuous service improvement. The commercial sector will often undertake thoroughgoing market audits, testing all aspects of the process from its inception. It may also be helpful to distinguish between strategic control, which looks at the broader aspects of marketing strategy and performance, and with the more day-to-day tactical control, which improves current marketing activity (Kotler and Andreasen, 1995, 598–614).

Closing the feedback loop, of course, takes us back to the importance of research. We need to know as quickly as possible if our marketing plans have resulted in service improvement. Has the increased promotion of a particular digital service increased its use? Over the last few years, usage monitoring of some commercially provided digital services has become much easier, enabling us to match usage to a promotion campaign. Has a targeted segment of your customers shown an increase in use and were the formats for communicating with them successful?

The need for continuous monitoring reinforces the need for longitudinal customer satisfaction testing. As an example of this from my own library and information service, feedback from satisfaction surveys showed significant levels of dissatisfaction with both the quantity and quality of student PCs available in our Library and Information Centre. In response to this, one of our main aims for service improvement over the last three years has been to increase the number of student PCs and the reliability of the service. We now have around 40% of our study spaces as PC-based electronic workspaces and the student network has been upgraded, in terms of hardware, network operating system and applications. As a result of this, satisfaction with this area of service has increased by over 40 points in our rating scales, from an admittedly low base.

Conclusion

Marketing is a crucial activity for a customer-based service like a library. Although its techniques were originally developed for the commercial exploitation of products, the impact of the service economy has refined marketing concepts and they can easily be used as useful tools for library managers. Kotler's recent summary of the marketing process (1999, 30) can be used as an effective framework for a library seeking to formalize or to reinvigorate its marketing activities. Researching the needs of our customers is a self-evident starting point, and several standard mechanisms are now available, which have been tailored to library circumstances. The tactical stage of market segmentation and targeting, with the allied activity of positioning library services, will allow closer linkages between the range of services offered by libraries and the often divergent information needs of their customer groups. Concepts related to the marketing mix (the value, costs and convenience of library services to our customers and how we then communicate these to them) are essential elements in service provision. The implementation stage reinforces the need for an effective marketing process, requiring both individual and group responsibility. Finally, the control or feedback stage loops back into the research process, to create a mechanism for continuous service improvement and innovation.

It is noticeable that we tend to adopt other managerial techniques without question in areas like strategic planning, finance and human resources. The two-way process of communicating with our customers is an equally important activity and we need the conceptual techniques to enable us to do this effectively. In a world dominated by the sophisticated marketing of services to a media-aware audience, we have no choice in this matter.

References

Benjamin, A. (2001) Read alert, *Guardian*, (13 June 2001).
Brewerton, A. (2001) Inspirational marketing, *SCONUL Newsletter*, **24**, 18–24.

British Library of Political and Economic Science (2001) *Annual report 2000–2001*, LSE.

Brophy, P. (2000) Performance indicators for the electronic library: the EQUINOX project, *SCONUL Newsletter*, **21**, 25–8.

Brophy, P. (2002) Strategic issues for academic libraries, *Relay*, **52**, 4–5.

Cannon, T. (1992) *Basic marketing*, 3rd edn, Cassell.

Cook, C. and Heath, F. M. (2001) Users' perceptions of library service quality: a LibQUAL+ qualitative study, *Library Trends*, **49** (4) 548–84.

Coote, H. (1994) *How to market your library service effectively*, Aslib.

Creaser, C., Maynard, S. and White, S. (2001) *LISU annual library statistics 2001*, LISU.

Davies, M. (1998) *Understanding marketing*, Prentice Hall.

Dowlin, K. E. (1995) Distribution in an electronic environment, or, Will there be libraries as we know them in the Internet world?, *Library Trends*, **43**, (3), 409–17.

Elliott de Sáez, E. (2002) *Marketing concepts for libraries and information services*, 2nd edn, Facet Publishing.

Ford, G. and Revill, D. (1996) *User satisfaction: standard survey forms for academic libraries*, SCONUL.

Hayden, M. (1997) Satisfaction surveys using Libra software and focus groups. In Spiller, D. (ed.), *Academic library surveys and statistics in practice: proceedings of a seminar held at Loughborough University 2–3 June 1997*, LISU.

HEFCE (1993) *Joint Funding Councils' Libraries Review Group: A report for the Higher Education Funding Council for England, Scottish Higher Education Funding Council, Higher Education Funding Council for Wales and Department of Education for Northern Ireland, Higher Education Funding Council* (the Follett report), available at www.ukoln.ac.uk/services/papers/follett/report/.

Joint Funding Councils' Ad-Hoc Group on Performance Indicators for Libraries (1995) *The effective academic library: a framework for evaluating the performance of UK academic libraries*, Joint Funding Councils.

Kotler, P. (1999) *Kotler on marketing*, Free Press.

Kotler, P. and Andreasen, A. R. (1995) *Strategic marketing for nonprofit organizations*, 5th edn, Prentice Hall.

Kotler, P. et al. (1999) *Principles of marketing*, 2nd edn, Prentice Hall.

Leicester University Library (1994) *Priority Search survey*, unpublished.

Measuring service quality (2001), *Library Trends*, **49** (4).

Middleton, R. (2000) Full of eastern promise, *Library Association Record*, **102**, (9), 510–11.

Noon, P. (1994) Finding a strategic role for information specialists in academic libraries. In Bluck, R., Hilton, A. and Noon, P., *Information skills in academic libraries: a teaching and learning role in higher education*, SEDA.

Town, J. S. (ed.) (2000) *SCONUL benchmarking manual*, SCONUL.

University of Wales College, Newport, Library and Learning Resources (1998) *Survey of staff*, UWCN.

Van House, N., Weil, B.T. and McClure, C. R. (1990) *Measuring academic library performance*, American Library Association.

West, C. (2001) *Measuring user satisfaction: a practical guide for academic libraries*, SCONUL.

Winkworth, I. (2001) Innovative United Kingdom approaches to measuring service quality, *Library Trends*, **49** (4) 718–31.

6

Assuring quality

Bill Macnaught and Mary Fleming

Introduction

Local authorities in England are required to demonstrate that their public library services are of good quality. There is a growing need to be able to provide evidence of planned and actual improvement in the performance of libraries. Public library services sit within the framework of local government and are subject to the growing discipline of performance assessment and quality assurance within all local authorities. This chapter gives an overview of the current position facing public library managers.

Performance indicators

Under the 1992 Local Government Act, the Audit Commission was instructed to devise a set of national performance indicators for local authorities, arrange for local audit of the data, compare performance between authorities, and publish the comparative data annually. With the range of local authority services covered by the indicators increasing each year, a total of 240 performance indicators had been set by the year 2000. Following the introduction of Best Value, the government itself took over the role of setting performance indicators, and from 2000/2001 laid down approximately 170 Best Value performance indicators (BVPIs).

For library authorities, performance management includes:

- monitoring performance using the relevant performance indicators, for example number of visitors to libraries, number of items issued, etc.
- setting challenging and realistic targets for the next five years

- estimating performance for the current year
- modifying targets in light of that estimate
- modifying again in light of actual performance
- reporting Best Value indicators to the Department of Culture, Media and Sport through the annual library plan
- providing the Chartered Institute of Public Finance and Accountancy (CIPFA) with statistical information so that comparisons can be made between authorities.

Local performance indicators

The government also encourages authorities to agree local performance indicators and targets to drive forward council priorities. For example, a local priority might be to open two new libraries, or that the library service must undertake activities to support lifelong learning. Library managers must report their performance against these targets to the local council.

Library managers must also report direct to local people, on their performance against both the government's Best Value indicators and the local council's indicators and targets.

Comprehensive performance assessment

The overarching framework for local government is provided by the comprehensive performance assessment (CPA) approach, introduced in 2002 by the Audit Commission. Performance management is a rapidly developing area of local government and CPA is likely to evolve further. The approach seeks to combine the best of previous performance assessment regimes with new data sources in order to provide a rounded view of services provided by local authorities in England. CPA is based on five elements:

- the gathering together of quantitative performance assessments already in the public domain, including inspection scores from various inspectorates, scored audit judgements, performance indicators and government office assessments of various service plans
- targeted work to plug gaps in service knowledge in order to ensure that the outcomes of CPA are based on a full understanding of local government service performance
- an assessment of the corporate capacity of individual councils to plan, deliver and continuously improve the performance of local services
- the development of a data model which combines the above information in an objective and rigorous yet transparent way

- action planning by authorities and external regulation to support delivery of improvement following CPA.

The model will assess performance on two levels: the quality of current services and the local authority's proven capacity to improve those services. Current and past performance, as well as future plans and targets, will be combined to categorize councils in one of the following ways:

- high performing
- striving
- coasting
- poor performing.

The performance of public libraries directly affects the CPA score for the local authority. Under the broad heading of 'Cultural services', public libraries provide a number of performance indicators, which will feed into the assessment-scoring machinery. The quality of the annual library plan will also affect the CPA score. The annual library plan is a document that systematically sets out an authority's plans for its library service. It is still a relatively new device and each year the methodology has been altered nationally in search of a more effective process for local authorities to follow. The government continues to seek improvements in the procedure.

Best Value

Before the comprehensive performance assessment was developed, the government introduced Best Value as a compulsory system for checking methodically the performance of every part of every local authority. It provides a robust framework for reviewing current services to look for improvements. Best Value is one of the most significant issues facing local authorities and affects everything they do. It means that authorities must ensure that:

- services are of a high quality
- the needs of local people are met
- local people can be assured that their money is being spent wisely
- services are developed in partnership with local people and users
- services are delivered by well trained and committed staff.

The review process is thorough and fundamental, and it is verified by the Audit Commission through external inspectors. Review managers need to demonstrate that they have looked at radical solutions to achieve improvements in line with the wishes of customers and elected members. Best Value puts pressure on local authorities to drive costs down as well as delivering improvements in services.

Every review needs to produce a five-year action plan for improving services, demonstrating how the local authority performs against the 'four Cs' of the Best Value process. This means that local authorities must:

- challenge why and how a service is being provided
- compare how the authority performs with other authorities' and service providers' performance, to see how services could be provided in better ways
- consult local people, service users, partners and the wider business community about what they want to get from services
- compete wherever practicable, fairly and openly to provide the best services.

Reviews must lead to better services that continuously improve.

Each authority also needs to produce a Best Value performance plan annually, setting out its targets and achievements in performance. Best Value provides a statutory basis for quality assurance because every authority must provide evidence that they are providing the right services, at the right level of provision, at a price acceptable to local people. That evidence needs to be the result of proper consultation. As with more general forms of quality management systems, the starting point is to be clear that you are providing what the customer wants.

Library performance management

Performance measurement is becoming an increasingly important factor in service management, and library managers along with managers of other services, must show that public money is being put to good use and that public services continue to improve.

Performance measurement is necessary on the basis that (Osborne and Gaebler, 1992):

- If you don't measure results, you can't tell success from failure.
- If you can't see success, you can't reward it.
- If you can't reward success, you're probably rewarding failure.
- If you can't recognize failure, you can't correct it.
- If you can demonstrate results, you can win public support.
- What gets measured gets done.

There are six recognized principles of performance measurement (Great Britain. HM Treasury, Cabinet Office and National Audit Commission, 2001):

- *focus:* on the organization's aims and objectives
- *appropriate:* to, and useful for the stakeholders who are likely to use it
- *balanced:* giving a picture of the main areas of the organization's work
- *robust:* in order to withstand organizational changes or individuals leaving
- *integrated:* into the organization's business planning and management processes
- *cost effective:* balancing the benefits of the information against the costs.

European Foundation for Quality Management (EFQM)

EFQM, the European Foundation for Quality Management, provides a widely accepted general approach to quality management. Founded in 1988, EFQM arose out of the need to develop a European framework for quality improvement to enable businesses to make better products and improve services. By the use of quality management principles in day-to-day operations and in their relationships with stakeholders, organizations are able to become more efficient and effective, to secure competitive advantage, and to gain long-term success (European Foundation for Quality Management). Currently, EFQM has 800 members in over 38 European countries, including Britain.

The EFQM Business Excellence Model is not only widely used in the private sector, but also increasingly so in the public sector, as an organizational assessment tool and as a fast track to service-quality improvement. The Model is a tool, which allows an organization to consider all aspects of its business.

The British Quality Foundation

As the UK arm of EFQM, the British Quality Foundation promotes the Business Excellence Model to UK organizations, many of which are using it to plan improvements and monitor progress. The UK Business Excellence award, introduced in 1994, is awarded to organizations demonstrating outstanding performance against the Model, the aim of the award being to toast the UK's most successful organizations, identify best practice, and promote competitiveness in the UK. The Model is a proven improvement tool, and so far, more than 200 organizations have applied for the Business Excellence award, and there have been 20 award winners. All government departments are now required to use the Model to improve their businesses.

The Model is based on nine criteria for excellence, shown in Figure 6.1. The five 'Enabler' criteria relate to what the organization does, and how it runs. The four 'Results' relate to what the organization is actually achieving, in the eyes of its stakeholders, i.e. customers, employees, the community and funders.

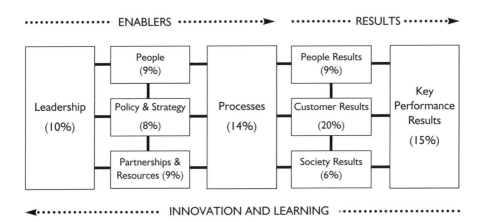

Fig. 6.1   *The Business Excellence Model*
(The Model is a registered trademark of the EFQM)

Figure 6.1 demonstrates clearly the Model's dynamic nature: The 'Enablers' make the 'Results', i.e. excellence in terms of performance, customers, people and society is achieved through leadership, policy and strategy, people, partnerships and resources, and processes. Innovation and learning drive and improve the 'Enablers' to produce improved 'Results'. The Model itself is not just another initiative, but rather the means by which existing initiatives (including Best Value, Investors in People, Charter Mark, ISO9000, NVQs, etc.) can be seen in their true context (UK Excellence Federation, 2001), can be better understood and more usefully and appropriately applied within the workplace.

At the heart of the self-assessment process lies the logic known as RADAR: Results, Approach, Deployment, Assessment and Review. The logic of RADAR states that an organization should: determine the **R**esults it is aiming for; implement an integrated set of sound **A**pproaches to deliver the required results; **D**eploy the approaches systematically; **A**ssess and **R**eview the effectiveness of the approaches (European Foundation for Quality Management).

The first step in the process is for the organization to undertake a self-assessment against each of the nine criteria, to identify its strengths and areas for improvement. This involves gathering evidence as to how the organization is performing and should include collecting feedback from people working inside the organization. Once this quality assessment activity is complete, areas for improvement can then be identified and prioritized according to the impact on people and the business. Systems will then be developed to find solutions which will subsequently be fed into business plans to ensure they are acted upon.

As Figure 6.1 shows, all the activities of the organization are grouped into the nine criteria, each of which is given a weighting or value according to its significance (UK Excellence Federation, 2001). For example, points scored for leadership account for 10% of the Excellence Model, while points awarded for customer results account for 20%. The organization's self-assessment should provide evidence of its performance against each of the nine criteria.

Leadership (10%)

Leaders develop the mission, vision and values and are role models of a culture of excellence. They are personally involved in ensuring the organization's management system is developed, implemented and continuously improved. They are involved with customers, partners and representatives of society and they motivate, support and recognise the organization's people.

Policy and strategy (8%)

Policy and strategy is based on the present and future needs and expectations of stakeholders, and information from performance measurement, research, learning and creativity-related activities. They are developed, reviewed and updated, deployed through a framework of key processes, and communicated and implemented.

People (9%)

People are involved and empowered, and rewarded, recognized and cared for. People resources are planned, managed and improved. People's knowledge and competencies are identified, developed and sustained. People and the organization have a dialogue.

Partnerships and resources (9%)

External partnerships are managed. Finances, buildings, equipment, technology and materials are managed. Information and knowledge are managed.

Processes (14%)

Processes are systematically designed and managed. They are improved, as needed, using innovation in order to fully satisfy and generate increasing value for customers and other stakeholders. Products and services are designed and developed based on customer needs and expectations. They are produced, delivered and serviced. Customer relationships are managed and enhanced.

Customer results (20%)

This relates to how well the organization is satisfying the needs and expectations of its external customers, and includes the customer's perception of the organization's products, services and customer relationships.

People results (9%)

This is about what the organization is achieving in relation to its people, and the people's perception of the organization, specifically motivation, satisfaction, involvement and services provided.

Society results (6%)

Self-assessment should demonstrate the organization's performance in meeting the needs and expectations of the local, national and international community, as appropriate.

Key performance results (15%)

The organization should show how it performs against its business objectives and against the needs and expectations of financial and other stakeholders.

Case studies

Gateshead Libraries, Arts and Information Services

The Business Excellence Model has been used to help to promote a culture of trust and empowerment. Focusing on the 'People Enabler' has helped the service to drive forward improvements in employee communication, consultation and involvement. The results so far include a more useful, relevant and informative weekly newsletter, and the setting up of focus groups and working groups to tackle issues of particular concern to employees, for example the reorganization of library services to accommodate a greater number of public access computers, the usefulness or otherwise of current online subscription services, and the need for employee support systems. Work on 'people results' has driven forward improvements in communication with external customers, increased and improved the opportunities for customer involvement in library operations, and generally prompted more frequent and regular consultation with local people. For example, customers have been consulted on the range of library services available, the pattern of opening hours, and the Public Library Standards.

Stockton Borough Libraries

Stockton is in the process of applying the Business Excellence Model to its spoken word service for the visually impaired. Library managers hope that at the very least, this will result in a written policy on the provision of the service (which has been in existence for 20 years), and at best will see the wholesale review of the provision of large print and spoken word from budget allocation through to disposal of old stock. This should tie in neatly with compliance with the Disability Discrimination Act – again hopefully resulting in a better service to the public.

Charter Mark

Like the Business Excellence Model, the aim of the Charter Mark scheme is to help organizations to make real improvements in service delivery and to show that they truly place the customer at the heart of their business – that they put their customers first.

Charter Mark is a key component of the government's drive to modernize public services by redesigning them around the needs of citizens. There are four key principles (Cabinet Office, a):

- setting high national standards
- empowering front-line staff to encourage diversity and creativity
- flexibility of employment and incentive
- promotion of greater choice for consumers.

The Charter Mark scheme is primarily about promoting and celebrating excellence in public service. Through the Charter Mark process, public sector organizations are encouraged 'to be the very best, to focus on customers, to constantly improve and to give value for money' (Cabinet Office, 2001).

Charter Mark is a results-based scheme, as it focuses specifically on the service the customer receives. It has two key uses: (a) as a customer service standard and (b) as a tool for improving service quality. The significant benefits the scheme offers include improved staff morale, improved performance, and recognition among peer organizations as an excellent service.

Again, like the EFQM Business Excellence Model, Charter Mark is a framework for self-assessment designed to help organizations identify both their strengths and any areas for improvement.

Any public sector organizations that deal directly or indirectly with the public can apply for a Charter Mark. Voluntary organizations providing a service to the public and receiving at least 10% of their income from public sector funds may also apply. The scheme is also open to sub-contractors 'as long as they provide a service to the public which is provided elsewhere by another public sector organisation' (Cabinet Office, a).

To achieve the award applicants must demonstrate that they meet these ten criteria: (Cabinet Office, a):

1 *Set standards*. Set clear standards of service that users can expect, and monitor and review performance and publish the results, following independent validation, wherever possible.

2 *Be open and provide full information*. Be open and communicate clearly and effectively in plain language to help people using public services, and provide full information about services, their cost and how well they perform.

3 *Consult and involve*. Consult and involve present and potential users of public services as well as those who work in them, and use their views to improve the service provided.

4 *Encourage access and the promotion of choice*. Make services easily available to everyone who needs them including using new technology to the full, offering choice wherever possible.

5 *Treat all fairly*. Treat all people fairly, respect their privacy and dignity, be helpful and courteous and pay particular attention to those with special needs.

6 *Put things right when they go wrong*. Put things right quickly and effectively, learn from complaints, and have a clear, well publicized and easy-to-use complaints procedure, with independent review wherever possible.

7 *Use resources effectively*. Use resources effectively to provide best value for taxpayers and users.

8 *Innovate and improve*. Always look for ways to improve the services and facilities offered, particularly the use of new technology.

9 *Work with other providers*. Work with other providers to ensure that services are simple to use, effective and co-ordinated, and deliver a better service to the user.

10 *Provide user satisfaction*. Show that your users are satisfied with the quality of service they are receiving.

Following submission of the organization's evidence of meeting the above criteria, a team of Charter Mark scrutineers will assess the applications for the award. In addition to this, an assessor will actually visit the organization to discuss the application in more detail with key personnel, and to collect further evidence of the organization's performance against the criteria. The assessor will also speak to front-line employees, as well as customers. Following the assessment, the organization is given detailed feedback on its performance against each of the criteria, and will be told whether or not it has met the standard.

Case studies

Gateshead Libraries, Arts and Information Services

Working through the Charter Mark process has brought about some simple, yet very effective changes in the way the Libraries, Arts and Information Services does things. For example, under the criterion 'Consult and involve', Gateshead acted upon feedback from customers who told them they were confused by their Bank Holiday stamping dates. Often, borrowed books and other items would be stamped 'due for return' on a different day of the week to the one on which they had been issued, because of Bank Holiday closure. Gateshead now ensures that items borrowed on a particular day of the week are stamped to be due for return on the same day of the week, even if this means extending the loan by several days more than the normal three-week period.

Improvements under the 'Be open and provide full information' criterion include the introduction of name badges for all employees, and 'senior on duty' photographs which are prominently displayed in public areas.

Under 'Put things right when they go wrong', a sample of customers who have previously submitted written complaints is now contacted at a later date to check to see if the complaints were satisfactorily dealt with at the time.

These changes, along with others implemented as a direct result of using the Charter Mark framework, and collecting evidence against each of the criteria, have been welcomed by Gateshead customers and praised by Charter Mark assessors.

Southwark Arts, Libraries & Museums Service

Charter Mark has also been a key factor in and indicator of strongly customer-focused services. Over the past three award periods several major customer care systems and quality standards have been developed. Central to Southwark's customer care policies is the Talkback system of customer comment/complaints forms, which are responded to within ten working days. A year ago a database was set up to enable the monitoring and analysis of Talkback responses and their links with service developments, which was highly praised by the Charter Mark assessor.

Southwark are now nearing the end of their Best Value review, which has been a touchstone for developing more sophisticated and varied means of consulting users and non-users of Library and Culture & Heritage services. These have included questions to the People's Panel and Young People's Panel (focus groups set up to seek and gain comments on the library service), the establishment of a Young People's Council at the Livesey Museum for Children (which involves nine-to-12-year-olds in programming, evaluating new exhibitions and designing promotional materials), community focus group interviews and library and street surveys.

London Borough of Sutton Library Service

Charter Mark assessors commented specifically on several benefits to users, which are a direct result of using the Charter Mark framework and working towards meeting the ten criteria. Assessors praised 'the high quality of care offered to your users throughout all your libraries, including your mobile libraries. Help was willingly offered, especially in using the computers and to children.'

Sutton Library Service prides itself on its customer care, which has been in evidence since at least their first Charter Mark award in 1995. As a result of the Charter Mark process, the following services were improved and singled out for commendation by the assessors:

- the DCMS/Wolfson-funded Travellers' Outreach project, which developed a resource collection for use with the Traveller community
- the special mobile library, which visits residential homes and day centres as part of the service to the housebound and elderly
- the special collection of books to encourage reading among young people with dyslexia
- storytime and activity visits (partnership with Mencap) to children with learning difficulties and to children with cancer at the Royal Marsden Hospital
- free access to the internet at all libraries
- LearnIT public computer centres, which enable residents to learn new job-related skills (free to residents of the two housing estates)
- web pages containing community information
- 24-hour reference library links to useful sites.

Specifically, the assessors' report had this to say: 'You have made commendable efforts to increase access to your service by users who would otherwise perhaps not use it regularly, for instance to Travellers, the frail and elderly and children with special needs. You also use IT to very good effect to increase the range and efficiency of your service for your users.'

The Health Promotion Library, Scotland

This is the library service of the Health Education Board for Scotland. The library is a free national health information resource for health promotion and consumer health information. Services are open to the public, health professionals and anyone involved in health education work in Scotland. For library managers the Charter Mark application process provided a structure and focus for development, which helped them in the areas of performance standards and measurement, customer care, value for money, user satisfaction and planning improvements in the service.

Their application benefited greatly from involving all staff and many users, with everyone playing an important role. Working through the process created a sense of ownership and made all involved much more aware of the importance of excellent customer service, user feedback and providing services that are used and valued by readers. Managers believe customers now benefit from an improved service. For example, staff have worked hard at improving customer care to everyone and especially in the area of disability awareness and accessibility to services.

Working towards Charter Mark was also found to be an effective team-working exercise, as everyone depended on each other for support and ideas. Teambuilding with readers encouraged staff to look at services through readers' eyes and to use their suggestions to make improvements. For example, for some time a box of toys and games had been provided in the Library to help entertain users' children. Following encouragement from users, Library services for children were expanded to encourage them to feel more welcome. Bean- bags, a blackboard, many more games and books, as well as a children's notice board are now available. Many readers are delighted with this improvement.

Winning the Charter Mark raised the profile of the Library service both within the Health Education Board for Scotland and outside the organization. It also resulted in a great sense of achievement and pride, with everyone working for the service delighted at the recognition and reward for their hard work. What's more, it has given everyone a common goal – to maintain an excellent customer service – and the motivation to work towards this goal.

National Vocational Qualifications (NVQs)

In order for an organization to be able to provide quality services in the first place, and then to be able to measure its performance against frameworks such as Charter Mark and Business Excellence, the people working in it need to possess a minimum level and range of skills and knowledge. NVQs are work-based qualifications awarded to those individuals who can demonstrate the required level of competence measured against agreed technical occupational standards. The NVQ system provides practical standards which give a framework for a comprehensive training and development strategy, and is seen to improve performance and aid consistency in service delivery. The standards set out the way in which work may be best carried out, reflecting best practices nationally, within Europe, and internationally (Dakers, 2001, 4).

In the UK, there are over 160 sets of NVQs covering almost every kind of work available. NVQs are offered at five levels, ranging from a basic minimum standard at Level 1 involving routine or predictable work activities, to a highly complex standard at Level 5, involving activities requiring the ability to analyse, diagnose, plan, execute and evaluate.

The ideas behind the NVQ system originated in the 1980s, and stemmed from the government's observation that as a country the UK was competing very poorly with its economic rivals, and that its future economic success probably depended upon better training and qualifications. The NVQ framework became a key component of the government's drive to improve the skills of the UK workforce, and provides a basis to link with other national and international qualifications (Dakers, 2001, 12). The National Qualifications Framework (see Figure 6.2) produced by the National Council for Vocational Qualifications (NCVQ), shows how NVQs loosely compare with national academic qualifications.

Employers value NVQs because of their potential to improve work performance, increase productivity, promote employee flexibility, benefit recruitment and retention, and articulate a national standard of competence across all sectors and at all levels of the workforce. (NVQ standards are increasingly being used in staff recruitment, appraisal, and as the basis for job profiles.)

From a political point of view, NVQs are an effective quality system because they improve access and enable greater participation in learning, encourage pro-

NVQ Level 1	GCSE
NVQ Level 2	A level
NVQ Level 3	A level
NVQ Level 4	Degree level
NVQ Level 5	Higher degree (Post-graduate diploma)

Figure 6.2   *The National Qualifications Framework (Source: NCVQ)*

gression and transfer between vocational and academic routes to learning, and take account of future needs with regard to technology, markets and employment patterns (Dove, 1998, 5).

NVQ certificates are issued by awarding bodies such as City and Guilds, OCR and Edexcel, who perform three key roles: the development and provision of assessment procedures for NVQs, the verification of employers' and training providers' assessment systems, and quality assurance (Dove, 1998, 6). The NVQ quality assurance scheme requires rigorous assessment of candidates against the national standards, by fully qualified assessors, internal verifiers and external verifiers. These individuals, along with the organization, have distinct but complementary roles to play in quality assurance. Internal verifiers provide an important link between the assessment processes and the quality assurance of the awarding body (Qualifications and Curriculum Authority, 1998).

In the context of public library service development, many services now have, in place of professionally qualified librarians, 'senior library assistants' or equivalent managing service points. To maintain quality, these employees need support and development in their extended role and additional responsibilities. NVQs in Information and Library Services are available at Levels 2, 3 and 4, providing an effective framework for ensuring all the required areas of work are covered, and encouraging employees to take an active part in their own learning and development. For example, employees are urged to develop an 'active attitude', to think about quality of services, plans and targets, as well as their own contribution to achieving higher quality outputs.

Managers find that NVQ achievers tend to be better motivated, more knowledgeable in such matters as health and safety and other legal and statutory obligations, and possess a higher level of corporate awareness than those who have not undertaken NVQs.

Case studies

Gateshead Libraries, Arts and Information Services

Information and Library Services NVQs, since their introduction in 1996, have provided employees with numerous opportunities to increase their knowledge and gain a better understanding of the range of services available, not only in Libraries, Arts and Information Services, but throughout the council as a whole. This has enabled them to offer better advice and information to users.

NVQ candidates have grown and developed in the way in which they fulfil their roles and responsibilities within the workplace. Both new and established employees have been able to develop new skills, and as a result, contribute to enhancing service provision. This comes from an increased awareness of what is required from them and how their actions affect the quality of service provided.

For new employees, an NVQ is an excellent induction-training tool, as it ensures that all aspects of library work are covered, and that everyone (both new and experienced employees) is providing the same level of service. Specifically, they ensure that employees are more customer focused because all units are customer driven, i.e. in order to achieve an NVQ, candidates need to demonstrate that they are consistently providing a high level of customer service. For example, Information and Library Services NVQ Level 3 includes such units as 'provide information/material to users', 'solve problems on behalf of customers', and 'maintain a supportive environment for users', all of which involve working with internal customers to meet the needs of external customers. As one candidate puts it, 'NVQs promote team work which naturally contributes to better customer service as everyone is pulling in the same direction'.

Numerous service improvements and additional services have arisen as a direct result of employees undertaking NVQs. One such example is of a candidate being asked to provide some children's novels that were also available on audio-cassette to a teacher working in the Bilingual Support Team. The candidate researched and provided a list of all the novels within the library network that were also available on cassette. She then distributed this list across the authority, and in doing so, introduced a new and subsequently very popular service. As part of this new service, she will now match books and cassettes for loan, on request, which greatly aids the teaching of English to the children of asylum seekers.

A number of Level 4 candidates embarking on 'user-education' units have developed excellent projects focusing on improving customers' ICT skills, producing related training materials to be used across the library network. These projects include internet taster sessions, word-processing, and website awareness, for customers of all ages, background and ability. This has expanded and developed ICT training programmes to library customers, and in the process made ICT facilities much more accessible to local people.

Some NVQ units have also been mapped to the New Opportunities Fund (NOF) ICT Training Programme for Public Library Staff. NOF has laid down a set of criteria covering skills and knowledge that employees must achieve under the terms of the funding. Mapping the NOF criteria to the performance criteria of appropriate NVQ units has enabled Gateshead to ensure that training received under the NOF programme is actually and relevantly applied within the workplace through specially designed projects, as employees must provide evidence of demonstrating (to the benefit of users) their learnt skills and knowledge.

Hartlepool Borough Libraries

Hartlepool Libraries are involved in an ongoing process of maximizing the skills of management-level employees so that they can provide advice and support for the implementation and development of quality systems. The service has a number of time-served, experienced employees whom senior managers consider would benefit personally and professionally from working through the Information and Library Services NVQ at Level 4. This level offers the opportunity for first-line managers to develop skills and knowledge in their work role as they learn.

Senior managers are confident that achieving the qualification will produce competent managers who possess flexible work-based skills, the confidence to support the senior management team, and the ability to develop junior employees. In short, the qualification affords a key link in the building of a strong staffing structure, which is directly evident in the quality of services received by library users, who can expect:

- employees who are familiar with the services available and methods of accessing them
- employees who are capable of flexible thinking and the ability to adapt what they know to particular situations
- employees who have the ability to monitor and suggest improvement to services and systems
- employees who have the skills needed to offer basic training in the ICT facilities available to users
- employees who are able to offer advice and help consistent with the level required
- employees who are sensitive to the well-being of colleagues and users alike.

The Level 4 qualification has been used to develop a new tier of Library Managers, most of whom are still working through the units. One employee has completed Level 4 and has made the following observations: 'Undertaking the NVQ has endorsed my confidence in my self worth. It has broadened my knowledge of library practices and the management decisions behind them.'

Another Library Manager who has just started her Level 4 NVQ has also been sharing responsibility for 'acting-up' in a senior officer capacity. The NVQ culture has helped to acclimatize her to working in a management capacity.

Newcastle Library and Information Services

They have found NVQs to be an excellent quality system, because of the rigorous checking by assessors, internal verifiers and external verifiers throughout the whole process. Across the service, managers believe that Library and Information Services NVQs have been responsible for a noticeable improvement in employee customer-service skills, and that they have also helped to generate a greater awareness of the role of library and senior library assistants as information providers, and of the contributions they are able to make, as individuals, to the service.

NVQs have given employees the confidence to go 'that one step further'. They are now more proactive in recommending alternative and new authors, promoting ICT facilities, and mounting promotional displays and events. This has resulted in measurable benefits in some libraries, such as increased issues and visitor figures, and a greater use of ICT facilities by asylum seekers.

Managers involved in interviewing library employees for promotion have seen a marked increase in the confidence and knowledge of candidates who have completed the Information and Library Services NVQ. Throughout the interview process, these candidates display, from the quality of their application to their performance in the interview itself, an awareness of the aims and objectives of the service, the value of the customer service, and an assurance stemming from their proven ability.

Teesside University Library

Employees based in the Learning Resource Centre feel that a key benefit of undertaking Information and Library Services NVQs is that the process gave them an invaluable overview of how the whole Centre functions. The Centre is very large, with many of the bigger, more complex day-to-day tasks divided into smaller tasks, and shared among the team. This means that some staff routinely only experience carrying out one small part of the larger piece of work. As NVQ candidates must provide evidence of understanding the task as a whole, why it is necessary, and its importance in the whole scheme of things, working through the awards and gathering the required knowledge and performance evidence has enabled staff to see, experience and understand the bigger picture.

Candidates also found that they learnt to do many new tasks, despite having worked in the Centre for many years. This has brought more flexibility to the individuals' approach to work, and even though methods and processes may change, the principles behind the actions will remain the same.

The mandatory units focusing on customer care provided staff with opportunities to broaden their experience on the helpdesk. This increased employees' competence and confidence in dealing with other departments inside the Centre and the University, as well as with outside organizations.

NVQ Level 4 candidates in particular found that completing the award helped them to develop self-motivation and time-management skills, equipped them to better identify and support customer needs in a changing environment, and provided the opportunity to work at a more professional level within the department.

Candidates at all levels say that by undertaking the NVQs, they are now more aware of the customer's point of view, of how important it is to get things right, and the need to balance customers' needs with those of the organization. Customer services within the University Library have improved as a result. These employees feel they have achieved a worthwhile qualification and that customer-service standards will keep on improving as more of their colleagues complete NVQs.

Investors in People

Investors in People (IiP) is a further example of an employee-focused quality system. First developed in 1991 as a DTI initiative, IiP is now over ten years old and used in dozens of countries around the world. IiP is a national quality standard which sets a level of good practice for improving an organization's performance through its people (www.iipuk.co.uk). The IiP standard is a cyclical process, creating a culture of continuous improvement. It is based on four key principles (see Figure 6.3).

These four principles are subdivided into 12 indicators, which provide a framework against which an organization can assess its practice. At the heart of the IiP framework is effective investment in training and development of each employee to achieve the organization's aims and objectives. What people can

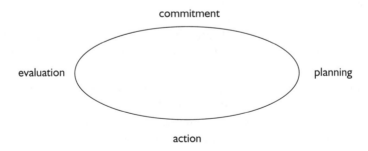

Figure 6.3 *The principles of IiP*

do and are motivated to do is matched against what the organization wants them to do.

The twelve IiP Indicators are:

1 The organization is committed to supporting the development of its people.
2 People are encouraged to improve their own and other people's performance.
3 People believe their contribution to the organization is recognized.
4 The organization is committed to ensuring equality of opportunity in the development of its people.
5 The organization has a plan with clear aims and objectives which are understood by everyone.
6 The development of people is in line with the organization's aims and objectives.
7 People understand how they contribute to achieving the organization's aims and objectives.
8 Managers are effective in supporting the development of people.
9 People learn and develop effectively.
10 The development of people improves the performance of the organization, teams and individuals.
11 People understand the impact of the development of people on the performance of the organization, teams and individuals.
12 The organization gets better at developing its people.

Used effectively, the IiP framework will enable an organization to improve the performance of its staff and to develop their skills, knowledge and qualifications. It will ensure that staff are aware of the organization's aims and objectives and what they have to do as individuals to meet them. Rather than merely recording the number of days spent on training courses, IiP provides a framework for examining what people actually get out of the training, how they apply in the workplace what they have learnt from the training, and what benefit it is to the organization.

Research shows that the benefits for employees include increased staff motivation, commitment, loyalty, confidence, job satisfaction and career prospects. Benefits for the organization include improved productivity, enhanced quality, reduced absenteeism and staff turnover, flexibility and response to change (Brefi Group). IiP is the most widely recognized tool for both public and private sector organizations to plan for current and future development of their staff to achieve organizational aims.

IiP is awarded by a national body – Investors in People UK – and delivered by a network of local organizations. Being recognized as an Investor in People raises an organization's profile in the eyes of current and potential employees, as well as those of its customers. By the end of December 1997, almost 9000 organizations recognized IiP, with a further 21,500 formally committed to the national standard. In total this accounts for around 30% of the people employed in Britain (Department for Education and Skills).

Case studies

Hartlepool Borough Libraries

Managers say that the Investors in People scheme has encouraged them to communicate better and to think about how their actions, or lack of them, or indeed inappropriate actions, affect other employees. The impact on the service has been to improve employee communication skills and communication methods, which in turn has helped to improve the delivery of information. Because employees are now better informed and better trained, morale has been raised, and employee attitudes towards the service and its customers have also become more positive.

Managers now have regular and frequent communications meetings where all employees are brought up to date with anything from the latest developments in e-government, to new staffing arrangements, to the effectiveness of Sunday opening. Rumours are squashed early, thus preventing potentially damaging information from becoming too much of a problem. The result is that teams now function more effectively and can offer a more efficient service to customers.

Stockton Borough Council

Stockton Council has found that as a result of adopting Investors in People, services are more customer focused and customer friendly. Employees are now more proactive in their dealings with customers as a result of the annual employee development interview, a key element of the process where training needs are recorded by line managers and are acted upon by the departmental training and development unit. This also results in staff being more highly motivated, better informed and generally more competent in their jobs.

North Tyneside Library Service

North Tyneside Libraries has used the IiP framework to develop training pathways for each post within the service as part of a long-term staff development plan. Due to this investment in staff, ensuring that they are part of any decision making, and as a result making them feel valued within the organization, the Library Service is able to pride itself on having a positive, helpful and knowledgeable workforce, one which encourages more and more visitors to their libraries.

The University of Exeter

The Library, IT Services and Staff Development Unit were jointly awarded IiP recognition in 1997 and this was successfully reassessed in 2001. In many ways the various processes of the award have formalized the activities already being undertaken, but they have also enriched many of these processes so that managers now have a clearer vision, for example of the importance of training (including a stated training and development plan which is known to all staff), feedback from staff and users and various appraisal mechanisms. As the academic services concerned are not converged, IiP recognition has also encouraged close working relationships on a formal basis with regular joint management meetings and common training forms and activities when appropriate.

As the standard has now changed, future reassessments may well involve an in-depth look at a specific aspect of work – perhaps the introduction of a new staff appraisal system – rather than a general examination of activities. Whatever, these University services remain committed to working to maintain the IiP standard through staff and service development.

The University of Portsmouth Library

IiP status was gained in 2001. Much of the IiP literature focuses on the benefits to the staff and the organization, and in the University's experience these were many – not least the visible commitment the process made to the importance of staff development. Managers feel the IiP experience has increased staff morale and this was backed up by the findings of a recent staff survey.

In the area of staff development practice it is helpful to have areas of good practice identified and recognized by an external agency. Also informal training is made overt and explicit as it counts as part of the process leading to staff who had considered that they had received little development realizing that this was not so. It has also led to increased confidence that the organization can provide good training without always going to outside bodies.

Ultimately it is the Library's customers who experience this benefit, as staff who feel valued give a better service. Staff have recently carried out an exit survey of 1500-plus library users, the results of which will be used as baseline data from which to plan further staff development and hopefully service improvement. Although the survey might well have been carried out regardless of IiP, managers are now confident that they have the systems in place to respond to the findings, within a culture that recognizes the importance of developing staff and services to better support customers.

Benchmarking

Benchmarking has been acknowledged as a powerful agent in the government's programme of reform to modernize public services, as set out in the White Paper *Modernising government* (March 1999). In benchmarking, the basis of the quality assurance system lies in working with others to approach mutual challenges and resolve common problems through the key principles of challenge, compare, compete and collaborate – all of which are vital to the development of modern public services.

In practice, benchmarking usually involves:

- continuously comparing performance against best practitioners
- identifying gaps in performance
- identifying and adopting new approaches to improve performance
- implementing improvements
- monitoring progress and reviewing benefits.

Benchmarking activities in many areas of the public sector have brought about significant improvements in the cost and quality of services (Cabinet Office, c). Nationally recognized benchmarks of good practice can be used to assess the performance of managers against the standard required to succeed today. By working with these standards, organizations can improve managers' effectiveness and therefore the overall effectiveness of the organization. Individual standards can be used as a framework for setting objectives for organizational development programmes (Brefi Group).

Some of the many benefits of using nationally recognized benchmarks to raise the quality of services provided to customers are:

- self-assessment against a good practice standard to determine how effectively the organization is performing
- the opportunity to share knowledge
- the opportunity to learn from other organizations
- greater employee involvement and motivation
- increasing collaboration and understanding within and between organizations.

Benchmarking may be applied in various ways (Public Sector Benchmarking Service):

- *Strategic benchmarking* is where organizations attempt to improve their overall performance by studying the long-term strategies and general approaches of high-performing organizations.
- *Performance benchmarking* involves organizations examining the performance characteristics of key products and services. Benchmarking partners are sought from the same sector.
- *Process benchmarking* seeks to improve specific critical processes and operations. Benchmarking partners are drawn from best practice organizations delivering similar services.
- *Functional benchmarking* involves organizations benchmarking with partners drawn from different business sectors or areas of activity to find ways of improving similar functions or work processes.
- *Internal benchmarking* involves partners from inside the same organization.
- *External benchmarking* involves benchmarking with outside best-in-class organizations.
- *International benchmarking* is used where partners are drawn from other countries because best practitioners are located elsewhere in the world and/or there are too few benchmarking partners within the same country to produce valid results.

In the UK public sector, benchmarking is recognized as one of the key drivers behind the improvements and changes needed to deliver modern public services. Benchmarking offers the incentive needed to ring the changes in the delivery of both core and non-core services, and to improve the quality of public services through the sharing of good practice. In theory, almost any activity can be benchmarked.

The Public Sector Benchmarking Service (PSBS)

The aim of this government body is to promote effective benchmarking and sharing of good practices across the public sector (Cabinet Office, b). Established in February 2001, PSBS has proved to be an effective knowledge management service, providing a range of information, advice and guidance on benchmarking and good practice to UK organizations wishing to deliver better public services. The PSBS database, accessible through their website, stores case studies of good practice from public sector organizations across the UK, including examples from Beacon Council scheme (see below) and Charter Mark winners, as well as Business Excellence (EFQM) and Best Value initiatives. Many of the contributions to the database are from public sector employees and Charter Mark assessors (Cabinet Office, c).

Service First Quality Networks

Quality Networks are run by groups from all areas and levels of public services, the aims being to share information on best practice, compare progress in areas of common interest, build partnerships between public service organizations and encourage problem sharing and solving. These local networks provide opportunities for organizations to discuss service quality issues, pool experience, and share and solve problems. Although they are largely self-financing, each Network is supported by the Cabinet Office, which plays a strategic planning and coordinating role as well as providing training for Network leaders. Cabinet Office and Network representatives meet quarterly at practice forums to discuss ideas and strategy for the Networks and to update and seek the involvement and views of the Networks on service delivery (Cabinet Office, b).

Beacon Council scheme

Beacon schemes were introduced in different parts of the public sector to identify and celebrate first-class performers, to enable others to learn from their knowledge and experience (Cabinet Office, b). The Beacon scheme is central to the government's agenda for modernizing local government. Its main aim is to help local government learn from other local authorities that have developed centres of excellence and quality service.

Each year, the government chooses themes for the Beacon scheme. In 2001–2002 Gateshead Council was awarded Beacon status for its work in 'Regenerating through culture, sport and tourism', one of only four councils in the country to receive this award. However, to obtain Beacon status councils also need to demonstrate good overall performance. The title is held for one year. In its role as 'Beacon Council', a council is committed to sharing best practice with other local authorities.

Each Beacon Council is required by the Government to draw up a dissemination plan for the year. In general, this takes the form of a series of learning activities such as open days, seminars, mini-visits and presentations. The purpose is to enable other authorities to improve their services by learning from the 'best'. However, through discussion of common challenges, there is also an opportunity for Beacon Councils to learn themselves (in particular from Beacon peers) to achieve further improvement for their own communities.

Feedback from participants at Beacon dissemination activities suggests that the main motivation for attending an event/consulting a Beacon Council is the opportunity to find out about practice elsewhere. A number of local authorities have utilized the scheme for benchmarking purposes. So for example, through comparison of practice, it can enable them to assess their own performance and develop plans for improvements.

Conclusion

Local authorities are required to demonstrate their public library services are of good quality and to provide evidence of planned and actual improvements. In facing up to this challenge, service managers have available to them a range of quality frameworks to develop a quality system appropriate to the organization's own way of working. These quality frameworks may be specifically employee focused, for example, National Vocational Qualifications, or Investors in People, or results focused, for example Charter Mark, or Business Excellence (EFQM). All are customer focused, based on good management principles and practice, and specify criteria to ensure that services meet customers' requirements. All have been found to be effective self-assessment tools, as well as proven tools for improvement. They provide standards against which the organization's performance can be measured, areas for improvement can be identified and prioritized, and systems can be developed to find solutions which will subsequently be fed into business plans to ensure they are acted upon.

Success in improving service quality depends heavily on people involvement – employees, customers, funders and all other stakeholders. Employee knowledge and competencies must be identified, developed and sustained. Customers must be consulted, involved, and found to be satisfied with the service provided. Quality objectives and emphasis on continuous improvement and monitoring of customer satisfaction provide the customer with increased assurances that their needs and expectations will be met.

References

Brefi Group, www.corporateconsultant.co.uk.

Cabinet Office (2001) *Charter Mark guide for applicants*, Cabinet Office.

Cabinet Office (a), www.chartermark.gov.uk.

Cabinet Office (b), www.servicefirst.gov.uk.

Cabinet Office (c), www.goodpractice.org.uk.

Dakers, H. (2001) *NVQs and how to get them*, Kogan Page.

Department for Education and Skills, www.lifelonglearning.co.uk.

Dove, P. (1998) *NVQs: an introductory guide*, University of Northumbria.

European Foundation for Quality Management, www.efqm.org

HM Treasury, Cabinet Office and National Audit Commission (2001) Choosing the right fabric: a framework for performance information. In Jones, D. *Using performance indicators*, Office for National Statistics.

Investors in People, www.iipuk.co.uk.

Osborne, D. and Gaebler, T. (1992) Reinventing government. In Jones, D. *Using performance indicators*, Office for National Statistics.

Public Sector Benchmarking Service, www.benchmarking.gov.uk.

Qualifications and Curriculum Authority (1998) *Verification of NVQs a guide for internal verifiers*, QCA.

UK Excellence Federation (2001) *Business excellence through action*, UK Excellence Federation.

7

Planning academic library buildings for customers and services

Professor Andrew McDonald

Introduction

If you build it, he will come.

Field of Dreams, 1989 (Director P. A. Robinson)

At the beginning of the new millennium, universities all over the world continue to build new academic library buildings and refurbish existing buildings with increasingly imaginative and varied designs.

In the last ten years, there have been more than 100 new academic library projects in the UK costing an estimated £350 million (SCONUL, 2002). This was largely in response to the recommendations of the influential Follett Report (HEFCE, 1993). In the USA, 30 new academic library building projects were completed in 1999/2000 alone at a cost of some $264 million. Fox and Jones (1998) suggest this reflects the continued importance of libraries for our well-being and future.

This is despite some almost reckless predictions about the end of libraries and their book collections, as a result of the rapid growth in networked electronic information and the use of the internet. While making suitable provision for information technology is very important, planning libraries is essentially about people, or rather it is about designing space in which people can interact with the collections, information technology and services they require. As Wu (1999) notes, 'the people-centred concept has come to dominate the philosophy of modern library architecture and will do so for the foreseeable future'. It is people who design libraries, people who deliver services and people who use them. Indeed, the library manager's vision and imagination should drive the planning process.

Creating new space is also a unique opportunity to change the culture of the organization and to provide customer-focused services.

The challenge is to create new 'scholarly' environments which encourage learning and inspire research. New libraries must provide improved access to both the traditional and electronic services that 'empower' people by 'connecting' them with the information and services they require. Libraries are becoming increasingly important social places for learning and scholarship, for culture and heritage, for recreation and citizenship, and, not least, for economic development. This is at a time of unprecedented change, not only in education, information technology and publishing, but also in economic fortunes, social attitudes and patterns of work. There are also influential architectural trends and changing attitudes to environmental and conservation issues.

But what should a new university library look like, how much and what sort of space is needed, and how will library services be delivered and used in the future? How can planners take account of the needs of current and succeeding generations of users and service staff?

This chapter discusses the managerial challenge involved in planning new academic libraries and explores the important qualities of academic library space, touching upon space standards and norms. The emerging trends in recent library designs are briefly reviewed, and the chapter concludes by contemplating the future of the library as a 'place' in the learning and information age of the 21st century.

Although the emphasis is upon academic libraries, it is suggested that the approach is just as relevant to national, public and other libraries. Indeed, the principles and qualities discussed go beyond traditional libraries and begin to define the nature of good learning space in general, an issue of some interest in the world of galleries, museums, archives and other public spaces for learning. The political and funding context will clearly be different in other sectors and domains.

The management challenge

A major building project remains a substantial managerial challenge, arguably the biggest the library director will face. Many library managers will only have one opportunity to plan a new building in their career and, even though large capital sums are involved, they will almost certainly have had little experience or training for managing such a project. But the librarian has a unique responsibility to ensure a good building which is capable of delivering high-quality services to generations of users. Indeed many librarians are planning buildings and important collections for posterity.

Vision

Library managers must have a strong vision for the new library and they have the important responsibility of communicating their vision to all those involved in the planning and design process. Indeed, this vision should actually inspire the design process (Bazillion and Braun, 1994).

Planning new academic libraries is about creating the physical environment necessary to facilitate the teaching, learning and research aspirations of the institution, not only for the immediate future, but also for succeeding generations of users. Space planning must be driven by the mission, ethos and culture of the institution, and it should be influenced by the newly emerging strategies for learning, research, information and estates within institutions.

Not only do managers require a broad vision, but they must also pay considerable attention to the detail of the project.

Strategy

Space is a precious and expensive resource that should be planned and managed within a strategic framework for the development of the library service as a whole. Unfortunately, it has sometimes received less professional attention than staffing, collection development, information technology, finance and the other resources that the librarian manages. Quite simply, good well-planned space enables the library to fulfil its mission and underpins the development of all other library resources. On the other hand, poor space often conflicts with what readers and library staff are trying to achieve and inhibits the library's ability to fulfil its aims and objectives in an efficient way. More seriously, it can constrain the development of the service.

Planning libraries is simply good management and, as Mason (1996, 14) reminds us, 'good management of the library building planning will make a better building'. He goes further and suggests that librarians 'must make sure they are in control of the management'. Like all management, space planning involves taking decisions, normally a large number of them, within a finite timescale and within the resources available. It is not primarily about architecture and taste, or about bricks and mortar, but it is about the responsible library manager seeking to create an attractive library that works well and lasts a long time. The new library must be delivered on time and within budget, and it must be affordable both in capital and recurrent costs. The new building should enhance the academic work of the institution and enable the service to respond to change.

Communication

A major project is a massive communications exercise. Library managers must communicate with staff within the library and the institution, and with the whole range of professionals involved in the building project. It is important to survey users' needs and to keep users informed of progress.

Change

> We shape our buildings, and afterwards, our buildings shape us.
>
> Winston Churchill

Planning new space is about creating a great deal of change in order to develop an entirely new service that can deliver better quality, greater efficiency and improved responsiveness. The librarian must provide the leadership and direction necessary to manage both library staff and users through a period of considerable change. On the one hand, this is about managing creativity and ideas, and on the other, it is about dealing with disruption and uncertainty. It is also an opportunity to change the culture and attitudes within the library and to influence the way in which both staff and users behave.

Risk

There are considerable political and professional risks involved. It is the librarian who will have the responsibility for providing library services to users in the new building, and it is the librarian's name that is invariably linked with the success or failure of the project. Well-planned new buildings stimulate demand for library services and these new levels of usage must be sustained. Poorly planned space will attract criticism from both users and external quality assessors and may have a profound effect on the morale of library staff.

Future-proofing

> All buildings are predictions. All predictions are wrong.
>
> Stewart Brand

One fundamental question is how far ahead we should plan. Any predictions about the size and nature of the buildings required for the future will be influenced by our view on how library services will be provided and used in the new information age. At one conference concerned with the impact of information technology on library buildings (Institute of Advanced Architectural Studies,

1995), it was suggested that the building structure should be planned for 50 years, the utilities for 15 years, and the fixtures and fittings for seven years. Lucker (2002) confirms that we are planning buildings for at least 20 years. These timescales may seem unduly short, but they reflect the pace of change in information and communications technology, higher education and society. Pragmatists might suggest that we should look as far ahead as we can, or perhaps as far as we can afford.

Architects

Both architect and librarian must bring their vision and respective skills to this creative process which, inevitably, has its creative tensions. It is worth remembering that there are no prescriptive solutions in planning library buildings; no one knows all the answers and no two projects are the same. Planning is a complex human process about which not everyone will or should agree. Indeed, different architects will often provide very different design solutions to a particular library brief.

Architects, particularly famous ones, tend to have a strong vision about the 'artistic interpretation of space'. The librarian must have an equally distinctive view about what is required and must articulate this clearly to the architect and all those involved in the project. The librarian must also make sure the design delivers what is required. Architects also comment on the differing and even opposing views among librarians. Unfortunately, architects and academics 'often use the same words, but with different meanings' (Mason, 1996, 16). Communication is vitally important and, as Bazillion and Braun (1994, 16) suggest, 'there is no reason why an architect who is willing to listen to his client cannot design an efficient, technologically-sound building that is also a credit to its creator'. Indeed, as a rule, the best libraries emerge when there has been a strong shared vision and good communication between all those involved in the planning process, especially between the librarian and the architect.

Qualities of academic library space

There are a number of important qualities of good academic library space that help define what managers should be striving for. They are the critical issues that managers should address in the brief and should discuss with the planning team, and they form a set of criteria against which design solutions can be assessed. Indeed they are the qualities that set academic libraries apart from other building types.

The qualities of academic library space were first defined by Harry Faulkner-Brown, a well-established British architect responsible for designing many library buildings around the world (Faulkner-Brown, 1979; 1998). He identified ten desirable qualities that became widely known as the 'ten commandments' of planning libraries. He suggested a library should be flexible, compact, accessible, extendible, varied, organized, comfortable, constant in environment, secure, and, economic. First published in the 1960s, the qualities have remained relevant to planning good libraries today, but it is not surprising that some of the words now have rather different meanings and that emphases have changed considerably. The qualities important for today's and tomorrow's new buildings relate to a new learning and information age in which higher education has been transformed and in which there has been rapid growth in networked electronic information.

I would now suggest that academic library space should ideally be:

- functional
- adaptable
- accessible
- varied
- interactive
- conducive
- environmentally suitable
- safe and secure
- efficient
- suitable for information technology.

The qualities are equally relevant to all space-planning exercises: a new library or extension, a refurbishment or adaptation, making better use of existing space, or, indeed, a mixture of these. Although the discussion concentrates upon university libraries, the qualities also have relevance to national and public libraries and they could be described as the qualities of learning space in general.

Clearly, the priority given to each of these qualities will vary according to the mission and culture of the university, and to the role and aims of its library service. The emphasis will be different when building a traditional library or a new learning resource centre, and when constructing new buildings in different countries around the world. They are intended as an indicative set of qualities and should never be taken as a prescriptive set of solutions. Inevitably, there are tensions and even conflicts between these qualities and also within each of them, and achieving them has resource implications.

An 11th and almost indefinable quality is best described as the 'oomph' or 'wow' factor. Skilful architects and planners will achieve an appropriate balance between all these qualities, creating inspiring buildings with distinguished features and satisfying spaces which capture the minds of users and the spirit of a university.

Each of these qualities is now explored in more detail.

Functional: *space that works well, looks good and lasts well*

McDonald (2000b) suggests that there are three key fundamental principles underlying the planning of new buildings: we should be aiming to design libraries which are functional, easy to use and economical to operate. Achieving all three of these attributes requires considerable skill on the part of all those involved in creating new academic space.

Functionally, the new space must enable the library to fulfil its role and must facilitate the delivery of high-quality services in support of university teaching, learning and research. Functional interests should take priority over any purely aesthetic considerations, but this is not to say that aesthetics are not important. Indeed, we want libraries that look good *and* work well, and a skilful and creative architect can achieve *both* of these requirements.

The design should recognize the crucial importance of people, books and information technology in modern library and information services, and the dynamic relationship and complex interactions between them. The building must also enable the library to develop, and provide services that are responsive to the changing library and information needs of the academic community.

Adaptable: *flexible space, the use of which can easily be changed*

Paradoxically, one of the few certainties in planning libraries is the almost guaranteed uncertainty relating to future use, particularly in relation to technology, organizational structure and user behaviour. It is important, therefore, to achieve a high degree of adaptability or flexibility in the building so that the use of space can easily be changed with the minimum of disruption merely by rearranging the furniture, shelving and equipment. However, achieving long-term flexibility in a changing and uncertain environment can be expensive, and may be more costly than delivering short-term functionality. Planners are now generally adopting a more pragmatic approach, and are choosing an appropriate balance between cost and adaptability requirements.

The most adaptable buildings are those with open, flexible space in which fixed elements, such as load-bearing walls and fixed fittings, have been avoided or at least restricted to areas like staircases.

It is generally held that in order to achieve a high degree of flexibility, the floor loading should be sufficient for bookstacks throughout the building. This high level of flexibility can only be achieved at the cost of building to the floor loading suitable for bookstacks throughout (6.5 kN m^{-2}). However, the growing use of information technology, often at the expense of bookstacks, has challenged this view. Some learning resource centres, housing predominantly IT-based resources, have been constructed to office, rather than traditional library, floor-loading standards. Savings can also be made by reducing the floor loading around the perimeter of the traditional library building where reader places, rather than books, will be accommodated. However, any potential savings should be carefully assessed against the loss of long-term flexibility.

Flexible provision for information technology is also important to enable a PC to be provided virtually anywhere in the library with access to all the networks required, but the necessary infrastructure provision can be quite costly. The development of electronic libraries has challenged our view that libraries should always be extendible.

Accessible: *social space that is inviting and easy to use, and promotes independence*

The library should be the central academic focus of the university and have a strong social role within the institution. New undergraduates may not have experienced a library of the scale and sophistication of a university library before. The service must be easily comprehensible to the growing diversity of part-time and lifelong learners from a wide range of backgrounds. It should, therefore, be as accessible as possible, encouraging and even inviting people to make full use of the services provided.

Access from the exterior into the building, and from the entrance to all parts of the library, should be as clear and straightforward as possible, requiring some but not too many additional signs and guiding. The layout should be self-evident, requiring little assistance from library staff, and it should facilitate independent study. The design of entrance areas is changing, particularly as libraries have become busier and have installed access control and self-service systems. The growth of 24-hour, seven-day services requires attention to the security and robustness of the building and its collections, furniture and equipment, and to the safety of readers and staff.

While great strides have been made in providing attractive, legible and flexible signage systems, some buildings still pay too little attention to guiding and others display an over-abundance of confusingly coloured signs. The use of mobile directory boards, multimedia guides and digital signs are all welcome developments.

It is crucial to make good provision for staff and users with disability and learning differences, not least because good design for disabled people is generally good design for the able-bodied. For example, the absence of internal doors in public areas facilitates the flow of book trolleys and wheelchairs alike, and automatic entrance doors have found favour with readers carrying books as well as with the disabled. Disability can range from physical to learning differences, and may be temporary or permanent. Adequate provision goes well beyond consideration of the mobility-impaired in wheelchairs who, in many libraries, continue to be unable to pass through the aisles, or to reach the books on the higher shelves, or to gain unimpeded access to counter services.

The design must meet the current legal requirements for access by those with disability. In the UK the Special Educational Needs and Disability Act (2001) confirms the legal obligations of all providers of education, training and other related services to those over the age of 16: discrimination against disabled students is unlawful. Institutions are required to make 'reasonable adjustments' to ensure access by disabled people and they will be acting unlawfully if they treat disabled people 'less favourably' or place them at a 'substantial disadvantage'. This applies in England, Wales and Scotland but not, as yet, in Northern Ireland. The Disability Rights Commission has published a Code of Practice to help define these concepts and clarify responsibilities. Its vision is to create a society where all disabled people can participate fully as equal citizens. The requirement is fully endorsed by both the funding and quality assurance agencies (HEFCE, 1999; QAA, 1999).

Burrington (2002) identifies a number of key areas: the approach to the library, the entrance, lighting, colour and colour contrast, horizontal communication, furniture, shelving and display, signage and guiding, vertical communication and assistive technology. It is also important to consider the design of computer interfaces.

Varied: *with a choice of learning environment and for different media*

The library should give readers some freedom of choice of study environment to suit different learning styles and the needs of researchers. Students should be encouraged to learn at their own pace and in their own time, with provision for quiet study, group work and independent learning, and the library should provide access to a wide range of traditional and electronic sources.

A variety of reader places is desirable, and these can range from single person to multi-person tables, casual seating, study rooms and group study facilities. Some readers like an 'active' or noisy social learning environment; others prefer a quiet study environment with good acoustic and visual privacy, and this can be achieved to different degrees with table dividers, book stands, mesh screens, partial carrels, and even fully enclosed carrels. Rooms and facilities are increasingly provided for seminars, information skills training and teaching purposes.

Some architects have a strong preference for specially designed furniture but this can prove both difficult and expensive to replace subsequently. Some libraries use standard tables for computers and equipment while others make use of special furniture. There are national standards for furniture in many countries recommending, for example, a standard height for tables.

Interactive: *well organized space that promotes contact between users and services*

It is important to achieve an appropriate level of interaction between the space given over to the collections, services, information technology and readers. Lucker (2002) suggests 50% for collections, 25% for readers and 25% for staff. The well organized library not only makes optimum use of the space available but also promotes human interaction and encourages use. Main counters and other service points where readers and staff interact require special attention, as do areas where readers themselves interact.

Conducive: *high-quality humane space that inspires people*

As the academic heart of the university, the library should convey a sense of quality and value. The ambience should be conducive to academic work and reflection, and should encourage and even inspire use. Readers, many of whom study for long periods and in increasing numbers, should feel comfortable and safe. The environment should facilitate access to information and the delivery of high-quality services and be responsive to user needs.

Imaginative architecture and varied internal spaces all contribute to the ambience of the learning environment, which can be further enhanced by paintings, sculptures, stained glass, internal gardens and other 'cultural artwork'. Once seen as an unaffordable luxury, cultural artwork is now often funded directly from building grants (The Arts Council of Great Britain, 1991). An investment in a high standard of furnishings and finishes will also create this sense of quality and will withstand heavy use over an extended period with the minimum of maintenance. The library should be much more than an unimaginative 'swotting shed' with a high density of regimented study places.

Noise, particularly from computer clusters and readers themselves, is an increasing problem in libraries. Planners are paying considerable attention to the management of noise in new buildings. Ironically, this is even more important in libraries where talking is permitted, because effective noise management enables users to interact with each other without disturbing others unnecessarily. Every attempt should be made to 'design-out' the effects of noise and, wherever possible, to 'zone' activities in order to keep potentially noisy activities away from quiet study areas. Blocks of shelving are often used to screen noisy areas from quiet areas. The suppression of noise can be achieved by attention to finishes, especially ceiling and floor finishes, and planners have sensibly begun to engage acoustic engineers to advise on ways of reducing noise in the building. Carpet is generally regarded as the best floor finish in this respect, but there have been concerns about the health problems associated with carpets in some countries, especially the underestimated effect on asthma sufferers. The choice of internal colours may even have an effect on behaviour, for example blue may have more of a calming effect than red and so may be more suitable in a reading room. One fundamental dilemma is the design of the staircases in the library. Some buildings are designed around an open central staircase for transparent access and airflow considerations. In others, planners have contained the inevitable noise associated with readers moving up and down the building by enclosing the staircases.

Environmentally suitable: *with appropriate conditions for readers, books and computers*

Suitable environmental conditions are required, not only for the comfort of readers, but also for the efficient operation of computers and the preservation of library materials. Ideally temperature, humidity, dust and pollution levels should all be controlled. The most suitable conditions for reading areas in libraries are held to be 20C and 50 to 55% relative humidity, but cooler temperatures, lower humidity and reduced light levels are better for the long-term preservation of books and other materials.

The 'intelligent library' has been defined as one which maximizes the environment for its occupants while at the same time allowing effective management of resources within minimum lifetime costs (Bisbrouck and Chauveinc, 1999). Any building or energy management system fitted should be designed to the lowest common denominator of building management. Universities often underestimate the real cost of running sophisticated systems and the need for properly trained maintenance staff.

The library should also be environmentally appropriate and sustainable. There is an enhanced awareness of the importance of conservation: many universities now have environmental policies and architects themselves are often taking the necessary initiatives.

Despite the continued close attention of architects and planners, the design of lighting systems sometimes still falls short of providing a consistent standard of illumination throughout the building. Ambient lighting, whether natural or artificial, should be sufficient both for bookstacks and for reader places, and must take account of the growing use of computer terminals by readers and library staff. Faulkner-Brown (1999) suggests 400 lux at the working plane throughout public areas but lower design levels are now commonplace. Fluorescent downlighting remains the most economical form of artificial lighting but it must be well diffused to prevent glare on computer screens. Where the lighting follows the direction of the shelving (as opposed to being at right angles or diagonal to the shelving), flexibility can be improved by arranging the lighting on tracks so that it can be moved should ranges be added or removed. Shorter, well-diffused tubes, which operate at higher frequencies and cause fewer headaches, are increasingly common.

Uplighting can create an attractive 'feel' in the library and reduce problems of glare. Lights can be automatically controlled in the stacks by photocells, but there are concerns about cost, reliability and personal security. Task lighting or individual table lights have traditionally been used to upgrade the lighting at the reader's desk, but they often suffer from vandalism and lack of maintenance. However, it may be the only way of providing illumination at night in tall glazed reading rooms where there are no artificial lights overhead.

New window and glass technology mean exterior vistas and natural daylight are now possible without many of the familiar hazards to people and paper. Double and even triple glazing, tinting, solar film, blinds or architectural shading are necessary to alleviate the worst effects of noise, solar gain and solar glare. Ways of cleaning huge glazed areas must be considered.

Although reader tables are normally placed around the perimeter beside the windows, library staff accommodation is sometimes planned in such a way that staff do not enjoy a similar privilege. However, there is a legal obligation in some countries to provide natural light for library staff.

Safe and secure: *for people, collections, equipment, data and the building*

The chained libraries of the past serve to remind us that security is not a new problem. Indeed, security and vandal resistance should be considered at an early stage of the planning process, and there are security risks associated with the building, the people using it, the collections, the equipment and also the data (Quinsee and McDonald, 1991). Every precaution should be taken to ensure personal safety and security, and the design must be in accordance with current health and safety legislation. Particular attention may need to be paid to non-standard working hours and to securing computers.

Unfortunately, good security measures can often be in conflict with convenience, aesthetics and even safety.

Efficient: *economic in space, staffing and running costs*

Libraries must be as efficient and economical to operate as possible. It is a well-rehearsed principle in library planning, as in other spheres, that the considerable capital sums involved in new buildings should be spent in such a way as to ensure that recurrent running costs, especially staffing costs, are controlled and, where possible, unit costs are reduced. Clearly, more staff will normally be required in expanded libraries, but the challenge is to meet the additional demand without a proportionate increase in staffing levels.

Considerable skill is needed in designing efficient library staff areas. This involves interpreting the complex workflow patterns and adjacency requirements of library staff in reader service areas, service counters, technical service areas, loading bays, and other important areas where library staff work. Although some architects may disagree, universities would stress the need for special attention to be given to planning for minimum running and maintenance costs. Some library managers are now required to meet these costs from devolved budgets. Space efficiency and life-cycle costs have come under close scrutiny, and projects are often required to demonstrate value-for-money in relation to the large capital sums made available for them.

Universities often consider the economics and desirability of extending and refurbishing existing buildings as an alternative to constructing new libraries (Fox and Cassin, 1996; McDonald, 1993). Existing buildings may have an emotional, symbolic or architectural significance within the university, and refurbishment may be consistent with campus plans (Jones, 1999). Planners may also consider the economics and convenience of housing certain collections in on- or off-campus stores, and have begun to compare the relative life-cycle costs of developing electronic and traditional libraries.

Suitable for information technology: *with flexible provision for users and staff*

One of the major challenges is creating space with appropriate provision for information and communications technology (McDonald et al., 2000). Although the definition of an 'intelligent building' may be a matter of discussion (Bisbrouck and Chauveinc, 1999), the new building must allow the library and its users to benefit fully from rapid advances in electronic information networks, e-learning materials, library automation and automated building management systems. Indeed, we should be planning buildings to surpass the demands of the internet generation (Fox, 1999). Even though only 18% of reader places in university libraries in the UK have computers at the moment (SCONUL, 2001), the number of computers and peripheral devices used in libraries continues to grow at a significant rate, and readers are also bringing in their own portable machines. The ultimate challenge is to have the capability of a fully networked computer at virtually any point in the building and to provide a conducive environment suitable for the use of that computer.

Effective planning relies on the combined wisdom and experience of architects, librarians, and computer specialists and networking experts. A suitable proportion of the building budget, typically 5–10%, should be devoted to information technology provision to fund the cabling, active equipment, connections and hardware required, together with suitable safety, security and environmental measures. Future-proofing in a relatively new and rapidly changing situation can be difficult, but it is clear that IT-based services are increasingly heavily used in libraries and that the cost and disruption of trying to make suitable provision at a later date may be prohibitive.

Most new academic library buildings have been fully wired-up. Provision must be made for getting cabling into the building to a data communications cabinet or hub room, and then for distribution to the various floors through risers, and finally across each floor to clusters and individual machines. Trunking is required for the distribution of power, data and telephone cables around the building. The trunking should reach as much of the floor space as possible and alternative routes included around the perimeter wall of the building, across the ceiling, under the floor, to pillars and to individual rooms. Large accessible cable trays are needed to accommodate any changes of cables that may be necessary during the life of the building. A structured cabling system will ensure future flexibility and minimize the need for rewiring.

Planners often choose to wire up a certain proportion of the reader places, not least for reasons of cost. Indeed, some institutions have developed a ratio for the number of PCs per student in the institution as whole, following the 1:8 ratio recommended in the Nelson Report (Computer Board for Universities and Research Councils, 1983).

Computers on tables arranged around the perimeter can easily be served from the wall. It is customary for tables to be positioned at right angles to the wall, but in some cases a continuous perimeter bench has been fitted where readers face outwards and the computer screens inwards. PCs are sometimes placed in the centre of the building to avoid problems of solar glare and gain.

In many libraries computers are simply placed on ordinary tables, and this gives the most flexible arrangement. Special computer tables are available from furniture suppliers, and architects and interior planners often design special computer tables for new libraries. There is a wide variety of designs, but common features include VDU shelves and some sort of secure enclosure for the central processing unit, sometimes located beneath the table to give more space at the work surface. The design of workstations for both readers and library staff should take account of the appropriate health and safety regulations, such as issued by the European Community (1990) and by the Health & Safety Executive (1992) for work with visual display equipment. The large number of wires in networked libraries makes wire management in the furniture a necessity, both for safety and for aesthetic reasons, and IT workplaces should be provided with fully adjustable chairs.

Planners should consider the merits of distributed PC provision, with proximity to the collections and other information sources, and separate clusters of machines, with the benefit of centralized management and support. They should also consider arranging machines in separate rooms or in open plan areas. PC clusters are now commonplace in libraries and have been given a variety of interesting names – Barn Cluster, Tarn Cluster, Apple Orchard, IT Shed, IT Pit, PC Terrace and Information Commons. They often double up as teaching clusters too. In designing the layout, there is an inevitable tension between achieving the maximum number of machines and creating an attractive space that is conducive to learning. Some libraries have used Y- or star-shaped tables, where one or two computers are placed on each wing with shared drives or printers located in the centre. It is suggested this gives a greater density of workstations and a welcome relief from more rectangular and formal arrangements. Large clusters can produce a surprising amount of noise and heat, and care must be taken to ensure fire protection and security.

Self-services and smart cards

Self-services are increasingly being offered in academic libraries as a way of meeting the growing demand from users and of extending opening hours while, at the same time, of avoiding the risk of repetitive strain and stress injury to library assistants. Self-issue and return systems have the potential to radically change our approach to designing entrance areas and counters since readers can undertake these circulation transactions themselves virtually anywhere in the library. Smaller counters may be required to deal only with those transactions where staff intervention is really necessary, and the design should encourage the interaction between users and staff rather than the circulation of books. Indeed, some automated services could even become available on a hole-in-the-wall basis. The use of card-entry and smart cards for entrance control and cashless financial transactions also have design implications.

Space standards and norms

There are space standards or norms for academic libraries in many countries. These usually indicate the amount of space required for readers or bookstock, or give an appropriate number of reader places in relation to the size of the user population.

According to the Atkinson norms approved some 26 years ago by the then University Grants Committee (1976) in the UK, the net size of a university library should be based upon 1.25 m² per full-time equivalent student. It recommended a ratio of one reader place for every six full-time equivalent students with an allowance of 2.39 m² for each reader place based on a reader's table measuring 900 x 600 mm.

These norms have been widely adopted by universities and government departments for planning and bidding purposes. But some universities regard them as an irrelevance because the level of funding necessary even to approach these minimum standards has never been made available. Indeed, even now after a significant investment in buildings in the 1990s, the average space provision in UK university libraries is still only 0.9 m² per full-time equivalent student (SCONUL, 2001).

It is widely accepted that these norms are now outdated and no longer reflect the real pressure for library space (McDonald, 1996b). Recent projects have found it necessary to make a more generous space allowance of around 4 m² per reader space (with a reader's table measuring 800 x 1000 mm) largely as a result of increasing information technology provision. However, improved space utilization in universities rather than space norms is likely to dominate the thinking of the Funding Councils.

Recent design trends

Standards of design continue to improve, and we are seeing a growing diversity of wonderful new library buildings in which exciting architectural expression, satisfying internal spaces and good functionality have been successfully combined. Each building represents a particular vision of what a new library should look like and in doing so contributes something to our thinking about the planning and design of academic library space.

Deep-plan cubes

A number of university libraries built in the 1970s and 1980s were designed as modular, deep-plan cubes with narrow or slit windows. The modular design successfully provides the required open flexible space with the minimum number of fixed elements. The architect, Harry Faulkner-Brown (1979), argued that the deep-plan cube, presented on a number of levels, provided a compact efficient building in which the vertical and horizontal travelling distances were theoretically much shorter than in a linear building of the same size, particularly when readers entered on an intermediate level. Typically, the arrangement was open-access bookstack in the centre of the building and study places around the perimeter. The interiors needed to be skilfully designed so as to breath life and colour into what could be rather bland open spaces. The small windows usefully reduced the glare on computer screens.

The designs were said to be efficient in their use of energy by virtue of the low window-to-wall ratio and the low wall-to-floor area. However, these large deep-plan buildings required an artificial environment, characterized by fluorescent lighting and forced ventilation, and they were normally sealed buildings in which the windows could not be opened. Since then attitudes have changed and many designers have preferred differently shaped buildings with larger windows and natural ventilation, particularly in view of the generally poor performance and reliability of air-conditioning systems in the UK.

Different shapes

In the 1990s, library buildings showed a refreshing trend towards more imaginative architecture, breaking away from the conformity to deep-plan cubes and sealed artificial environments of the previous two decades.

We have seen a growing variety of interesting and curvaceous shapes, often with much larger windows and greater use of height in the architecture, with a consequent improvement in the variety and ambience of the interior. Some of these 'glazed envelopes' were perhaps inspired by the simplicity of the form of barns and hangers and give wonderful views of the surrounding areas. These buildings demonstrated that good functionality and aesthetics can be achieved even where sites and budgets are restricted. Height and increased fenestration have been used to create a welcome variety of internal spaces, the ambience of which has been enhanced by a range of lighting and by attractive cultural artwork. The greater use of information technology has been supported by improved trunking and wire management, and clusters of PCs are often differentiated from other areas in the library. A concern for noise management and for improved access for those with disability are further important trends.

Learning resource centres

Some new universities have built impressive new libraries to improve the quality of their learning support services. These 'premier' buildings are often the most distinguished on campus and some have been designed by internationally renowned architects. Many are conceived as learning resource centres, reflecting their role in supporting learning (Brewer, 1997). Some are 'converged' library and computing services, in which there is a greater emphasis on providing reader places, information technology and a wide range of learning media, rather than on traditional printed collections. Some also house media centres, information skills laboratories, learning development services, curriculum support units and other learning facilities. Others provide teaching accommodation and seminar rooms.

Some planners regard learning resource centres as a new building type with distinctive qualities (Higher Education Design Quality Forum, 1995). In practice, most forward-looking library and information services are 'hybrid' services, providing both traditional and electronic services, whether in support of teaching and learning, or of research, or both (McDonald, 1996a).

People-centred buildings

Recent design trends emphasize the people-centred approach to planning as much as providing an environment suitable for the preservation of library collections and for information technology (Faulkner-Brown, 1999). Users of new library buildings are enjoying the variety of daylight and sunlight and welcome views of the outside world. Natural ventilation systems are replacing the totally artificial environments, and users frequently have more direct control of their environment. The buildings themselves often exploit thermal mass and free night-time cooling. Atria can introduce welcome light and natural ventilation to the centre of large buildings, but can also form obstacles to movement around the building. Open central staircases facilitate transparent access to all floors of the library and make buildings easier to ventilate, but they can also allow the penetration of unwelcome noise throughout the building.

Some university libraries have extended their opening to 24 hours a day, seven days a week, either to PC clusters or to the collections and study places too. Continuous use presents a number of challenges for designing buildings and services that are both secure and robust. Greater attention is being paid to removing the physical barriers that make it impossible or unreasonably difficult for disabled people to effectively access library services in order to comply with the Special Educational Needs and Disability Act (2001). As well as designing conducive environments for large numbers of PCs, libraries are giving over more space to IT support, printing services, information skills training and distance learning services. Current developments include the provision of high- bandwidth networks throughout the building, the introduction of faster wireless connectivity at reducing costs (despite concerns about reliability and security), and the increasing use of flat screens, laptops and portable devices.

Interior design

Interior designers recognize that even in the digital age, libraries are 'human-centred environments' that should have a strong sense of place, and there is considerable interest in innovative design spaces both for private and social learning in galleries, museums, libraries and other public places. In some cases, the library may become more like the living room, providing the emotional space for social interaction within the community. Trends in retailing suggest that library design will be influenced by entertainment and technology and the need for 'food with everything'. Kugler (2002) suggests that different lighting, noise levels, temperature zones and seating styles can be used to create a variety of flexible and comfortable learning spaces. She points out some of the complex design issues, for example the tension between creating flexible and well-defined space, and between personal and social space in libraries.

Joined-up libraries

Many new academic libraries remain 'standalone' projects but, as academic institutions increasingly work in partnership with other bodies to broaden participation in learning, we are likely to see more innovative 'joined-up' building projects. In the USA, some academic libraries have been built with student services and other academic buildings and also with public libraries and health centres (Fox and Jones, 1998). Joint university and public libraries have been built in Scandinavia and are planned in the USA. New learning centres in the UK have been created in companies, shopping malls, churches, football clubs and other places convenient for lifelong learners (McDonald, 2000a). Exciting new joint amenities are emerging from the closer working relationship between libraries, museums and archives. There are significant funding, political and design challenges in planning these multipurpose 'places'. There is likely to be a general trend towards more learner-friendly design in workplaces, public places, shopping centres, libraries and other buildings. The Department for Education and Employment (1999) sees this as important in creating a new learning culture in which lifelong learning can flourish.

Conclusion

The future of the library as a physical 'place' has been a matter of considerable professional speculation and debate. Despite some hasty predictions about the imminence and inevitability of the virtual electronic library, universities around the world continue to build libraries in which teaching, learning and research can be pursued often, as it happens, with growing printed collections. Many countries are also building new national libraries, recognizing 'that libraries are becoming indispensable social and cultural institutions' (Wu, 1999).

These new buildings still provide the 'place' where people can come together, preferably without disturbing each other too much, to undertake a number of important activities. They come in increasing numbers to study, learn, reflect and exchange ideas. They consult the collections, retrieve information and use the equipment and computers provided. They seek the assistance and support of trained information professionals, and they make use of the whole range of managed services provided. Increasingly, they learn information skills and use other learning development services. Importantly, libraries provide access to information and information technology for the information 'have-nots'. The buildings are the hub for distributing networked services to off-campus scholars and learners, and they continue to house growing traditional collections and special collections of important research and heritage materials. Although the balance between these activities is likely to change, the library building remains the important 'place' where all these essential services can be conveniently provided, even in the virtual age (Hurt, 1997). It is interesting that many of the most automated libraries in the world are still buildings and most often very pleasant ones too.

Libraries remain among the most socially inclusive, enduring and well-used 'places' in modern society, and creating good new library buildings is critical not only to the future of our universities but also to the intellectual capital of our countries. In planning and designing these important new 'places', the library manager must have a clear vision of what is required, communicate this to all those involved and play a leading role in the planning process. This vision must embrace a whole range of issues, but it is reassuring that the people-centred approach has come to dominate modern designs. As Dowlin (1999, 205) confirms, 'the magic of libraries is in connecting minds . . . and successful library buildings in the 21st century will enable those connections to happen'. By planning new space with customers and services at the core, the library manager can enable our new libraries to play their full part in the teaching, learning, research and reachout activities of our universities within the emerging information and learning age.

We are witnessing unprecedented and dynamic change in society, higher education, technologies and management. These trends, and the considerable challenges they present to planners, are likely to continue at an ever-increasing pace. Tomorrow's libraries will look and feel very different 'places' from yesterday's buildings. However, the building shells we create today will remain lasting tributes, whether in stone or brick, or now more likely in glass, to the managerial vision, leadership and influence of the librarians responsible for their planning.

References

Arts Council of Great Britain (1991) *Percent for art: a review*, The Arts Council of Great Britain.

Bazillion, R. J. and Braun, C. (1994) Academic library design: building a 'teaching instrument', *Computers in Libraries*, **14** (2), 12–16.

Bisbrouck, M.-F. and Chauveinc, M. (eds) (1999) *Intelligent library buildings: proceedings of the 10th seminar of the IFLA Section on Library Buildings and Equipment, The Hague, Netherlands, August, 1997*, Saur.

Brewer, G. (1997) A new learning centre at the University of Derby, *Standing Conference of National and University Libraries Newsletter*, (Summer/Autumn), 20–4.

Burrington, G. (2002) Design and adaptation of libraries and services. In Hopkins, L. (ed.), *Library services for visually impaired people: a manual of best practice*, Resource, Council for Museums, Archives and Libraries, available at www.nlbuk.org/bpm/chapter12.html.

Computer Board for Universities and Research Councils (1983) *Report of a working party on computer facilities for teaching in universities*, Computer Board (the Nelson Report).

Dowlin, K. E. (1999) San Francisco public library. In Bisbrouck, M.-F. and Chauveinc, M. (eds), *Intelligent library buildings: proceedings of the 10th seminar of the IFLA Section on Library Buildings and Equipment, The Hague, Netherlands, August, 1997*, Saur, 117–209.

European Community (1990) Minimum safety and health requirements for work with display screen equipment, *Official Journal of European Community L Series*, **156** (14), European Community (Directive No. 90/270/EEC).

Faulkner-Brown, H. (1979) The open plan and flexibility, *Proceedings of International Association of Technological University Libraries*, **11**, 3.

Faulkner-Brown, H. (1998) Design criteria for large academic libraries, *World Information Report 1997/98*, UNESCO.

Faulkner-Brown, H. (1999) Some thoughts on the design of major library buildings. In Bisbrouck, M.-F. and Chauveinc, M. (eds), *Intelligent library buildings: proceedings of the 10th seminar of the IFLA Section on Library Buildings and Equipment, The Hague, Netherlands, August, 1997*, Saur, 9–31.

Fox, B.-L. (1999) Structural ergonomics, *Library Journal*, **124** (20), 57–69.

Fox, B.-L. (2000) Strength in numbers, *Library Journal*, available at www.libraryjournal.com/architecture2000/index.asp

Fox, B.-L. and Cassin, E. (1996) Beating the high cost of libraries, *Library Journal*, (December), 43–55.

Fox, B.-L. and Jones, E.J. (1998) Another year, another $543 million, *Library Journal*, **123** (20), 41–3.

Great Britain. Department for Education and Employment (1999) *Creating learning cultures: next steps in achieving the learning age: second report of The National Advisory Group for Continuing Education and Lifelong Learning*, Department for Education and Employment (Chair R. H Fryer).

Great Britain. Health & Safety Executive (1992) *Display screen equipment work – guidance on regulations*, HMSO.

Great Britain. University Grants Committee (1976) *Capital provision for university libraries: report of a working party*, HMSO (the Atkinson Report).

HEFCE (1993) *Joint Funding Councils' Libraries Review Group: A report for the Higher Education Funding Council for England, Scottish Higher Education Funding Council, Higher Education Funding Council for Wales and Department of Education for Northern Ireland, Higher Education Funding Council* (the Follett report), available at www.ukoln.ac.uk/services/papers/follett/report/.

HEFCE (1999) *Guidance on base-level provision for disabled students in higher education*, Higher Education Funding Council for England.

Higher Education Design Quality Forum (1995) *Learning resource centres for the future: Proceedings of a conference organised by the Higher Education Design Quality Forum, Standing Conference of National and University Libraries, and Royal Institute of British Architects*, Standing Conference of National and University Libraries.

Hurt, C. (1997) Building libraries in the virtual age, *College & Research Libraries News*, **58** (2), 75–6, 91.

Institute of Advanced Architectural Studies (1995) *Building libraries for the information age: proceedings of a symposium on the future of higher education libraries held at the King's Manor, York, April 1994*, Institute of Advanced Studies.

Jones, W. G. (1999) *Library buildings: renovation and reconfiguration*, Association of Research Libraries, Office of Leadership and Management Services.

Kugler, C. (2002) Spaced-out design in the digital age. In Clark, B. (ed.), *Future places: reinventing libraries in the digital age: proceedings of the 12th international seminar of the IFLA Section on Library Buildings and Equipment*, Saur.

Lucker, J. (2002) Critical issues in library space planning for the 21st century. In Clark, B. (ed), *Future places: reinventing libraries in the digital age: proceedings of the 12th international seminar of the IFLA Section on Library Buildings and Equipment*, Saur.

McDonald, A. C. (1993) The refurbishment of libraries – what should you be looking for?, *Aslib Information*, **21** (1), 32–5.

McDonald, A. C. (1996a) Some issues in learning resource centre accommodation and design. In *Learning resource centres for the future: proceedings of a conference organised by Higher Education Design Quality Forum and the Standing Conference on National and University Libraries, held at Royal Institute of British Architects, 1995*, Standing Conference of National and University Libraries, 23–42.

McDonald, A. C. (1996b) *Space requirements for academic libraries and learning resource centres*, SCONUL Briefing Paper, Standing Conference of National and University Libraries.

McDonald, A.C. (2000a) Lifelong learning and the University for Industry: the challenge for libraries in the United Kingdom, *Advances in Librarianship*, 23, 207–38.

McDonald, A. C. (2000b) Planning academic library buildings for a new age: some principles, trends and developments in the United Kingdom, *Advances in Librarianship*, 24, 51–79.

McDonald, A. C. et al. (2000) *Information and communications technology in academic library buildings*, SCONUL Briefing Paper, Standing Conference of National and University Libraries.

Mason, E. (1996) Management of library building planning, *Journal of Library and Information Science*, 22, 14–28.

QAA (1999) *Code of practice for assurance of academic quality and standards in higher education: students with disabilities*, The Quality Assurance Agency for Higher Education.

Quinsee, A. C. and McDonald, A. C. (eds) (1991) *Security in academic and research libraries*, Newcastle University Library.

SCONUL (2001) *Annual library statistics 1998–99*, Society of College, National and University Libraries.

SCONUL (2002) *Library building projects database*, Society of College, National and University Libraries, available at www.lgu.ac.uk/deliberations/sconul/

Special Educational Needs and Disability Act (2001) Stationery Office. (Great Britain. Acts)

Wu, J. (1999) *New library buildings of the world*, International Federation of Library Associations and Institutions.

8

Developing a service culture through partnerships

Maxine Melling and Joyce Little

Introduction

Library and information services have a well-documented history of partnership activity, ranging from document supply to access agreements. Many examples of partnership, such as interlibrary loan services, are well established, while more recently active collaboration within and between different sectors has grown and has moved onto the political agenda.

The motivation for collaboration can be driven by a desire to improve basic services to library users, seeing this approach to service provision as of general benefit by making scarce resources go further or by providing access to a wider range of resources than would otherwise have been possible. However, increasingly, service providers are also motivated by external pressure, brought to bear by government and/or funding incentives. As scarce resources come under increasing pressure, and as technological advances make it possible to offer electronically distributed national collections, pressure is growing on libraries to collaborate more actively at national, regional and sectoral levels.

But what of the users of our services? Most will be rightly ignorant of delivery mechanisms and systems, whether they result in locating a book or periodical article or in gaining access to an electronic database. For customers, the critical issue is one of access to help and resources, regardless of who funds them or where they may originate. Increasingly, partnership working is the invisible thread that enables customers of libraries to gain access to a nation's resources from one library service.

This chapter aims to provide an overview of partnerships in library and information services and to consider this provision from the viewpoint of the user. It will offer some definitions of partnership as currently understood, examples of the types of partnership work taking place across the sector, and consider the barriers to partnership. The basic premise of this chapter is that partnership working, supported by agreed principles and approaches, provides better and more comprehensive services to library and information service (LIS) users than can be achieved by any library service working in isolation. The outstanding question is whether partnership activity can and should develop beyond what has already been explored in the examples provided.

Definitions

Words used to describe partnership activity tend to be interchangeable and rather vague. As discussion about this area of activity increases and as examples of good practice are shared across the LIS sector some consistency is beginning to emerge. Perhaps one of the most useful set of definitions has been provided in a report carried out in the higher education sector (Higher Education Consultancy Group and CHEMS Consultancy, 2002). This report suggests a hierarchy of activity which moves from the informal to the formal and which exists at a number of different levels. The hierarchy includes:

- *Co-operation:* defined by the report as a 'basic level of working together' and seen as weaker than collaboration.
- *Collaboration:* defined by the report as 'joint working which involves a conscious and shared approach to planning, implementing and reviewing aspects of LIS services'. This definition does not necessarily include the commitment of any significant resource.
- *Partnership:* defined as a more 'formal and explicit approach to collaboration' possibly involving contractual agreements.
- *Resource sharing:* defined as ways of working together that involve the 'sharing of resources, whether finance, staffing, services, accommodation and infrastructure support, or collections'.
- *Deep-resource sharing:* defined as 'collaboration between or among libraries in which institutional autonomy in service provision is in some degrees surrendered, and which involves some degree of risk'. Interestingly, an alternative and more restrictive definition of deep-resource sharing has been provided by Law (2002) as 'the treatment and management as a single collection, of the collections of several institutions'. What both definitions have in common is the move away from joint working to the merging or combining of resources in order to provide a richer end product.

These attempts at providing a hierarchy of definitions relating to joint working are helpful, not only in providing a shared vocabulary but also in articulating the range and depth of possibilities. The main content of this chapter lies within partnership and collaboration, as described above. Reference is made to the possibilities offered by resource sharing and so-called 'deep-resource sharing'. However, as part of a practical guide to managers regarding what is currently possible, this chapter accepts that both the benefits and the barriers of deep-resource sharing require greater exploration.

Types of partnerships

The clarity of the definitions provided above can mask the complexity of the range of partnership activities taking place across LIS. Partnerships can be profit or non-profit making with the latter in the majority. Library services may work in partnership with other libraries in their sector or cross-sectorally (academic, public, special, health) and cross-domain (libraries, archives, museums). They can be restricted to a local community, work within a metropolitan or rural area, or be regional, national or international. Libraries will work in partnership with library suppliers, publishers, booksellers and book promotion agencies. In joint purchasing consortia journals and books can form part of a specification alongside library systems and furniture. Externally, there is a myriad of partnerships with public sector services such as education providers, community agencies, communications access providers and private companies to provide income generation and information and communications technologies (ICT) services for networking, content development or publicity. Partnerships can be inter or intra institutional.

Formal cross-sectoral collaboration in the UK dates back to the setting up of the nine regional library bureaux in the 1930s and the creation of the National Lending Library for Science and Technology in 1957. It subsequently evolved, following merger with the National Central Library, into what is now known as the British Library Document Supply Centre (BLDSC). Other established partnerships, primarily in the academic sector, deliver consortia purchasing and licensing agreements. In public libraries, school library services have long been the result of close working between library and local education authorities and have been the basis of the development of homework clubs, after-school clubs and curriculum support. Work with other information providers has increased access to information for active citizenship and provided additional support for vulnerable people in the community. Campaigns to increase personal achievement, promote healthy lifestyles and deliver learning opportunities have been possible through collaborative partnerships with education providers, health authorities and voluntary organizations.

Newer forms of partnerships are delivering content and content development for library networks. Consortia of libraries, library systems suppliers and ICT companies are delivering projects that are creating the foundations for national access to catalogues and resource discovery across libraries, archives and museums. In addition, such joint working creates new access to rare and valuable items with the added benefit of sustainable preservation of materials.

Public libraries can often be agents for inclusiveness. For example, long-standing partnerships with social services, disability organizations, charities and voluntary organizations have enabled improvements to the delivery of services for people with disabilities. Similar partnerships for the fostering of library services for black and other racial minority groups, the unemployed, single parents, the elderly and the very young have provided individuals and organizations within the community with services that improve the quality of life. These social benefits are not always recognized as an outcome of the provision of a public library service.

Within the local authority context the most obvious and demonstrable form of partnership is where the library service is managed within an education or cultural service. It can be argued that public libraries are the original lifelong learner support mechanism. Links with local education services have provided excellent means of delivery to those receiving compulsory education, as have initiatives such as Connexions, Sure Start, Bookstart and Adult Learning Plans. As part of this type of joint working public librarians often sit on the Strategic Lifelong Learning Partnership and have been invited on to the board of Learning and Skills Councils, as well as working with the Adult Guidance Partnerships for the delivery of career and training guidance for adults.

The UK is not alone or at the forefront of such collaborative consortia. In the USA the Association of Specialized and Co-operative Library Agencies (ASCLA), a sub-division of the American Library Association (ALA), represents state and specialized library agencies, multi-type library co-operatives and independent librarians (www.ala.org/ascla/org). Co-operative collection development and document delivery have been at the heart of consortia arrangements between public and academic libraries in a number of states for a number of decades. Perhaps the greatest single public/private partnership was the Gates Foundation which, in 1998, made a $20 million grant to over 1000 US libraries for computers, technical assistance and training to provide public library users access to the internet.

Why collaborate?

Self-motivation

Library services have traditionally fostered joint working and the sharing of knowledge, expertise and advice. This culture of collaboration was acknowledged in a review of information co-operation undertaken by the APT Partnership (1995, 1.1) which concluded that 'Cooperative activity currently represents a comparatively small, but vitally important, part of total library and information activity, ... [and that] library cooperation forms a part of the value system and organizational culture of those who work in library and information services'.

Up to the 20th century, the inter-lending services which developed from the 1930s were, in the broadest sense, the greatest added-value service provided by libraries of whatever nature and wherever located. Libraries maintain large and irreplaceable collections most of which are catalogued, listed and made available to their customers. Partnership working through interlibrary loan and document delivery replaces the need for ownership of materials with access to materials. Inter-lending provides library services with a win–win situation that benefits the service and the user to equal effect. The extent and depth of the interlibrary loan and document supply services available in the UK are, to some extent, taken for granted by library and information services and possibly by their users. Interestingly, the Higher Education Consultancy Group and CHEMS Consultancy report (2002, 51) puts forward the view that these services are viewed in countries such as the USA as a primary example of 'deep-resource sharing'.

Developments in ICT have provided a further self-motivating influence which offers opportunities to customers of services while presenting libraries with significant benefits. Within the academic sector the development of the Joint Academic Network (JANET) which links higher and further education institutions, has enabled a level of joint working across the sector that would otherwise have been impossible. Resource discovery, facilitated by ICT innovations, and new partnerships with ICT providers, have resulted in clumping projects at national, sub-regional and local level. Technical obsolescence and the need for innovation in information and communications technologies provides a driver to seek external partners to deliver networked services in this rapidly changing environment.

From the point of view of the service provider, partnership working also stimulates research and can provide a clearing-house for information. Standards and service guidelines resulting from joint working can provide the basis for other libraries to introduce similar or parallel developments. Library professionals rely heavily on benchmarking and networking in order to develop new approaches to service provision.

Most justification and explanation of partnership working centres on cost-effectiveness and management requirements and the desire to work with other library sectors, other domains (museums and archives) or with statutory and voluntary organizations as well as the private sector. Often omitted are the needs of the customers as analysed in the People Flows report (Mynott et al., 1999). The research team for this report focused on adult use of public and academic libraries in two metropolitan areas and the data demonstrated the clear need to develop partnerships across these two sectors to promote access to collections and to save customers' time. This report includes some pragmatic ways forward to promote partnership working and was a key source for the later government response to the Empowering the Learning Community report (Great Britain. Department for Education and Employment and the Department for Culture, Media and Sport, 2001).

The People Flows report indicated that learners do not necessarily see themselves as users of one particular library or type of library. The data provided showed that approximately two-thirds of the university and college respondents and just over half of the public library respondents had used other libraries in the year before they were surveyed. Interestingly, in spite of these high numbers, very few of the respondents were aware of any co-operative library agreements, they simply took access for granted. These findings suggest that library users are ahead of some service providers in their assumption that libraries should be open to anyone according to need.

It can be argued that adult learners have the most to gain from the results of partnership working and this is supported by strategic agencies involved in overseeing the delivery and development of library and learning services. The Library and Information Commission listed benefits for learners at home and work, citizens, community members and businesses in their model of strategic frameworks (Library and Information Commission, 2000). Access to distance learning and online resources, improved access to public information, enhanced library services and business access to collaborative networks could result from partnerships whose purpose is to develop electronic networks in libraries, community centres and other public buildings.

External influences

External pressure to increase performance and cost-effectiveness has certainly resulted in a growth in collaborative partnerships. In public libraries for example, demonstration of partnership working or collaboration that provides improvement in services is central to the government's drive for best value and has led to a growth in the measurement of service with the customer's requirements in mind. Under Comprehensive Performance Review and in Best Value reviews public library authorities are called upon to challenge the purpose of a service, consult with the community, compare performance with other authorities and provide competition where appropriate. The aim is continuous service improvement measured through customer response and monitoring and evaluation against other authorities. In a similar way evidence of public and private sector partnerships is specifically required in local authority annual library plans and must be demonstrated to achieve national quality standards such as Charter Mark and Beacon Council status.

Resource, the Council for Museums, Archives and Libraries, which was launched in the UK in 1999, was established to build on commonality in the different sectors for the benefit of communities and to link into the growing regional agenda. Regional development agencies, regional cultural consortia, regional government offices and regional assemblies, the forerunners to proposed devolved regional government, were all established in the UK in the 1990s to meet regional needs and aspirations. One of the core values of Resource is that partnership and co-operation are essential components of success (www.resource.gov.uk).

The establishment of single regional agencies to deliver a common agenda for museums, archives and library services for each of the nine regions of England is driving cross-domain collaboration beyond the voluntary nature of previous liaison and co-operation for project development. The expectation that the single regional agencies will be central to grant making and grant aid funding assessments is placing this new regional structure at the apex of strategic planning for these key cultural institutions. The establishment of regional access and learning support units will provide links between the three domains and the learner, initially through effective partnerships and the establishment of electronic networks and support. Local authority cultural strategies encompass library services within the cultural agenda and linkages with the arts, heritage, museums, archives, media, sport, tourism and the creative industries. Among other aims, these strategies are intended to identify cultural needs, the demands and aspirations of local communities and encourage new and holistic solutions to providing cultural services and identify opportunities to meet local needs (www.culture.gov.uk). The UK government expects to see a strategic approach to their provision with collaborative working and partnerships a keystone to the approach.

In the academic sector a number of reports have advanced the cause of collaboration. For example, the Atkinson Report (Great Britain. University Grants Committee, 1976) put forward the idea of the so-called 'self-renewing library' which removed little-used material in order to create space for new acquisitions. This approach could only be successful with the back-up of the British Library as a library of last resort. More recently, in 1993, the Follett Report (HEFCE, 1993) and Anderson Report (Joint Funding Council, 1996) encouraged collaboration between institutions as a way of ensuring support for both teaching and research. The consultation process for the Research Library Support Group (RSLG) has made it clear that UK researchers are not best served by over 130 independently managed university and college libraries (Follett, 2001). Instead, a national strategic framework which delivers one national distributed research collection is seen as the most cost-effective alternative.

Particular emphasis was placed by Professor Michael Anderson, in the group set up following the Follett Review, on the need for universities to collaborate in avoiding unnecessary duplication. One very practical outcome was the provision of funding to a number of research-based university libraries, via the establishment of 'Access Funds' which are intended to recompense such libraries for use by researchers from across the UK and to ensure that access is guaranteed.

Principles

Examples of existing collaborative practice in library and information services suggest that service providers need to be convinced of some basic principles before embarking on joint ventures, whether they be in the self-motivation or the external pressure categories. The main principles are:

- that the home service provider is primarily responsible for providing information needs to its user base
- that collaboration brings mutual benefit
- that pragmatism and consensus are needed.

The home service provider is primarily responsible for providing information needs to its user base

This key principle is central to the majority of collaborative agreements currently in place and is critical to their success. In higher education the 'modernization' of universities in the 1990s and the reduction in unit funding has led to a much more open culture of competition in the sector. Well-developed quality assurance systems in higher education, which include close scrutiny of library services and a high priority placed upon reported student experience, ensure that academic library services prioritize provision to local fee-paying users above any collaborative arrangements. Although competition between sectors is less significant the need to protect local fee-paying customers is still present. The Education and Libraries Task Group (Library and Information Commission, 2000, 34) recognized this tension in its recommendation that:

> cross-sectoral funding arrangements should be established [to] include an element which is measured against progress towards closer cross-sectoral community partnerships.

The devil, as they say, is in the detail. However, it is inevitable that funding streams and culture affect the extent to which library services can make all facilities and services accessible to the wider community.

Collaboration brings mutual benefit

The policy of the Consortium of Academic Libraries in Manchester (CALIM) states clearly that one of its governing principles is that of 'co-operation in the spirit of enlightened self-interest' (www.calim.ac.uk/info.htm). This approach mirrors a definition of collaboration provided by the APT Partnership in its report (1995, 1.1) as 'the creation and operation of equitable, that is mutually "fair", collaborative arrangements between libraries and information providers which enhance the common good through making information available to all potential users (without obstacle to access by reason of cost) which is more extensive or more valuable to the user and/or is of lower cost to the collaborating providers'.

Where collaborating partners have very different strengths and weaknesses, for example a consortium with a mix of research-based and teaching-based academic library services or a city-centre public library service and an out-of-town academic institution, the partners must see mutual benefit in collaboration. One reason why some library services are wary of active collaboration is the fear of 'swamping', with unsustainable pressure being placed on resources that have been purchased for local users. There is certainly a belief that resources of the home institution are of more interest or benefit to potential users than are those of other partners, a case of the grass being greener on *this* side of the fence. Evidence from the UK Libraries Plus Scheme (www.uklibrariesplus.ac.uk) and from established consortia such as the Libraries Access Sunderland Scheme (LASh) (www.lash.sunderland.ac.uk) suggests that cross-use of libraries within consortia tends to be of equal balance across members and to have a relatively low impact. Of course, the impact measured by these schemes is based on physical access to buildings and/or borrowing within very strict control mechanisms, in other words on very clearly defined and controlled parameters. The impact of more open collaboration, for example in so-called 'deep-resource sharing' would be far greater and has yet to be fully modelled or tested.

Pragmatism and consensus

A healthy dose of common sense and shared values lies behind many of the current successful collaborative arrangements. The M25 consortium of over 40 university and higher education institutions in the UK cites the principle of pragmatism and consensus as central to its success (Enright, 2001, 20). The group reports that developments have often started with small pilot projects that are do-able and, if successful, can then be scaled up. Similarly, the Hatrics co-operative lists both a shared vision and an ability to adapt over time as critical success factors (Hatrics and Capital Planning Information, 1999)

The principles listed above are, of course, presented from the viewpoint of the service provider. Some alternative principles have emerged from both the service user and from government sources which challenge what might be seen as a collaboration-by-stealth approach. The main stated principle that lies behind increasing pressure by the UK government for library collaboration is that of developing a 'learning society in which everyone is able to learn and upgrade their skills throughout life' (Great Britain. Department for Education and Employment and the Department for Culture, Media and Sport, 2001, Foreword). The implementation of the People's Network, establishing ICT Learning Centres in over 4000 public libraries, is designed to ensure compatibility with the National Grid for Learning, developed primarily as a means of providing new digital content for school children. These joint developments will significantly enhance access to resources for lifelong learners.

Partnership agreements

The examples cited above support the view that good working practice demands the drafting of an agreement clearly stating the nature of the partnership, the parameters and the expected outcomes. It is also recommended that guidance be provided in the case of the dissolution of the partnership. Whether the agreement is a memorandum of understanding (Kopp, 1999) or a legally binding contract, all parties should have a clear understanding of the objectives of the partnership and the benefits to the organization and customers.

Funding, administration and management of any partnership are key to the facilitation of effective delivery to encourage sustainability. Consistency of approach through the production of documentation and the establishment of management committees may appear bureaucratic but will produce a more effective partnership. All grant-making organizations will require monitoring and evaluation during project/programme progress and systems must be established to deliver management and performance information.

In developing working agreements it is important to resolve issues such as stated aims and objectives, funding sources, capacity for possible expansion, marketing, and evaluation. Decisions such as who will act as the chair of a collaborative group can be fraught with political and personal issues which can distract from the worthy intentions behind joint working. Most existing partnerships have developed formal working agreements and some have agreed annual subscriptions that fund a joint secretariat or joint development programme. Many partnerships continue to work within existing mainstream budgets. However, as cross-sectoral and cross-domain working develops and as the deliverables of partnership work become more evident, there is evidence that some commitment to a working budget is needed. The Competitiveness though Partnerships with People Report (Great Britain. Department of Trade and Industry & Department for Education and Employment, 1997) is useful in providing guidelines on successful partnership, which it presents in terms of five paths to sustained success; shared goals, shared culture, shared learning, shared effort and shared information.

Collaborative possibilities

A number of relatively straightforward and beneficial immediate gains can be achieved through collaborative partnerships. Those included as examples below have been achieved largely through a pragmatic approach and, often, within existing funding regimes. These approaches meet the needs of many LIS users and pose no threat to the autonomy of the member institutions.

Access

The findings of the People Flows report (Mynott et al. 1999) make it clear that many library users see access as a first priority and, in truth, the provision of access to facilities in member institutions is one of the easy wins of collaboration. Most collaborative partnerships in the UK have started with access, often by mapping the strengths of the different collections, and agreeing to allow each other's members to make reference use of the various libraries. A typical access statement such as the one shown in the Southampton Libraries in Co-operation scheme – 'providing access to their libraries and the information within them (subject to any publicized restrictions) and permitting borrowing to registered users' (available at www.sconul.ac.uk/Meetings/SOTON.pdf) – assures physical access, with local restrictions that are usually linked to licensing and network protocols for electronic resources. Borrowing is becoming more common but is still largely restricted to registered users, with the exception of a range of reciprocal borrowing schemes in higher education for staff and researchers.

Cross-sectoral access agreements exist across the UK, with some well documented examples in the cities of Liverpool (www.liv.ac.uk/Library/llgroup/llg.html), Sheffield (www.shu.ac.uk/sinto/), and Sunderland (www.lash.sunderland.ac.uk).

Examples of national academic library agreements can be seen in both the UK and Australia. The UK Libraries Plus scheme allows borrowing for part-time, distance and sandwich students, based on the host institution's external borrower regulations and allowances. As with most schemes, UK Libraries Plus places the responsibility for the actions of users on the host institution. Membership of UK Libraries Plus grew slowly at first but now covers the majority of higher education institutions. In Australia, a pilot national borrowing scheme for university students and staff has shown early promise. The Council of Australian University Librarians (CAUL) National Borrowing Scheme is open to students and staff of member universities of the Australian Vice-Chancellor's Committee who are not otherwise eligible to borrow from another university under relevant regional borrowing schemes. Membership of the scheme is for the current calendar year, no matter when an individual joins. The scheme operates alongside regional borrowing schemes in the country.

National licensing agreements and local network restrictions tend to result in access arrangements being limited to print services and facilities. Ironically, the person walking in off the street has less access to many basic reference tools now than might have been the case ten or 20 years ago when print copies of key textbooks and journals were available on the shelves.

Resource discovery

Resource discovery tools invariably facilitate improved access. Many collaborative schemes have initially provided simple printed and online resource guides based on subject and location, which have developed into mature resource discovery tools, often facilitated by technical solutions. For example, the M25 Consortium offered online resource guides in 1995, which have gradually developed into a suite of resource discovery tools that the Consortium has called InformM25. In a paper to a Capital Planning Information seminar in October 2001 Suzanne Enright (2001, 24) described this suite of tools as:

- virtual cross-catalogue searching across the Consortium (this was developed from an eLib Phase 3 'Clumps' project)
- a web-based library location guide
- a virtual union list of serials
- the development of a new online guide to help learners identify individual eligibility and entitlement to physical access and other services (e.g. borrowing).

The M25 Consortium hopes to secure funding to add the catalogues of non-higher education organizations and sectors to InformM25 in order to develop a cross-sectoral resource discovery tool.

The provision of technologically advanced resource discovery tools, supported by clear access arrangements, acknowledges the rights of customers of library services to ask questions about the availability and location of stock, and to make decisions about travelling to use material in other libraries.

Staff development and training

Joint training and development programmes are common among established consortia, providing obvious benefits such as shared expertise, cost-effectiveness and networking opportunities. Training and development events also help raise awareness and understanding of collaborative partnership arrangements among the full range of staff involved in service provision. This helps avoid the nightmare scenario of partnership work, where the person staffing an issue or reception desk professes complete ignorance of any of the carefully crafted collaborative agreements so close to the hearts of senior managers. The Libraries Together Partnership in Liverpool, a partnership of public, higher and further education libraries, has carried out joint training since the early 1980s and also runs an annual conference which covers topical issues of joint concern. The CALIM consortium has a joint staff development programme made possible by pulling together the expertise and resources of the member libraries and offering events in the north west of England which staff might otherwise have to travel much further to benefit from. The CALIM website (www. calim.ac.uk/info.htm) describes the benefits of its staff development programme as pioneering:

> programmes for consortial staff development which have delivered substantial cost savings and increased added value over conventional training routes. The programme provides a forum, not only for interactive learning, but also for sharing of experience and exchanging expertise on professional issues of joint concern. Such a programme also provides an opportunity for professional relationships to develop which are consolidated through the work of CALIM's specialist groups of library staff.

User support

For the purposes of this chapter the main area of user support under discussion is that of digital reference. A number of forms of digital reference support are available including e-mail, web-based help forms, chat reference, and web call centres. Some of these technologies allow only for asynchronous interactions (i.e. a delayed interaction, as with e-mails and web-based enquiry forms). Other internet options allow synchronous interaction that attempts to mirror the face-to-face support provided at a library help desk. The latter have borrowed technology from online customer services, providing chat software such as Human Click, that allows the user to interact in a live setting with the librarian, and enables the librarian to control the user's browser, providing live demonstrations of database searches while discussing the best approach to an enquiry. Interest in such technologies in the UK has developed alongside improved bandwidth capability and the need to support increasing numbers of distance learners, as well as the recognition that many library users want to access services from their own desktop.

The ELITE project (www.le.ac.uk/li/distance/eliteproject/project/elite.html) at the University of Leicester carried out a trial of a range of such technologies in order to meet the needs of the University's own distance and other learners who required electronic access to library services. ELITE concentrated on the needs of users at one university library; however, it also featured examples of how the development of the digital library is affecting service provision in a number of ways, not least in relation to collaboration. ELITE highlighted both the advantages of being able to share expertise in collaborating over digital reference provision, and also of being able to offer 24-hour support by collaborating with partners in different time zones. The practical exploration of 24-hour support is being tested through a number of projects, not surprisingly in countries rather larger than the UK. In the USA these include the Collaborative Digital Reference Service (CDRS) (www.arl.org/newsltr/219/cdrs.html), which aims to provide a network of digital reference provision across public, academic and national libraries, and 24/7 Reference, a project run by the Metropolitan Cooperative Library System (MCLS) in California which is an association of 31 city and special public libraries (www.247ref.org/portal/access2.cfm?lib=Public).

In an online paper about the 24/7 Reference project, Karen G. Schneider (2000) referred to the cultural change involved as less like 'a paradigm shift' and more like 'a shove'. Schneider highlighted one of the critical mindsets in providing online reference: 'One of the cardinal and transformational rules of online reference is that the user isn't remote; the librarian is . . . it's the librarian's job to meet the users where they are, to seek them out, to market in language intelligible and attractive to our target communities, and to customize services based on the users' needs, preferences, and timetables.'

This new approach to service provision, through collaborative and user-focused digital reference services, identifies a key place for library and information staff in the so-called 'Google environment' where intermediary services are seen as less and less relevant as users rely on apparently comprehensive and easy-to-use search engines.

Resource sharing

The potential for collection management through partnership working has been recognized for some time and has resulted in the mapping of collections and the staged introduction of implementing collection policies across member libraries. Such maps often identify the weaknesses and strengths of partner library collections, saving users valuable time and effort in wasted journeys. Interlibrary loan and document supply may be achieved regionally but local agreements may extend or replace this, particularly where electronic access to web-based catalogues provides the location and status of material.

This sort of mapping conforms with the key principles of mutual benefit and consensus described above. It offers the opportunity to combine access to collections without challenging the autonomy of each of the member institutions, presenting no real threat to the priority given by each institution to its own members. Recent discussions about the possibility of greater resource sharing in the British higher education sector have started to challenge these key principles. It has been suggested that resource sharing and deep-resource sharing, as defined above in this chapter, offer possibilities to make real cost savings and to enrich the collections made available to users. Examples of this type of resource sharing, where ownership and/or autonomy are surrendered, are few and far between. There are some voluntary, subject-based agreements within the higher education sector and some project-based work has been carried out, mostly under the auspices of the Research Support Libraries Programme (RSLP). However, barriers to this level of resource sharing are strong (see below) and evidence of real benefit has yet to be provided.

Cost-effectiveness

Partnership working can be seen to provide clear benefits to customers by achieving more than would otherwise have been possible within local budgets. External pressure for collaboration has also resulted in welcome funding incentives, especially for cross-sectoral collaboration, for example through the British Library Co-operation and Partnership Programme (BLCPP) which 'encourages and facilitates partnership and collaborative activity in the key areas of access, collection development, preservation and record creation and bibliographic services'. The purpose of this funding is clearly stated as 'to optimise use of resources' as 'no library is now able to meet the existing and future information needs of all users' (www.bl.uk/about/cooperation.html).

The Joint Information Systems Committee (JISC), the strategic organization working on behalf of the UK higher and further education funding bodies, also works in partnership with the research councils. JISC directly runs projects for the institutions either individually or as part of a greater consortium to support the take-up and development of information and communications technology (www.jisc.ac.uk). Additional grant aid for higher education institutions has been available from the RSLP to deliver collaboration, particularly in the area of collection management, and sharing in the use of the research infrastructure (www.rspl.ac.uk).

These national organizations are actively facilitating partnership working for the benefit of customers whether through separate library sectors or with the BLCPP actively encouraging cross-sectoral partnerships.

Social inclusion

Libraries are often at the forefront of the promotion of social inclusion in both rural and urban areas through community development work and supporting sustainable neighbourhoods. Poverty, age, gender and sexual orientation, race, ethnic origin, disability or social background should not be a barrier to access to library services including information, learning opportunities or cultural and recreational activities. Libraries have long provided specialist services and staff to support the most vulnerable in the community, and formal and informal partnerships have evolved with charities, voluntary organizations, schools and other local authority service providers to make libraries open to all. The library is recognized as a safe, non-political and neutral space and has been used for meetings, information exchange and social interaction for many years but mainstreaming services to tackle social exclusion still requires effective strategies and funding.

Physical access to buildings, specialist signage and interpretation, perhaps through specialist software, is provided for people with disabilities. Formal and informal partnerships to assist access to materials in alternative formats such as Braille, spoken word and signed films exist in many parts of the country. National charities and more recently Resource have taken partnerships to a new level to improve access through Share the Vision (www.resource.gov.uk), the collaboration between the Royal National Institute for the Blind and Resource.

Specialist collections in community languages have been the basis of co-operative schemes for some years to support black and other racial minorities. Partnerships may be geographically distant when serving minority groups and subscription services rather than partnership may be the foundation of the relationship.

Drawbacks and barriers

Barriers to access

Barriers to access are often practical, relating to geographical boundaries, different approaches to classification, cataloguing and signing, or simply to psychological difficulties associated with going into an unknown environment. Non-customers may find a lack of information regarding membership criteria and general usage of the library that is visited, and it may not be seen as a priority to supply information to non-customers of the home institution. The Libraries Together Partnership in Liverpool has attempted to address these issues by ensuring that all member libraries have a common display in the entrance to the buildings, where the same posters are exhibited and the Partnership's leaflet is available. Although a relatively simple approach, it helps users of the services to spot something familiar and to feel that they have a right to be there. Staff knowledge and understanding of any collaborative agreements is obviously crucial, especially as an increasing number of academic library services have introduced card-access systems which mean that anyone other than local students needs to present themselves to a member of security staff in order to gain access. Having found one's way to a remote campus and got through the front doors of an imposing building the final straw can be a person in a uniform who professes to know nothing of a local agreement and acts as if you're here to steal the family silver.

Barriers relating to culture and/or attitude are of course much more difficult to address and are often associated with fears of 'swamping' by users of other libraries or that a competitive edge may be lost. Evidence provided by the People Flows report and discussed elsewhere in this chapter suggests that this fear is largely unfounded (Mynott et al., 1999). However, there may be instances where small specialist collections may be under pressure should unlimited access be made available or where local public and academic libraries may find themselves acting as the sole provider for students from an institution which has developed distance learning provision or has built accommodation for students away from their own library service. In such instances local agreements may need to be amended to acknowledge genuine concerns.

Barriers to resource sharing

The Higher Education Consultancy Group report (2002) found little evidence of active collaborative collection management in the UK, although there are many examples of strengths in different libraries being 'taken into account' as part of local collection management policies. The major barriers to any more proactive collaboration through, for example, relinquishing autonomy over particular areas of a collection or sharing the costs of expensive subscriptions lie at the heart of each institution's funding and management structures. It is probably also fair to say that many libraries – and their parent organizations – still place significant emphasis on the size of the local collections. The number of volumes owned is still a key performance indicator. Giving up ownership of materials that have been developed at great expense and over considerable time, is for most librarians, their parent organization, and many users, still a collaborative step too far.

Some evidence behind the perceived reluctance to deep-resource sharing has been provided by the Glasgow Allied Electronically with Strathclyde project (GAELS). One of the key aims of the GAELS project was to afford one excellent collection of engineering materials by removing overlap in journal provision, providing joint electronic services, and setting up a document delivery service to facilitate use of the collections at both institutions as if they were one. In describing the outcomes of the GAELS project, Law (2002) referred to difficulties in embedding the principles of deep-resource sharing because of systemic and cultural barriers within higher education institutions. In essence, academic researchers see library collections as a huge investment that is not to be surrendered lightly. Law's view, influenced by the outcomes of the GAELS project, is that deep-resource sharing is not possible in the current culture and that effort should be concentrated on collaborative projects and on the development of a national electronic resource. The GAELS project provides a very interesting example of a brake to active collaborative activity being applied by users of a service rather than by the providers.

Barriers to ICT

Developments in information and communication technology offer some of the greatest opportunities and drivers for partnership and collaboration. The so-called 'clumping' projects have provided models for the active removal of barriers through providing one common search protocol. There are examples in the UK of successful cross-sectoral clumping projects in both the Co-East (www. Co-east.net/) and the Liverpool Libraries Partnerships (www.liv.ac.uk/Library/llgroup/llg.html). However, it is also the case that some of the greatest barriers to partnership working are also linked to ICT, either for legislative, technical or financial reasons.

The academic sector has benefited greatly from nationally negotiated licences for content-based services, such as the National Electronic Site Licensing Initiative (NESLI) and the Distributed National Electronic Resource (DNER). However, restrictions imposed by the suppliers of content mean that access is only provided to registered members of each institution. As library services migrate increasingly to electronic information sources, access is actually becoming more restricted.

There are possibilities for collaboration in the purchase of expensive items such as library management systems. Issues of autonomy still apply, but in addition the complexity and timescales involved often make it impossible for several libraries to migrate to a new system at the same time. In addition it's fair to say that local control of the specification for a system remains very important to library staff.

Barriers for management

Many of the examples of best practice in partnership work and collaborative activity are the result of the enthusiasm and commitment of individual library managers. In a local area the success of a collaborative group can rely on something as simple as the ability of the local directors of service to get on with each other. The opposite can also hold true, with reluctance in one organization presenting real barriers to partnership work. Concern over existing staff workloads or of staff resistance to change can also present difficulties. It is arguable that the skills and abilities associated with partnership work, such as excellence in networking, clarity of purpose, clear strategic thinking and excellence in management skills, still require development across the profession.

Conclusion

The collaborative achievements cited in this chapter are indicative of the range of widespread projects which have succeeded in delivering benefits directly to service users. Much of the existing collaborative activity stems from an LIS culture that accepts partnership and collaboration as of mutual benefit through widening access to existing resources. In addition, partnership work is accepted as a method of showing a willingness to address the stated agendas of government and funding bodies. Pressure on resources, the possibilities offered by ICT, and the development of a regional agenda in the UK have all played a part in encouraging a more formal approach to the existing tendency to work in partnership and to articulate collaboration across sectors and domains. A very useful outcome has been the development of models of collaboration, with collaborative initiatives that have often developed from a good idea and enthusiasm becoming embedded as good practice.

The main outstanding issues for library and information services are probably best articulated in the Empowering the Learning Community report (Library and Information Commission, 2000) which highlighted the need for regional cross-sectoral co-operative agreements, the establishment of cross-sectoral funding arrangements, the development of regional 'access maps', and the co-ordination of joint training. The government response to this report (Great Britain. Department for Education and Employment and the Department of Culture, Media and Sport, 2001) acknowledged the 'legislative, administrative and financial constraints in which the library community operates' and made it clear that a top-down approach was not going to be imposed. Rather, the relevant government departments favour the continuation of local initiatives and the encouragement of the benchmarking and implementation of existing best practice. It remains to be seen whether this approach will result in the expansion and development of the sorts of initiatives described in this chapter or whether systemic and cultural barriers will result in a continuation of current practice. It is welcome news for the users of our services that there is some indication that more formal approaches to cross-sectoral collaboration have begun to become embedded in practice. This is evidenced through initiatives such as the Society of College, National and University Libraries (SCONUL) and the Society of Chief Librarians (SCL) agreement (SCONUL, 2001) to the principle of access referral from public libraries to higher education libraries and the British Library. In addition the British Library's commitment to collaboration is evident in its strategic plan (British Library, 2001) in which partnership activities form one of its three key enabling strategies. Users of our services can surely only benefit from developments of this kind.

References

The APT Partnership (1995) *The APT review: a review of library and information co-operation in the UK and Ireland*, British Library Research and Development Report 6212, LINC.

The British Library (2001) *New strategic directions,* British Library, available at www.bl.uk/about/strategic/planfor.html

Enright, S. (2001) Partnerships for learning: the role of higher education in cross-sectoral collaboration in London. In Brewer, S. (ed.), *Empowering learners: libraries and cross-sectoral partnerships: proceedings of a seminar held at Stamford, Lincolnshire on 3 October 2001*, Capital Planning Information.

Follett, B. (2001) Just how are we going to satisfy our research customers?, *Liber Quarterly*, **11**, 218–23.

Great Britain. Department for Education and Employment and the Department for Culture, Media and Sport (2001) *The government's response to Empowering the Learning Community*, a report from the Library and Information Commission's Education and Libraries Task Group, DfEE and DCMS.

Great Britain. Department of Trade and Industry and the Department for Education and Employment. (1997) *Competitiveness through partnerships with people*, DTI and DfEE.

Great Britain. University Grants Committee (1976) *Capital provision for university libraries: a report of a working party*, HMSO (the Atkinson Report).

Hatrics and Capital Planning Information (1999) *The Southern Information Network information intertrading: successful partnerships in library and information services*, British Library Innovation Centre Report 158, Hatrics.

HEFCE (1993) *Joint Funding Councils' Libraries Review Group: A report for the Higher Education Funding Council for England, Scottish Higher Education Funding Council, Higher Education Funding Council for Wales and Department of Education for Northern Ireland, Higher Education Funding Council* (the Follett report), available at www.ukoln.ac.uk/services/papers/follett/report/.

Higher Education Consultancy Group and CHEMS Consultancy (2002) *A Report to the RSLP on: Barriers to resource sharing among higher education libraries*, Research Support Libraries Programme.

Joint Funding Councils' Libraries Review (1996) *Report of the Group on a national regional strategy for library provision for researchers*, HEFCE (the Anderson Report).

Kopp, J. J. (1999) Documenting partnerships: here a MOU, there a MOU, *Library Administration and Management*, **13** (2), 68–77.

Law, D. (2002) unpublished paper to a SCONUL/M25 Consortium Inter-consortia conference at the Building Centre, London on 19 February 2002.

Library and Information Commission (2000) *Empowering the learning community*, Report of the Education and Libraries Task Group, LIC.

Long, S. (2001) Library to library: global pairing for mutual benefit, *New Library World*, **102** (1162), 79–82.

Mynott, G. et al. (1999) *People Flows: an investigation of the cross-use of publicly-funded libraries*, Library and Information Commission and Centre for Information Research, University of Central England.

Pilling, S. and Kenna, S. (eds) *Co-operation in action: collaborative initiatives in the world of information*, Facet Publishing, 2002.

Schneider, K. G. (2000) *The distributed librarian: live, online, real-time reference in American libraries*, ALA, available at www.ala.org/alonline/netlib/ill100.html.

SCONUL (2001), *Annual review 2001*, Society of College, National and University Libraries, available at www.sconul.ac.uk/02.01.doc.

9

Virtual service

R. David Lankes

Introduction

Virtual service is a bit of an oxymoron. After all, an organization either provides service to customers or not. It may be good service or bad, but it is still service. Of course the reason we qualify any term with 'digital', 'virtual', or 'electronic' is to distinguish it from what many libraries have done in a physical space, or within the confines of geography. Some say the ultimate success of a 'virtual' service, be it reference, or resource access, is to drop the qualifier and simply call it reference, or service. However, I am not so sure.

Certainly, digital reference is simply just a type of reference, and virtual service is only part of a much larger concept of service. However, there is some analytical power to making the distinction between what we do on the internet and what we do in person. For one, we are relative novices at the online world (as are the vast majority of organizations). Secondly, things are simply different online. There are very different skill sets for patrons and librarians in the online environment, and concepts of identity and privacy are radically different.

Ultimately it is worthwhile to discuss virtual service, with the understanding that the ultimate success of any virtual service is its fit into the overall goals of the organization, virtual or not. In this chapter the author will discuss how electronic networks, with a special emphasis on the internet and the world wide web, can be used to create a 'virtual library branch' that better serves customers in cyberspace.

Defining virtual service

For the purposes of this chapter, let's define virtual services as a means of connecting the library to the public via an electronic network. While it might be easier to simply say 'through the internet', there is a wide range of electronic networks, from local-area networks connecting workstations and printers, to wide-area networks linking organizations around the globe. While this chapter, and the literature at large, will focus on the internet, it is important to understand that services may be offered within an organization, through a so-called intranet. These services share much in common with internet services, often utilizing the same software, but have marked differences. Intranets are defined by a greater degree of control (e.g., an organization can mandate a given piece of software, or a certain degree of training) and knowledge of the user population (i.e., knowing who has logged into a service, or knowing the exact computing platform of an organizational member). While this chapter will concentrate on internet services to the general public (or at least a population over which the library has low knowledge or control), where appropriate the author will point out intranet possibilities.

It is also worth a quick discussion of the term 'service' on its own. The author adopts a simplified definition of a library. A library is an organization that provides a user with a collection of materials and a set of services. These services are often tied to the collection, but may well exist in the absence of a collection. We'll adopt the term 'coupling' to describe how closely tied (tightly coupled) a service is to a collection or another service, or how independent, or operating in the absence of knowledge of a collection or service (loosely coupled), a service is. While at first glance it may seem the objective would be to tightly couple services and collections, this is not always the case. A few scenarios may be useful.

Scenario 1: Tightly coupled services

A library has a strong collection of local images, pictures and slides. In order to make this collection more accessible to local patrons, as well as scholars and interested users worldwide, the library digitizes the images. The digitized images are placed in a database and the database linked to a web server connected to the internet. Now with a simple URL, users can browse and search the images. The library adds a virtual service that allows an internet user to pay a fee and receive high-quality prints of the images as well. Finally, as a result of interest in the collection, the library begins to field questions from internet users via e-mail. This digital reference service helps users find relevant images, answers questions concerning copyright, and uses repeating questions to add a 'Frequently Asked Questions' area to the website as well as highlighting popular images.

Clearly these services (digitization, web access, print on request, digital reference) are tightly coupled. Any of the services would become quickly irrelevant if the original collection were to go away. However, many services are much more loosely coupled.

Scenario 2: Loosely coupled services

A library begins a list of useful web links on its web page. At first the set of links is organized as a simple list. Later the list is divided into subject headings (science, genealogy, local interest, travel, etc.). Abstracts are then added to links. Finally the library purchases web indexing software, and the links are actually remotely indexed over the internet, and patrons can search a special database of selected websites.

While these services are no less technically involved than the first scenario, they represent loosely coupled services. The sites being linked to, and later indexed are most likely unaware of the service being offered to library patrons. Indeed, the indexed services do not have to do anything for the service. Web search engines are examples of loosely coupled web services. Compare these with union catalogues where tightly integrated technologies such as Z39.50 must be employed. As a general rule the more tightly coupled the service, the more resources are needed to maintain and grow the services. Loosely coupled services, virtual or otherwise, are often fast to implement and more scalable.

And so now, with a fuller understanding of virtual services as being delivered through an electronic network along a continuum from loosely to tightly coupled, we can begin to explore how virtual services can be used to build a successful customer-centred culture.

Advantages and disadvantages of the virtual environment

As we proceed with our look at how to offer virtual services we must realize that for every positive of using the internet to interact with customers, there is a negative. The trick is to balance the two to maximize the usefulness of the service to customers, while upholding the needs of the organization. For example, while users would love us to digitize large portions of our collections for access via the internet (certainly a positive for the users) the library can neither afford to provide such a service, or in doing so would violate licensing or copyright restrictions. The art of virtual service, where the user base is potentially enormous and the information environment that we're entering into is immense, is finding what a library can do most effectively for the customer to promote the mission of the library. It is quite possible that some services, while viable from a resource and economic perspective, may still be inadvisable in view of the mission.

Reaching customers through the web

A web page is not a digital library. A web page is a virtual service, but is not sufficient to be good service. These may be obvious statements to some, but many libraries and organizations use the web as a virtual library or as a poor cousin to real library service believing that only services in the physical library count as real. This bias towards physical, or traditional library service as real, and the web or network services as nice additions is dangerous. It leads to virtual services that both frustrate online users as well as diverting resources from other library activities. Simply stated, either the web is part of the services you offer, with the same level of commitment, or it is a liability.

It may seem heresy to suggest in these internet days not to have a website, particularly in a chapter about virtual services, but a rule of thumb is that a bad website is worse than no website at all. A website that leads to user frustration, presents the library in a bad light, or represents all that the library is against (bad organization, untimely information, lacking a human face) will do more damage to a library than simply concentrating on getting customers in the door and making sure they are satisfied with traditional services.

So, this leads to two questions: why is it worth building a website, and what makes a good website anyway?

Why the web?

There are, of course, a multitude of reasons to go to the web. Some are customer driven (providing information after hours, providing remote access to online materials) and some are purely organizational (the parent institution wants one, or some information is only provided via the web). Let me outline key forces and needs that can be met on the web.

Remote access to users

Clearly a primary advantage of the web is providing access to digital information to customers outside the physical confines of the library. It is well known in information science that the resources that customers turn to the most are not predicated on quality or reputation, but convenience. Scholarly studies have even shown that academics will cite resources in their office first, the resources available to them in their physical department second, and those in an academic library a distant third. The promise of the web is to put the library 'into the office' or convenient proximity of the customer when they need the information.

Certainly not all the resources of a library can be sent down a modem, but at the very least their existence can be made plain and obvious. The point is to put the library 'in the face' of the user. This is more than simply putting a website on the internet, it involves placement of the site. How close is the site to a user when they first bring up their web browsers? Is it their home page? In an academic setting is it linked from the top page of the college or university? Is it a simple URL that users can remember? Never underestimate the power of a good URL. For example to get to my local public library I must type in the following URL: http://www.ocpl.lib.ny.us/. However to get to the Boston Public Library it is http://www.bpl.org. Also, how will users know this URL? Do they have bookmarks? Pamphlets? Newsletters? E-Mail newsletters? The point is to make the library truly ever present.

As stated earlier, with every positive is a potential for substantial negatives. One of the factors that must be considered for remote access is a potential expansion in the population you are serving. Like it or not, the web is a worldwide phenomenon. Once you have a service on the web, anyone can get to it unless you deliberately prevent access. Preventing access can be through some form of IP filtering (restricting access based on the internet address of a user's computer), username and password or some existing means of access restriction such as a library card or student ID.

Expansion of service in time

When the Library of Congress first put their catalogue online (way back in the days of Gopher) the site was available 9–5 Eastern Standard Time. I'm not making this up. While this may have been to provide quick support if a server went down, or if a patron needed assistance, it was still very odd. The internet is about having information any time, anywhere. Users expect to have web servers waiting for them, not the other way around. Certainly in the case of providing remote access to digital information, there is little reason not to provide access 24 hours a day. In many libraries customers can put hold on items, search the catalogue and databases, and access web-based applications regardless of the time of day. This allows the library to serve its customers beyond the limitations of staffing and security.

Unified interface

The web was revolutionary. What first caught people's attention was the embedding of images in text. The second thing that captured our imagination was hyperlinking. Yet, the true revolution lay in the web's expandability. Unlike previous internet protocols, the HyperText Transfer Protocol (HTTP) built a single protocol that could transmit text, images, video, sound and software. In essence, if the browser could read it, and the server could send it, you could do it via the web. This may seem like a very technical view, web as general transport layer, but don't underestimate the power of a good protocol. Because the web (once again, more technically, HTTP) could ship almost any binary information, it was quickly adopted by software developers and service managers as a platform-independent interface.

In the old days software developers would have to develop a piece of software two to three times, once for each computing platform it was going to run on. So one CD-ROM search interface program was developed for Windows, one for Mac, and one for the mainframes or minicomputers still very much present in libraries today. Not only would they have to develop the end-user software, often they would have to do special development if the application was networked in some way (one for Z39.50, one for telnet access, etc.). With the web, these development problems quickly vanished. Now developers could write one piece of software for a server, and just assume a web client could handle the end-user interface. Not only that, but the interface was often as simple as HTML text files that could be altered in seconds.

This led to the wide-scale adoption of the web as an application environment. CD-ROMs were costly not only to libraries, but vendors as well. A vendor had to create a separate CD for each platform, then had the added cost of producing and shipping a physical product and added to that was the cost of staffing helpdesks and providing technical support for the product. With the web: program it on one server, and let the libraries access the product through a web browser the library supplies and supports. Also, on the web there are no space limitations, as were common with CDs. The end result is that today vendors who used to sell CDs are making a rapid transition to web-based applications.

Libraries can take advantage of this transition as well. The website can be more than simply a place to post hours and programming, it can become a unifying interface for other library services. Now the hundreds of electronic resources the library provides can be linked from a central web page. Moreover, the library can supply value additions to this access, providing customers with help in selecting the best online source, online tutorials or, as will be discussed later, real-time assistance. What's more, this need not only be a unified interface for online users, it can provide some valuable co-ordination of access for in-library use as well. By making the same interfaces available on the library's intranet the web can become a central point for disseminating news, maps and pathfinders. Just as in-library users used to see the search interface of the online catalogue, now they can see the library's home page, giving the library an opportunity to present the user with a larger view of what the library does. The web allows a library to more tightly couple the diverse offerings of electronic information it offers to customers.

A diversity of unification

There is another unique situation created by the migration of information to a web interface. The web interface need not be exactly the same for all users. I know this seems contrary to my previous point, but stick with me. What the web has done is disconnect the interface from the underlying information. The web does not expose the database a user is searching, nor does it prescribe exactly how information is displayed in the browser. We've all experienced the fact that a page can look one way in Netscape, and quite a different way in Internet Explorer. This can work for you.

Once you have created a single access point to electronic resources, you can have multiple views of that access point. So you have a graphic-intensive interface within the library where you know you have high-powered computers and fast network access, and stripped-down interface for the outside world, or an image-free interface for blind users, or even foreign language instructions and tutorials for target language groups. You are still providing a single point of entry for customers, but you take the differences of your customers into account. I call this approach the 'one-stop, any-stop' approach.

The concept is that the user only has to go to one interface (one web page) to get to all the services your library offers, but that page may exist in different forms (or on different servers) for different user communities. So, a library can create an expert interface to the online catalogue showing all the indexed fields and Boolean operators. They can also create a novice interface with one big search box and some online help. Both pages will search the same catalogue (the one stop), but users can choose their preferred interface (any stop).

Branding of information

The unified one-stop, any-stop approach to interfaces through the web also leads to an important new ability of the library, to brand access to electronic resources. Access to information is a rather invisible entity – so invisible we take it for granted. When a customer is in a library accessing information there is little doubt as to who provided that access. The chair the customer sits on, the computer in front of them, all of these are branded as part of the library because of the constant physical reminders as to where the user is. Online, these obvious cues are gone, and all the user is left with is the web page on their screen.

Often in today's web-based interfaces libraries provide web access to online information by simply linking the user from the library's web server to a vendor's server. The user is left with a very valuable resource that is only identifiable from the branding of the vendor. Add to this the ability of the user to bookmark resources, and the user will often use the resource with little thought to who is paying for this access, or any other role the library played in the access. There are no walls to remind the customer who provided the access.

As discussed before, the web can be the solution. HTML pages are easily modified with the logo of the library, or a link back to the library home page. Because modifying web interfaces is relatively easy, vendors are normally very open to making modifications indicating the library's role in the transaction. The point is to not only brand the information with the vendor who has compiled the resource (the visible portion of a resource), but with the library that is providing access (the often invisible contribution of a library).

So what makes a good web service anyway?

There are many books and websites devoted to what makes good websites. They explore aspects of the web including aesthetics and design, response time and proper HTML coding. I will not try and summarize all the advice here. Rather I will concentrate on what makes a good *library* web. Certainly those things that make a good website apply, such as pleasing design and responsive load times, but I feel there are unique aspects to a library on the web that must be maintained. These aspects are the hallmark of any good library service, simply transferred to the web.

Interactive

The point of a library is not simply to collect a set of information and warehouse it in some structure, often with columns. Rather a library, as we all know, is a living interactive information provider in the community it serves. The website of a library should be no different. People come into the physical library to interact with information, not be confronted with it. The same should hold true on the web. Rather than having a simple site with hours of operation and a phone number, give the users some means of interacting. Let them search the catalogue or databases. Give them some collection of data they can use in research. Don't ask them to change medium (web to phone) to accommodate the library, rather meet the user at the point of service (a discussion that will be continued as we explore digital reference further along). Having a face on the internet is more than mounting a logo and a list of hours – that would be like having the patrons use the library through a mail slot in the door ('push in your requests and we'll push out the answers').

The point is to make the website a destination, not simply another form of placard outside the library walls. A library website should not be a poster or brochure, but more of a branch. It should have services and collections that can be used. Anything less is a bad reflection on the library and a very loosely coupled service to the physical services. If you are going to require the user to come to your physical facility to get information (which makes sense with special collections), at least give the user a strong reason to get out of their office (home, car, etc.) and come in to your library.

Representative of the library collection and services

If your library offers reference services, advice for readers, an extensive genealogy collection and a great popular fiction collection, why does your web site simply list the catalogue? Use the web to showcase your good work and more importantly, your good librarians. Put a human face on the library's presence in cyberspace. If you are not ready for a real-time reference service, how about a collection of reference sources compiled by an information professional? Take a theme you know will be important to your community (holidays, issues under discussion, a local election) and craft part of your web to lead people through the catalogue. Demonstrate that a library is more than a collection, but a set of experts to make sense of all of the information. Have your librarians sign the pages they put online. Let the customer know a real person is working on this web.

Another way to represent the spectrum of services you have is not to try and cram all of those services on to a single website, but create a unique site for each customer type. The public library of Charlotte and Mecklenburg County (www.plcmc.lib.nc.us/) lists no fewer than nine unique websites it hosts for special customer types. From business to health to kids, they all have a home that looks and feels like home.

Maintained and updated

A great library should have a great website. If you don't have a great library, feel free to save money on your website. Of course, we all aspire to being great libraries; don't let the web drag you down. For a number of libraries that are obsessed with an inviting physical facility and excellent desk service, the web simply becomes a far distant second in terms of priorities. I cannot tell you the number of library websites I've been to that list events that occurred in the past. News releases from over three months ago are litter, not information. The point is that libraries are in the business of informing their communities, we pride ourselves on our currency of knowledge and skills – an outdated website in the information medium of the web is a clear statement that we are not practising what we preach. Every page should have an update date on the bottom and it should be reviewed daily for updates.

This is not a call for a full-time webmaster. Actually the best way to keep a site updated and current is to make it part of all librarians' job responsibilities. The reference librarians should monitor and regularly update sections on ready-reference resources. The technical service librarian should be providing up-to-the-minute information on the catalogue and making sure online help is effective. Distributing the task of web development not only lowers the library investment, it builds ownership of the web on the part of the staff and leads to a better web presence.

Well organized and searchable

Just as out-of-date information is a bad reflection on library service, so is bad organization. If your customers get lost on the library website they will never come back. How you organize information on the web, what is commonly called information architecture, is a rapidly developing field. It is more than simply putting the Dewey classes on the home page. The web should be organized by how the customer is looking for information. This means that putting reference services under the heading 'Adult services' will often be misleading to the average customer (not to mention that adult services often have a *very* different context on the internet). Use the language of the customer. The web is a very different world from that of traditional library cataloguing. The web is meant to be flexible, with frequent changes and rapid evolution.

In addition to making the website browsable with a clear and common language classification system, it must be searchable. Today a search function is simply an absolute requirement of a web. Not just a search of the catalogue (that is often segregated to another search), but of all the materials on the site (help files, welcomes from the director, digitized resources).

The point is to make the web presence not just an information outlet for the library, but a tightly coupled service for the customer. If users can pay bills online, order a book from Amazon and get groceries with the click of a mouse, they had better be able to get at your services just as easily. The web really needs to become a branch library. That is not to say that all internet services need to involve the web.

Other virtual services related to the internet

Calling the internet the web is often convenient, but is simply wrong. The internet is a set of computers connected together with a common networking protocol, IP. It existed long before the web and still has many services that cannot be accessed via the web (defined by the protocol HTTP). The recent attention to music-sharing services such as Napster and Morpheus is quick proof of this. A user could not use Napster with a web browser. Rather they need to download a special program that allows them to share files with other users. Libraries tend to concentrate on websites because they have a far reach (almost everyone with an internet connection has a web browser) and are relatively simple to mount (the software comes shrink wrapped or already on many computers).

However, there are other virtual services that a library can offer. E-mail is an obvious example. While a customer can access e-mail through the web, the infrastructure for the service is completely independent of the web. A library can offer e-mail accounts to its customers. While that may seem outside the mission of a library, it is still an invaluable means to access information. The library has a vital role to play in providing a stable e-mail address as customers may change schools, internet providers or jobs and lose other e-mail addresses.

Libraries can offer chat services, or bulletin boards. These services offer the closest analogue to the library's role as social centre or information commons for a community. Users can express opinions about issues in the community, or even information-specific activities (e.g. customers reviewing books on the library's catalogue).

Libraries can also offer networked services to non-computer users. Personal digital assistants (PDAs) such as Palm Pilot devices have become widespread. The library can provide e-books and current events to be downloaded to PDAs in wireless networks for example. The point is to be where the users are.

Reaching customers through digital reference

As stated before, a library can be seen as a group of collections and services. However, one of the invaluable resources in a library setting is a librarian. Trained information professionals constitute a unique source of information and set the library apart from every other information provider. Yet this expertise and unique human touch are often lacking in the virtual environment. How can a library network presence be truly representative of the library collection and services if reference is considered a 'physical only' activity?

The recognition of this has led to an explosion in activity concerning digital or virtual reference services. For the purposes of this paper, digital reference is defined as human-intermediated assistance offered to users through the internet. Today, libraries are offering this service at an ever-increasing rate. Research by Janes and his colleagues (Janes, 2000) found that 45% of academic libraries and 12.8% of public libraries in the USA offer some type of digital reference service. Stephen Francoeur (2001, 190) reports that as of April 2001 he was able to identify, 'a total of 272 libraries [that] were being served by a chat reference service, 210 of which (77 percent) were served by one of eight chat reference consortia'. However, digital reference services are often ad hoc and experimental. Janes and McClure (1999) found that for quick factual questions, librarians using only the web answered a sample of questions as well as did those using only print sources. Many libraries conduct digital reference service in addition to existing obligations with little sense of the scale of such work or its strategic importance to the library.

The multiple faces of digital reference

Digital reference has many forms and names. Some refer to it as virtual reference, e-reference, electronic reference, real-time reference, chat reference, e-mail reference, but it comes down to a simple concept: put reference librarians at the point of need. More often these days, that point of need is not at a desk, but rather within electronic information sources such as an online database or catalogue. That means that even if the customer is located in a physical library facility, they may still need assistance at a computer. Asking reference questions 'on the computer' allows the user to keep their computer, keep their place in an online resource, keep their train of thought, and still get expert guidance.

The type of guidance is very dependent on the context of service. Let us take the example of the patron in the library. A customer is having difficulty finding a given book. They have the author's last name and a subject, but not the exact title of the book. Unfamiliar with the catalogue, and indeed fielded searching, they need help. To walk over to the reference desk would mean losing the computer they are on and their existing search results, and the delay in finding their way to a reference desk. Instead, the user clicks an 'Ask a Librarian' button in the catalogue, and the user enters into a real-time text chat with a librarian. After a quick discussion, the librarian actually shares the screen of the user and walks the customer through a search process, highlighting features of the catalogue and even printing the results of the search for the customer. This librarian may well have been sitting physically behind the customer, or half a world away.

Software is available today for libraries to implement the digital reference system described above. It requires a very fast network connection and having screen-sharing software loaded on both the librarian's and patron's computers (making it very operating system dependent). However, it is the perfect application for an intranet. Academic libraries and special libraries that work internal to an organization can build tightly coupled digital reference services that provide reference experts at point of need.

This is not to say that digital reference only works in intranet or intra-organizational contexts. Digital reference has become widespread, at least in the USA and Canada, in the public library sector. With software as simple as e-mail, libraries can begin to provide a 'human face' to the library's cyberspace presence. Years of practice have shown that it is important to have human-to-human communication in order to help users identify information needs and find the appropriate resources to answer those needs (Mardikian and Kesselman, 1995). According to the Library and Information Technology Association (LITA), a division of the American Library Association, putting a human face on the virtual (digital) library is a key need (LITA, 1999):

> It's time to put a human face on the virtual library. What's the crucial factor in the success of the nonvirtual library? The people who work there and serve the user! What do libraries emphasize on their Web sites? Resources, collections, facts with no human guidance or presence! On many library Web sites, the user is hard-pressed to identify the staff, whose names, if they're there, are five levels down. The human factor is still important.

The question in the LIS community is no longer whether to provide reference services in a digital environment, or whether to provide human intermediation services on the internet, but rather how best to provide such services.

Means of providing digital reference

There is a set of decisions that need to be made before setting up shop as a digital reference service. The first decision point is whether you want to provide an asynchronous or synchronous service. The second is the software you will use. The third decision is whether you will offer a local service, or become part of (or form or extend) a digital reference consortium. Let's take these decisions one by one.

Asynchronous versus synchronous digital reference

Asynchronous digital reference is simply having the customer enter a question and having a librarian provide an answer at two different times. The advantage to the customer is that they can ask the question at any time: two in the morning or three in the afternoon, the customer can ask their question and wait for the answer.

As digital reference has progressed there has become something of a 'real-time' peer pressure in the reference community to push to only doing synchronous reference, but studies (Lankes, 2002) have shown that so long as the user knows to expect a delay, asynchronous services receive high user satisfaction ratings and have distinct advantages over real-time services. For one, many users seek out these services so they can defer their answer – ask the question at one point when it arises, but knowing that they will not be able to use the answer immediately. This was the case in one study of rural school teachers' use of internet resources (Fitzgerald, Branch and Lovin, 2000). A study showed that primary school teachers had only 18 minutes in a day to ask questions and seek information online. These teachers would rather ask the question and get the answer later when they had time to deal with it. This time to process is also useful to librarians who can fully develop an answer without a patron waiting. Asynchronous services can also be very useful in larger, loosely coupled digital reference networks as will be discussed below. Asynchronous services also offer a lower initial resource allocation to get started, often being a matter of simply setting up an e-mail account.

Synchronous services, often referred to as real-time services, seek to more closely replicate traditional reference. They promote themselves as the best way to conduct online reference interviews because they offer the natural conversational give and take without the delay of sending e-mails around. Many services also augment this real-time 'chat' function with co-browsing (literally guiding a user through a website or websites) and transcripts of the session. The cost of entry is higher and there is greater difficulty in tightly coupling these services across libraries, but they do provide an excellent means of interacting with users who are looking for information right away.

Software selection in digital reference

Steve Coffman of LSSI provides an excellent framework for making synchronous software decisions in digital reference (http://quartz.ssyr.edu/ACRL/Software.htm). He lays out four basic software types for digital reference: e-mail, chat/instant messaging, remote control, and web contact centre software. While he takes this from the approach of buying software, these types of solutions could also be developed internally.

E-mail is the cheapest and easiest way to get into the digital reference game. This is not to say it is only for beginners. AskERIC, for example, runs an internationally distributed digital reference system for education on e-mail answering over 45,000 questions every year. The issue associated with e-mail is that the library will have to think through training and policy development to make up for the fact that e-mail was not designed explicitly for reference. For example, e-mail does not support the sophisticated statistical reporting one might like to use to evaluate a digital reference service, and the ability to build in automation (in routing of questions for example) is rather limited compared with other applications.

Chat and instant messaging solutions have been used in digital reference with a large degree of success. This software is widely available across platforms, very easy to learn, and cheap (normally free). The one significant difficulty with these applications is the ability to queue customers. As customers ask questions windows will pop up on the librarian's screen. Five users ask a question at the same time, five windows. It is also very difficult to have two or three librarians staffing the virtual reference desk at a time, because it is the customer who chooses where to send a question. Lastly, there is a dearth of standards to allow easy interoperability in the instant messaging software available. If the patron doesn't have AOL Instant Messenger, they can't send a question to a library that uses AOL IM.

Remote control software represents the technology used in our previous 'in-library' example. This software is very full featured and allows a librarian and customer to work together on a single computer. Some software features include the ability to use special tools like highlighters and onscreen annotations. With the recent inclusion of screen-sharing software as a standard part of Windows (in Windows XP it is called 'remote assistance') we may well see a rise in the use of this approach to digital reference.

Web contact centre software is really a migration of e-commerce tools to the library setting. Library integration companies such as LSSI and 24/7 have taken commercial helpdesk software and added library features. With these packages the patron clicks on a button and is taken to a 'split' screen. Down one side of the window is a chat session; in the other window is a web page that can be changed by either the user or librarian. This ability to 'co-browse' allows the librarians to guide the information seeking of the customer, visiting together any web page while talking to each other.

Obviously which type of software you choose will be strongly influenced by which type of service you are offering. E-mail software and web-forms for question submission will work for asynchronous services, while synchronous services will require chat, remote control or web contact software. The costs of these solutions vary widely, as do the demands on your staff to install and support these systems.

Local versus consortial digital reference

Another factor in which software solution to buy is who, if anyone, you want to share questions and answers with. A good deal of digital reference is happening at the local level, that is within a given library. Libraries are looking to connect to existing and possibly new customers that have come to see the internet as a main source of information. Local service is an opportunity to promote the library, motivate staff to try something new, and meet customers at point of need.

Some have said, however, that the true value of digital reference is through networking the reference function. By teaming with other libraries new service opportunities become available. Libraries have connected to peer institutions in different time zones to expand the service hours of reference. Libraries have networked with different libraries (public to special or school to academic) to increase the scope of reference services. Some libraries have teamed with other libraries, or library vendors, to expand the number of reference enquiries that can be handled. Still other digital reference networks have been formed to increase the overall quality of reference that can be offered, particularly with small libraries with few professional reference staff.

The network is often built on existing co-operative or consortial arrangements. However, some are totally new pairings. Two examples of large-scale digital reference networks are the Virtual Reference Desk Network and QuestionPoint (formerly the Collaborative Digital Reference Service). These networks take a very different approach to coupling digital reference service.

The Virtual Reference Desk Network in the USA is a loosely coupled service operating primarily on e-mail. Libraries become members of the Network and then can send in questions that will be routed to other libraries, a variety of expert answering services (so-called AskA services such as Ask-a-Teacher), and government organizations. The entrance to the network is very low (e-mail) and there is little in the way of administrative overhead.

QuestionPoint, on the other hand, is a very tightly coupled library digital reference network headed by OCLC and the Library of Congress. In this network a library joins by creating an extensive profile, and then agreeing to use an established web-based software package. Question Point has a governance structure, extensive policies, and soon a fee model. Both services aim to expand reference to include a scale and scope unachievable at the local level.

The power of reference authoring

Digital reference also allows for the tighter coupling of reference and the collection. Many libraries see the reference function as 'sitting on top' of the collection. The collection is developed (weeded, selected, organized) and then reference's job is to improve access to this collection. One of the fundamental realities of digital reference, however, can significantly change this view. A reality of working in a virtual environment is the creation of a 'transaction trail'. Be it transcripts in synchronous digital reference, or e-mail archives in asynchronous services, some electronic artefact or document is created as the result of each reference process. While this seemingly simple fact raises issues such as privacy, it also allows for the creation of a reference authoring process.

Reference authoring is collection building through reference. Reference archives and transcripts can be mined for statistics such as which library resources are most used, what internet resources are most used and what gaps exist in the collection. In the case of pointing to electronic resources, an answer in reference terms can be seen as a beginning, or stub cataloguing record (i.e. one with some, but not all, fields complete or checked for accuracy). The reference librarian (the cataloguing agent) identifies a resource (the location), some abstract or comment on the resource ('this is good for the following question') and can even add other basic cataloguing information such as resource subject. Reference then becomes a form of lightweight cataloguing. The answers provided by the reference staff can also be documents in and of themselves. Libraries have long constructed pathfinders to relevant information. A reference answer is a pathfinder. These pathfinders can be used in the library's web presence to aid in putting the human face on the website. By creating a tighter coupling between reference and technical services the library is a more responsive organization.

Conclusion

Virtual customers are customers. The web and digital reference give the library a set of powerful tools to serve customers. Whether putting catalogues on the internet, or librarians, the library must be fully committed to virtual customer service, that is interacting with customers in the mode they have chosen. Using the internet and networks as a means to persuade the user to switch modes from digital to coming to a physical facility is difficult in these days of innumerable information choices. Customers will select the source they find most convenient and there is no reason that libraries can't fill that role. As information organizations, libraries should quickly adopt to the internet not simply as a source of information, but as a means to expand current services to new audiences.

It is time to begin considering your library's virtual services as a sort of online branch. While it is arguable if you should staff it as such, users will begin to view websites and digital reference services as a home. For the increasingly connected patrons, the online branch may well be their first stop, only resorting to entering into your physical facility to retrieve a book on hold, or have an in-depth consultation with a reference librarian. The point is to meet the user at the point of need.

Entering into the online world is no longer the daunting task it once was. With increasingly ever-present internet connectivity and with out-of-the-box network solutions, simply having a presence online is easy. Having an online presence that is meaningful and most of all useful is still as difficult as ever. The point is not to have a library transform itself completely to an online entity, but rather to have its online virtual services meet the high standards of quality we have come to expect inside our buildings. The bottom line is don't bother being online if you are not committed to meeting customers' needs in an online mode. Don't bother being online to entice patrons into your buildings. Go online to make the online world better.

References

Fitzgerald, M. A., Branch, R. and Lovin, V. (2000) *The gateway to educational materials: an evaluation study*, available at
http://www.geminfo.org/Evaluation/Fitzgerald_00.09.pdf.

Francoeur, S. (2001) An analytical survey of chat reference services, *Reference Services Review*, **29** (3), 189–203.

Janes, J. (2000) Current research in digital reference: findings and implications, *Presentation at Facets of Digital Reference, the VRD 2000 Annual Digital Reference Conference, 17 October, Seattle, WA*, available at
www.vrd.org/conferences/VRD2000/proceedings/janes-intro.shtml.

Janes, J. and McClure, C. R. (1999) The web as a reference tool: comparisons with traditional sources, *Public Libraries*, **38** (January), 30–9.

Lankes, R. D. (2002) The necessity of real-time: fact and fiction in digital reference systems, *Reference and User Services Quarterly*, (Summer).

LITA (1999) *Top tech trends*, available at
http://www.lita.org/committee/toptech/trendsmw99.htm

Mardikian, J. and Kesselman, M. (1995) Beyond the desk: enhanced reference staffing for the electronic library, *Reference Services Review*, **23** (1), 21–8.

Index